Race and Class Matters at an Elite College

Race and Class Matters at an Elite College

Elizabeth Aries

TEMPLE UNIVERSITY PRESS
Philadelphia

Temple University Press
1601 North Broad Street
Philadelphia PA 19122

www.temple.edu/tempress

Printed in the United States of America

Text design by Erin New

∞ The paper used in this publication meets the requirements of the American
National Standard for Information Sciences—Permanence of Paper for Printed Library
Materials, ANSI Z39.48-1992

Library of Congress Cataloging-in-Publication Data

Aries, Elizabeth.
   Race and class matters at an elite college / Elizabeth Aries.
     p. cm.
   Includes bibliographical references and index.
   ISBN-13: 978-1-59213-725-1 (cloth : alk. paper)
   ISBN-10: 1-59213-725-3 (cloth : alk. paper)
   ISBN-13: 978-1-59213-726-8 (pbk. : alk. paper)
   ISBN-10: 1-59213-726-1 (pbk. : alk. paper)   1. Amherst College—Freshman—Social
conditions—Case studies.   2. Private universities and colleges—Social aspects—Massachusetts—
Amherst—Case studies.   3. Minority college students—Massachusetts—Amherst—Social
conditions—Case studies.   I. Title.
   LD156.A75 2008
   378.744'23—dc22

                           2008006412

2 4 6 8 9 7 5 3 1

Contents

Acknowledgments   vii

1   Becoming a More Diverse College: Challenges and Benefits   1
2   Investigating Race and Class Matters on Campus   13
3   First Encounters with Race and Class   25
4   Negotiating Class Differences   44
5   Relationships across Race and Class   64
6   Learning from Racial Diversity   87
7   Learning from Class-Based Diversity   109
8   Negotiating Racial Issues   131
9   As the Year Ended   154
10 Meeting the Challenges of Diversity   169

Appendix A. On-Line Survey Measures   185
Appendix B. Interview Questions   189
Notes   193
References   219
Index   231

Acknowledgments

I want to thank the many people who inspired, encouraged, and contributed to this work. Several years ago, as my interest in understanding the psychological implications of social class grew, I turned to a sociologist and long-time friend, Maynard Seider, for suggestions on literature to read. Our conversations about social class and identity led to our collaboration on a study of the interactive relationship between class identity and the college experience. The study described in this book builds upon the research I conducted with Maynard and extends it to include an analysis of race. I am deeply appreciative of the knowledge and insight Maynard has shared with me and his influence on my thinking.

A deep debt of gratitude is owed to the students who participated in this study. Their voices make up the heart of this work, and the richness of the story told here is due to their openness and honesty in sharing their experiences of race and class. I am particularly grateful to the participants who read drafts of the manuscript and gave me feedback on what I had written. Because of considerations of confidentiality, they cannot be named here. I spent many hours with them during the spring of 2007, the end of their sophomore year, discussing their reactions to the manuscript as they expanded on their on-campus experiences with race and class. They helped me see things through their eyes, more deeply and clearly, and in new ways. This book has very much been shaped by their insights.

Before approaching publishers, I turned to family, friends, and colleagues for their reactions to the introductory chapter. Thanks go to Ronnie Janoff-Bulman, Jane Levin, Nancy Aries, David Hall, and Maynard Seider for their comments and suggestions, and particularly for their enthusiasm about the book at that early stage. After completing a draft of the chapter on coping with racial issues, I solicited the feedback of Charri Boykin-East and Alan Hart. I am extremely grateful for their astute and perceptive comments.

A number of people at the college, both faculty and administrators, showed incredible kindness in agreeing to read and comment on the completed manuscript in its entirety. Special thanks go to Rose Olver, Tony Marx, and Jane Taubman in this regard. Rose Olver and I have been discussing issues of race and class for many years. She has been a constant source of friendship and support, not only throughout the writing of this book, but throughout my career. She offered great help to me, in particular, in dealing with the description of the research methods and formulating the conclusions. Thanks to Tony Marx's leadership as president of the college, opportunities for lower-income students to attend Amherst have increased significantly, and Tony continues to be dedicated to making the college more accessible to a diverse group of students, and to making it a better place for them. I am deeply grateful to him for taking time from his extraordinarily busy schedule to read and respond to my work, and for his support. I turned to a special friend, Jane Taubman, to get the reactions of a colleague from a very different field who has known and worked with students at the college over the years. Two days after I sent her the manuscript, Jane had completed a close reading and provided excellent editorial comments and suggestions. I could not ask for more from a friend and am deeply appreciative. I also want to thank Katie Fretwell and Tom Parker, whose leadership in our Office of Admission has enabled Amherst to identify, attract, and matriculate such outstanding and diverse students. I am grateful for their feedback on and support for this book. Thanks go to Mitzi Goheen for reading and commenting on Chapter 8. And, finally, I want to express my great appreciation to Nancy Aries. I sought Nancy's expertise in framing a discussion of how organizations need to change to meet the needs of a diverse student body. With incredible generosity and kindness, she immediately dropped everything and devoted herself to articulating the central issues, helping me organize a discussion of these issues, and providing me with additional literature to read.

The data for this project could not have been collected and analyzed without the help of many people. I want to thank the Teagle Foundation for providing the funds to make this research possible. Special thanks go to Janet Price, who worked with me for hours to help turn my fall and spring questionnaires into on-line surveys, teaching me how to use the necessary computer programs, helping to get the surveys up and running, and dealing with computer problems when the surveys were sent out. I am deeply grateful to Marian Matheson, Cate Zolkos, Gail Woldu, and Richard Berman for generously giving their time to serve as interviewers, and for their commitment to the study and their belief in its value. Very special thanks go to Southey Saul, my fabulous summer research assistant, who helped with the coding of the interviews and the organization and analysis of the data. She worked with enthusiasm, intensity, and competence. Thanks to her hard work and dedication to the project, more was completed over the summer than I had dreamed was possible. It was a delight to work with her.

I want to thank Ron Lembo for his encouragement about my work, for suggestions on reviewers to look at my book proposal, and especially for directing me to Micah Kleit at Temple University Press. I am extremely grateful to Micah, who was excited about and believed in this book from the start and helped see it through to production.

But by far the greatest thanks go to my husband, Richard Berman (Luke). He has been the love of my life, my best friend, and my partner in all things. Luke played a major role in every aspect of this project, from giving me wonderful suggestions for interview questions, to serving as an enthusiastic and skilled interviewer, to endlessly discussing the material with me, but especially in helping me with the writing. Luke is a gifted songwriter, and with a writer's eye he read draft after draft of every chapter of this book, offering detailed editorial suggestions about organizing the material, improving the clarity of the writing and word choice, and particularly presenting the ideas in a more engaging manner. As a storyteller, he is always looking for the narrative. He helped me enormously by showing me how to approach the writing from that perspective, and it is because of his suggestions that this story comes to life. Despite the fact that this book took over my life and consumed me for two years, through it all Luke never wavered in his belief in and support for this research. He was always there for me and was a constant source of help. I dedicate this book to him.

1

Becoming a More Diverse College

Challenges and Benefits

I f I had stood before the entering freshman class at Amherst College in the fall of 1967 (the first year for which data on race are available), almost all the 304 male faces looking up at me would have been white and affluent. How white? All but 12. There were no Puerto Ricans, no Chicanos. There was one Asian American student. Seven of the students were from abroad, including two from Canada. How affluent? Sixty-two percent of the class was receiving no financial aid, and for those who did receive it, many of the awards were nominal. Nearly a quarter of the class were legacies—that is, sons of Amherst alumni.

Fast-forward to Sunday afternoon, August 29, 2005. Katie Fretwell, director of admissions at the college, is about to deliver her welcoming speech to the 431 entering first-year students. The faces she looks out on are strikingly different from those of 1967, and the differences go well beyond outward appearance. As Dean Fretwell describes the class to it-self: "Fifty-two percent of you are women and 48% are not. . . . One-third of you have self-identified as students of color. . . . Twenty-nine of you are non-U.S. citizens. Twelve percent are first-generation college students [first in their family to go to college], and more than 47% are receiving financial aid from the college." Further, she noted, "For almost 15% of you, English is not your first language. You speak 31 different languages in your homes (one of you can actually sing in five)." She could have added that one in eight of the students before her was a legacy, compared with one in four in the class that had arrived 38 years before. One statistic had barely changed: the percentage of students from private schools (39% in 1967 versus 38% in 2005).[1] What had changed were the students selected from those schools. Today many of the students of color come to the college from private schools.

Although just over half of the students entering the college in 2005 were able to pay the full costs of over $40,000 a year without financial aid, the differences between the two classes at Amherst represented a sea change, and one with important social and educational implications. The vastly increased diversity in race and class in the student body not only afforded opportunities for social mobility to underrepresented minorities and students with less financial means; it also had the potential to increase students' understanding of those different from themselves and to challenge previous notions about race and class. But was that potential realized? And what challenges did students of different classes and races face in coming to live together in a diverse community? These two questions and their answers serve as the focus of this book.

How Admissions Policies Have Changed—and Why

Many currents coursing through our society over those 38 years contributed to redirecting admission to the college and thus transforming the Amherst community. Until the 1960s, elite private colleges and universities in the United States recruited their students largely from New England boarding schools, private day schools, and a select few public schools almost exclusively located in wealthy suburban communities. The students selected were affluent, white, and well-rounded, not one-sidedly intellectual. These schools gave preferential treatment to legacies and went to some lengths to develop policies to exclude Jews.[2]

The emergence of the civil rights movement in the 1960s brought with it a dawning awareness among leaders of government, business, and education of the importance of reaching out to underrepresented minorities. Amherst's efforts to diversify the student body were part of a larger pattern occurring at private colleges and universities. According to sociologist Jerome Karabel, the powers that be, including those in higher education, came to recognize that "taking strong measures to rectify racial injustice was not simply a moral imperative; it was also a matter of enlightened self-interest at a time when the existing order was under challenge."[3] Along with the movement to provide equal legal rights to minorities came the idea of "affirmative action," righting past racial wrongs by giving a leg up to disadvantaged blacks. In addition, the argument was made that more diversity on campus was to everyone's benefit, an argument articulated by former Harvard University president Neil Rudenstine:

> In our world today, it is not enough for us and our students to acknowledge, in an abstract sense, that other kinds of people, with other modes of thought and feeling and action, exist somewhere—unseen, unheard, unvisited, and unknown. We must interact directly with a substantial portion of that larger universe. There must be opportunities to hear different views directly—face to face—from people who embody them. No formal academic study can replace continued association with others who are different from ourselves, and who challenge our preconceptions, prejudices, and assumptions, even as we challenge theirs.[4]

In response to this shift in awareness, in the late sixties colleges such as Amherst began to reach out to underrepresented minorities and actively recruit students who, prior to the civil rights movement, had little access to these institutions. Minority students were given an admissions advantage at elite schools through race-sensitive admissions policies.[5] Other changes in admissions followed, including a decline in the preference given to students from prep schools and to legacies (the 431 entering freshmen at Amherst in 2005 came from 342 different secondary schools). The rise of the women's movement in the wake of the civil rights movement helped impel the admittance of women to formerly all-male institutions. Amherst admitted its first women students in 1975. Jews were accepted in increasingly large numbers, as were students from a broader range of public schools and a broader range of states across America and countries around the world.[6]

In addition to racial and gender diversity, in recent years elite colleges and universities have turned their focus to another underrepresented group, white students who have few financial resources or whose parents have never attended college. Arguments are being made for increasing opportunities for lower-income students based on the principles of promoting social mobility, social justice, and equity. Concern has grown at the elite schools that they are "reproducing social advantage instead of serving as an engine of mobility."[7] William Bowen, former president of Princeton University, and his colleagues argue that social mobility is an important societal goal, and that "the sense of democratic legitimacy is undermined if people believe that the rich are admitted to selective colleges and universities regardless of merit while able and deserving candidates from more modest backgrounds are turned away."[8] Lawrence Summers, former president of Harvard, argued that these schools have a "profound responsibility to help meet our national challenge of achieving equal opportunity."[9] The lack of access to elite colleges for students of lower socioeconomic status has also been framed as a problem of lost talent in the educational system.[10] Gifted white students with little if any financial means or from families with no experience with higher education have, until recently, gone unrecruited; quite likely, they have been unaware of opportunities to attend elite schools on scholarships—opportunities that are expanding. Thus, they never got the challenges and rewards afforded by those schools.

But concern for social justice is not the only reason advanced for admitting more students with little financial means. Another argument for this change echoes the one raised by Neil Rudenstine in support of racial diversity. Anthony Marx, president of Amherst College, in 2004 argued that if we do not increase opportunities for lower-income students, "we will neither prepare any of our students for the world, nor will we serve our role in that world."[11] In his 2006 Convocation Address, he told the entering freshmen: "The fact that we are not all the same is not merely a pleasant aspect of this college: it is an essential strength. We select and gather differences purposefully, and at some expense, precisely to build that strength. We build it because we learn more than if we were or behaved as if we were all the same. . . . Your differences are also your best gifts to each other. . . . How to build a community on the basis of diversity is the pre-eminent challenge of our world and our time. If we don't do it at Amherst, we'll find it only harder beyond here."[12]

Having set the goal of creating a diverse student body at the college, Amherst goes to great lengths to find and attract students from all walks of life, from all over the United States and beyond. High school advisors, family and friends, Amherst alumni, and surveys and rankings of liberal arts colleges such as that of *U.S. News & World Report* have put Amherst on the map for some students. But in the increasingly competitive world of college recruitment for racial and economic diversity, these passive approaches have been supplanted, at Amherst and other wealthy institutions, by enormous investments of time, personnel, and money in active recruiting. The Office of Admission at Amherst uses its substantial budget to bring the college to the attention of those whom it seeks to enroll in its attempts to diversify its student body. It not only sends staff out to schools in search of students, but also brings students it wants onto campus, often in groups, sometimes individually. In recruiting black students to Amherst, programs such as Prep for Prep[13] and A Better Chance[14] are invaluable, and many minority students at the college have been in these programs or similar ones. These programs identify and work with gifted and motivated minority students from an early age (10 years old, in the case of Prep for Prep) to get them prepared for and enrolled in private preparatory schools from which they can go on to colleges that are actively looking for well-prepared minority students. In recent years Amherst has subscribed to the services of QuestBridge,[15] which finds and then matches intellectually gifted and financially needy students of all races with colleges looking for economic as well as racial diversity. Students accepted through QuestBridge are guaranteed full scholarships for their four undergraduate years.

When Anthony Marx spoke of selecting and gathering differences "at some expense," he was understating the resources that have been put into play to create a truly diverse student body at Amherst. The work of the Office of Admission is just the beginning. The class that entered Amherst in the fall of 2005 received over $5.5 million in scholarships and grant aid that academic year from the college, with an average amount of almost $28,000 (out of the over $40,000 tuition) for each of the 47% of the students getting aid.

Benefits, Costs, and Challenges of Diversity

Considerable social science theory and research back up the belief expressed by Anthony Marx and other educators that a diverse academic community can change its members' attitudes, beliefs, and behaviors.[16] Most of the work is directly concerned with race but is arguably applicable to social class as well. In 1954 Gordon Allport, an eminent Harvard social psychologist, wrote in his classic *The Nature of Prejudice:* "Prejudice (unless deeply rooted in the character structure of the individual) may be reduced by equal status contact between majority and minority groups in pursuit of common goals. The effect is greatly enhanced if this contact is sanctioned by institutional supports . . . and if it is of a sort that leads to the perception of common interests and common humanity between members of the two groups."[17]

Other social scientists have found support for Allport's contact theory and have enumerated additional factors that enhance the impact of contact: greater diversity in terms of numbers belonging to the different groups increases the likelihood of social interaction across racial lines; the contact should be regular and frequent; it should occur across a variety of settings and situations; it should be personalized and allow sufficient time for development of cross-group friendships.[18] Given the pattern of segregated housing and schooling in America, many students enter college from communities that have given them little experience with peers from diverse backgrounds, whether racial or socioeconomic.[19] This lack of experience is truer for whites at Amherst than for blacks, as many of the black students have gone to predominantly white private high schools and thus have experience with the world of white wealth.[20]

The social science literature suggests that people in an in-group (e.g., the majority) tend to see members of an out-group (e.g., the minority) as homogeneous and lacking in variability, while seeing themselves as more heterogeneous.[21] This sets the stage for stereotyping. Getting to know those in the out-group, however, gives in-groupers an opportunity to develop cognitive empathy, which entails taking another's perspective, and to reduce prejudice as they learn about the out-group and come to understand out-groupers' differing world views, norms, values, beliefs, and perceptions of the in-group.[22]

Judging from Allport's contact theory and the subsequent research, a college campus such as Amherst that has committed to creating a diverse community of students seems ideally suited to break down stereotypes. Students live on campus and interact across a variety of settings and situations. They are housed together in dormitories, eat together in a common dining hall, attend classes together, and take part in sports and other extracurricular activities on an equal-status basis. They have repeated contact on campus over a long period of time. They work cooperatively in numerous endeavors toward common goals, collaborating on group projects in class, competing as teammates in sports, rehearsing for musical or theatrical performances, publishing a magazine or newspaper. The college provides students with the opportunity to reconsider their attitudes toward those from a different social or economic class, a different race, or both. Such a community also encourages students to think about their own race and class in society. According to psychologist Nancy Cantor, such experiences "set the stage for replacing unfair stereotypes, even the favorable ones, with something more individual and realistic."[23]

While a diverse college campus seems like an ideal place to interact across the boundaries of race and class, the social science literature suggests that there are obstacles to be overcome. A college may bring together black and white, rich and poor, but psychologists Patricia Devine and Kristin Vasquez argue that students have few guidelines for "how to do the inter-group thing well."[24] Students are aware of implicit rules about speech—for example, that racial or ethnic slurs are inappropriate—but they have few guidelines for which types of actions are appropriate. Most students lack experience in producing positive inter-group interactions, and as Devine and Vasquez put it, "There is a great deal of potential for miscommunication that arises out of the expectations and concerns that both majority and minority group members bring to the interaction."[25] Students in the majority tend to discuss difficulties arising in an inter-group encounter only with members of their own group, and not with minority group members, missing the opportunity to work through their difficulties as interaction partners.[26] In describing his experience as an undergraduate at Harvard, Ross Douthat, an associate editor at the *Atlantic Monthly,* observed that "unsuspecting eighteen-year-olds are packed together in tiny spaces with people vastly different from anyone they have ever known before, relieved of adult supervision, and asked to learn from one another's differences. The nation's future, Justice Powell would say, depends upon such experiments."[27] Yet for the most part, on most campuses, the faculty and administration leave it to them to find their way.

laisser-
faire
approach

The literature suggests that all students, black and white, lower-income and wealthy, face challenges in a diverse community. Lower-income first-generation white students face class-related difficulties at college because they differ in economic, social, and cultural capital[28] from their more affluent white counterparts and have a harder time achieving a sense of comfort and belonging.[29] One study found that these difficulties were more acute at an elite college than at a state college because of the greater disparities in economic, cultural, and social capital there.[30] The same study found that lower-income white students, and, in particular, first-generation students, who were most lacking in cultural capital, reported feelings of intimidation, discomfort, inadequacy, deficiency, and exclusion; they worried about deficiencies in their linguistic skills, clothing, and knowledge of how to act in certain social situations.

Concerns have been raised about costs of affirmative action to racial minorities at selective institutions.[31] Dinesh D'Souza, a fellow at the Hoover Institution at Stanford, claimed in his book *Illiberal Education*, "American universities are quite willing to sacrifice the future happiness of many young blacks and Hispanics to achieve diversity, proportional representation, and what they consider to be multicultural progress."[32] Sociologist Joe Feagin and his colleagues found that blacks at a predominantly white university faced stereotyping, hostility, and discrimination, and reported "an environment filled with racial obstacles and hurdles created not only by other students but also by white instructors, other staff members, and security personnel."[33] Other evidence, however, shows that race-sensitive admission has not harmed the beneficiaries.[34] Based on data from 28 academically selective colleges and universities, William Bowen and Derek Bok, former presidents of Princeton and Harvard respectively, found that the more selective the institution blacks attended, the lower the dropout rate, the higher the likelihood of graduating and earning an advanced degree, the higher their satisfaction with their college experience, and the higher their eventual salaries.[35]

Bowen and Bok's data do not cover the day-to-day experiences of blacks on these campuses.[36] Nor do we have much data about the challenges faced by wealthy black students, who have lived in a largely white world, when they are expected to connect to other blacks on campus. Even affluent whites, whose wealth, in the past, might well have assured them status, face challenges on a campus where values and norms are changing.

The Research Study

What, then, actually happens to students at Amherst? What is the return to the college community on its enormous investment in diversity? As noted

earlier, Amherst College president Anthony Marx told students, "Your differences are your best gifts to each other." Are those gifts actually used? Does
having racial, ethnic, and class diversity at Amherst result in people interacting in ways that enhance their understanding of those different from themselves, as Allport's theory would suggest? Or do students self-segregate? Do
previous notions about race and class go unchallenged and unchanged? And
what price, if any, is paid for those gifts? What challenges do students from
distinct racial and socioeconomic worlds face in coming to live together at
Amherst?

The chapters that follow show the results of a study conducted at Amherst College over the 2005–2006 academic year involving 58 students in
their first year, the year that an increasing body of evidence points to as critical to overall success at college.[37] The study was designed to discover the effects, if any, of living in a diverse community over the course of students' first
year at the college, and what challenges they faced based on their race and
social class. The day-to-day experiences of students with their peers were
explored, bearing in mind the finding of Alexander Astin, professor emeritus
of higher education and organizational change, that "the student's peer group
is the single most potent source of influence on growth and development
during the undergraduate years."[38]

The students were selected from four distinct groups: (1) affluent whites,
(2) affluent blacks, (3) whites with high financial need, limited family education, or both, and (4) blacks with high financial need, limited family education, or both. Through on-line questionnaires and face-to-face interviews at
the beginning and end of their freshman year, the 58 students (roughly 15
from each group) laid out their notions of race and class, their past experiences with diversity, their experiences with diversity during their first year at
Amherst, and what challenges and changes, if any, these experiences led to in
their thinking or behavior.

Students had many stories to tell as they became part of a diverse community and faced the challenges that entailed. Their responses were as varied
as the students themselves. Some embraced those challenges; others paid little attention to those different from themselves. This book will take a close
look at these 58 entering freshmen and explore what they actually experienced and learned about race and class on their journey through their first
year. For example, Emily, a young white woman from a small farming community, spoke of being raised in a world that was almost exclusively white.
Blacks were routinely referred to as "niggers," she reported in her fall interview, and folks in her community, including herself, carried stereotypes of
blacks gleaned from television. During her first weeks at Amherst, Emily was
sitting at a table in the dining hall when three male students of color came
and sat with her. "I was very uncomfortable because I just didn't know how

to interact with them. Because I hadn't met them, I didn't know anything about them. . . . So I was just sitting there, trying to think of what to say or how to begin a conversation while trying to stay politically correct." How would this diverse world she was now entering affect her? Would she achieve a degree of comfort? Would she remain worried about what words might come out of her mouth? Would she come to feel some rapport with and understanding of students of color, people so unlike those with whom she was raised?

And what about Matthew, an affluent prep school legacy? Asked if social class would make a difference in choosing friends at the college, he answered: "A little bit. It sounds insensitive to say, but college is so much about making connections and your relationships with people. It is about learning, but the most important thing is networking at college. Period. And the networking will help you get the jobs or know people or whatever, and the people who are more likely to help you get the jobs you're looking for are of a certain class. That's not to say that kids of another class won't extend this, but say the probability that a relationship is going to help you later down the line is going to be much higher if it's a person from a higher class than another." Would this young man's experience at Amherst make him view class and his classmates differently over time? Would he develop friendships with students from class backgrounds different from his own?

Brianna, a low-income black student, the youngest of many siblings and the first and only child in her family to graduate from high school, came to Amherst carrying the un-asked-for burdens of early success, of being held out as an example to the younger children in her extended family, of great expectations and vicarious triumphs. "I'm representing my whole race, and I don't like that, 'cause it's like I shouldn't be made to represent my whole race. . . . If I don't become this world-renowned doctor, then I kind of feel I didn't meet [my family's] expectations because that's what they wanted me to do." She carries much greater pressures to succeed than the average affluent white student. Would these added pressures be too great a burden? How would she fit in among predominantly white, affluent students?

William, a black student from a wealthy family, could not at first find his place at Amherst. "Black people made jokes about me being lighter skin . . . so I felt at first I couldn't fit in with them. . . . And then white people, I mean, I don't completely fit in." He spoke of an additional challenge posed by his race: "At nighttime, people will see you, especially a big male such as myself, being black, as potentially a sex offender, or an attacker. I've noticed that sometimes when I come back late from the gym, people, girls especially, will avoid eye contact and be kind of shy around me." Would he find a comfortable place on campus with blacks and whites? Would other students recognize and get beyond the stereotypes they hold about him?

Robert, a white student with high financial need, spoke of his sense of not belonging as he listened to a wealthy white friend talking with others in the dorm about things like "summers in the Hamptons and he takes his friend's yacht over there every summer. To me, this is something that I used to see on TV. A summer in the Hamptons, it's something you read about in magazines. I don't feel comfortable chipping in because I don't know what they're talking about." Would he continue to feel excluded from conversations? Would he likewise feel excluded from activities because he lacked sufficient discretionary funds?

Overview

In the chapters that follow, I provide details about the study I conducted, drawing heavily on the voices of the 58 students to convey the results of my research. These students spoke openly and candidly about the very pressing but politically charged issues of race and class, and they expressed in compelling ways why race and class matter and require our attention. In Chapter 2 I describe how the participants in the study were selected, their backgrounds, and their prior experiences with race and class. I go over how the data were collected at the beginning and end of the academic year, and then analyzed. The next seven chapters present the results of the study.[39]

Chapter 3 focuses on students' expectations about the year and their initial experiences on campus. How aware or concerned were they about the possessions they brought with them, about their clothes and appearance, their knowledge of and experiences in the world? What did students perceive to be the advantages or drawbacks of their race and class status over the early weeks at college? I will examine the nature and extent of the concerns they voiced about the expected role of race and class in their experiences in the year ahead.

In Chapter 4 I look at the complex issues students faced in coping with class differences on campus. They were confronted daily with great disparities in wealth and had to find ways to handle these differences. This chapter opens with an analysis of students' understanding of their own position on the class spectrum and its consequences. It considers the extent to which students desired to hide their class backgrounds: affluent students, black and white, wanting to hide their privilege out of guilt or fear of being stereotyped negatively by classmates; lower-income students wanting to hide what they lacked out of feelings of inadequacy or inferiority. How salient was social class in their daily lives as the year progressed? Finally, I discuss the benefits students with high financial need, black and white, derived from relationships with other students from a similar class background.

Chapter 5 looks at the extent to which students segregated themselves by race or class or formed cross-race and cross-class relationships.[40] Did the students in the study get to know students of another race and class well? I look at the challenges entailed in reaching across race and class lines, the value placed on doing so, and the extent to which this occurred. I examine whether students felt left out based on social class from interactions such as eating out, spring break trips, or off-campus activities and describe the types of efforts students made to bridge race and class differences and be inclusive.

In Chapters 6 and 7 the focus shifts to what benefits, if any, students gained from diversity both inside and outside the classroom. Race is the focus of Chapter 6 and class the focus of Chapter 7. Inter-group contact on campus fulfilled the optimal conditions Allport described in *The Nature of Prejudice* and thus had the potential to reduce prejudice. Further, according to social psychologist Thomas Pettigrew, inter-group contact can lead to "learning about the outgroup, changing behavior, generating affective ties, and ingroup reappraisal."[41] These chapters address two vital questions. Did students gain a new understanding of their own racial or class group or of other races and classes over the course of the year? Did they become more aware of and sensitive to other people's lives?

I examine the race- and class-based stereotypes students held and then look at whether informal interaction helped break down stereotypes and revise assumptions and misconceptions about members of different races and social classes. I look at the extent to which students engaged in meaningful, honest conversations about racial and class issues, and what they learned from these conversations. I examine issues of classroom diversity, a term used by social scientists to refer to both learning about diverse groups through the formal curriculum and learning by interacting with diverse peers in the classroom.[42] I report on whether students took courses that addressed issues of race and class, and what, if anything, they learned from hearing in class the personal perspectives of students from a different race or class. I look at classroom issues that arose for black students: feelings about being the only black person in a class, about being called upon to present the "black" perspective, and about hearing insensitive or racist comments or negative stereotypes presented in the classroom.

Chapter 8 explores some of the unique issues blacks faced on campus.[43] The blacks in the first-year class were an extremely heterogeneous group, differing, for example, in their class backgrounds, in whether they self-identified as African American, Caribbean American, biracial, or mixed-race, in the degree to which race was central to their self-definition, in their attitudes and beliefs about how African Americans should live and interact with society, and in the darkness of their skin. I discuss the benefits blacks gained from connections to and bonding with other blacks on campus, as well as the issues that arose as they negotiated their differences among themselves. I look at questions black students faced about not being "black enough," or of "acting white"—not because of their academic achievement, but because of their speech, clothes, tastes in music, skin tone, or choice of friends. I examine the expectations many black students felt to hang out with black students rather than whites, to join the Black Student Union, or to date blacks, and the sanctions they experienced for not meeting these expectations. I then move on to the complexities of black-white relationships, the racial joking on campus, the difficulty of building trust in black-white relationships, the problem of handling racist comments, and what language was appropriate and which terms might offend.

In Chapter 9 I examine the extent to which race and class were related to students' self-reports about their academic experience and their social and psychological well-being at the end of the year. In the academic realm, were there differences along racial and class lines in how well students felt they had been prepared for the academic challenges at college, in their academic confidence, and in their academic success, as measured by final grades? Students from families with high financial need and/or limited family education were now on a trajectory of upward social mobility. What costs, if any, might accompany the benefits of an Amherst education? I consider the ways in which these students were changing, including their perceptions of the families and communities they were leaving behind.[44] Having opportunities that their parents and siblings lacked could be a burden, as such students carried high expectations from immediate and extended family members.

In the final chapter I summarize the study's findings about race- and class-based diversity, looking at the challenges that were faced and the learning that occurred. The college has made great strides toward becoming a diverse community and allowing students to learn from these differences, but more could be done to take full advantage of the opportunities that such a diverse community offers. While students are being asked to adjust to the culture of an elite college, are there adjustments that the college must make to incorporate a more diverse student body? This chapter suggests ways in which administrators and educators might better facilitate students' learning from differences and support them around matters of race and class.

2

Investigating Race and Class Matters on Campus

In the fall of 2005, I invited four groups of entering first-year students at Amherst to share with me their experiences with diversity over their first year of college. As described in the previous chapter, these four groups included students who were either: (1) affluent white, (2) affluent black, (3) white with high financial need and/or limited family education, or (4) black with high financial need and/or limited family education. Before describing the findings of the study, we need to take a step back and examine in more detail how those students were selected for the study, how the groups might be more fully described, and how the data were collected and analyzed.

Selecting the Participants

In the summer of 2005, before first-year students arrived on campus, I turned to the Office of Admission to help me identify potential participants. The Office of Admission had information from students' applications about race: students had been given the opportunity on the application form to identify themselves with a particular ethnic group. Application forms also included information about whether or not students would be applying for financial aid, and about parental occupation and education. I drew on this information, used by the Office of Admission in identifying students from underrepresented groups, to determine students' races as well as which ones came from families with high financial need or limited family education, and which were affluent. Thirty entering students (7% of the class) who self-identified as "White or Caucasian" had high financial need and/or limited family education (i.e., the parents had not completed college), while 116 students (27% of the class) who self-identified as "White or Caucasian" indicated that they did not intend to apply for any financial aid.[1] These two groups of students served as potential participants for the two white groups.

In the entering class of 431 students, 33% self-identified as students of color; of those, 41 students (9% of the class) self-identified as "African American, Black." Another 7% of the class self-identified as "multi-ethnic." Some of those students may have been part African American or black, but they were not included as potential black participants for the study.[2]

Establishing two black groups that were parallel to the two white groups posed a complexity. Most of the entering black students were middle class. Only 12 of the entering black students were coded by the Office of Admission as having very limited financial resources and/or limited family education. As for an affluent sample, all but six of the 41 entering black students indicated that they would be applying for financial aid. Some of the black families who applied for financial aid were not found to qualify, thus meeting the criteria for the affluent group and bringing the potential group of affluent blacks to 14. I could not assume that every student recruited for my study would agree to participate, and so I faced two choices. I could go with rather small groups, set by the number of black students available, limiting the power of my study, or I could slightly broaden my definition of affluence or having high financial need and/or limited family education in order to attain a slightly larger sample size by including students close to the criteria for financial status and family education. I chose the latter alternative. I was able to identify some additional black students from each end of the class spectrum and add them to the lists of potential black participants. In the data analysis I paid careful attention to whether the responses of these additional students were different from the majority of students in their respective groups with respect to their class experience on campus, and found that not to be the case.

For ease of identification, both black and white students with high financial need and/or limited family education will be referred to as "lower-income." "Lower-income" should *not* be taken to mean "lower-class," as students in these groups ranged from lower class to middle class, as will be described below. Having high financial need must be understood in the context of the comprehensive fee for tuition, room, and board at the college, which for entering students in the year of the study was $43,360. Additional fees for student activities, health insurance, books, supplies, and personal expenses potentially added $4,000 to $6,000 to the overall cost for the year.

The parental contribution toward tuition and fees can weigh heavily on middle-class families, particularly those with more than one student attending college.

The lower-income groups, both black and white, spanned a wide range and included, for example, first-generation college students; students from working-class families in which a parent had later gone to college and now held a middle-class job; students with immigrant parents who were highly educated but worked low-prestige, lower-income jobs; students whose parents worked service jobs; as well as students whose parents were not in the workforce. The designation as "lower-income" indicates "lower" socioeconomic standing in relation to the affluent students. Compared with the affluent groups, the lower-income groups were also "lower" with respect to parental educational attainment. As was the case with the lower-income groups, the family incomes of the affluent students spanned a wide range that encompassed some families with considerable wealth.

Recruiting the Participants

In late August 2005, on the day the first-year students arrived on campus for a week-long orientation, I sent an e-mail invitation to a sample of potential participants in each of the four groups. I let them know that they were being invited to take part in an interview study of a diverse group of first-year students on the role of race and social class in students' experiences at Amherst College. I stressed that their participation in the interviews and the surveys administered at the beginning and end of the year would afford them the time and space to reflect on their experiences, and that their willingness to share their personal accounts would provide information that might make Amherst College a better place for future students.

Many students immediately agreed to take part; a few declined; and some did not respond. Follow-up e-mails were sent to the nonrespondents. If there was still no response by midweek, I sent out invitations to other students on my list as needed to attain the goal of recruiting approximately 15 participants per group by week's end, with each group balanced by gender.

Affluent whites. In picking a sample of affluent white students, an equal number of males and females were randomly selected to get a final group that was balanced by gender. Twenty white students were invited to participate, and 14 agreed (70%). The final group included 8 males and 6 females.

Lower-income whites. Twenty-one students were invited to participate in this group. A total of 16 students agreed (76%), of whom 6 were male and 10 were female.

Affluent blacks. Sixteen students were invited to participate in this group, and 14 (88%) agreed, including 6 males and 8 females. During their interviews these students presented their racial identification as follows: 10 described themselves as African American, one as black, one as African American of mixed race, and 2 as biracial.

Lower-income blacks. A total of 20 students were invited to participate in this group, and 14 agreed (70%). The final group included 7 males and 7 females. During their interviews, 3 described themselves as black, 7 as African American, one as black (Haitian American), one as West Indian American, one as biracial, and one as mixed race.

Total sample. The total sample included 58 first-year students; 27 were male and 31 were female; 16 were lower-income white, 14 lower-income black, 14 affluent white, and 14 affluent black. The overall response rate was 75%, meaning that the participants were likely to be representative of the groups from which they were chosen. When the second data collection began in the spring, 3 of the original students in the study were on a nonacademic leave from the college and were no longer on campus (2 lower-income white females and one affluent black male). One of those students agreed to complete the spring interview by phone and to fill out the on-line survey. Thus 56 of the 58 students (96.5%) served as participants in both the fall and the spring.

Data Collection

During the first week of classes in September 2005, students filled out an on-line survey, and over the following two weeks they were interviewed face-to-face. I conducted half the interviews, and four other middle-aged people (two white women, a black woman, and a white man) also served as interviewers. Each interviewer was assigned an equal number of participants in each of the four groups to control for bias. To further ensure consistency and standardization across interviewers, interviewers were instructed to read the questions. They were encouraged to ask follow-up questions to make sure that they fully understood what participants were trying to communicate. The fall interviews ranged from 20 to 90 minutes, with most lasting about 40 minutes. Many of the interviews with affluent white students were shorter than those with students in the other three groups, since many of the interview questions centered on students' concerns about the role that race and class might play in the year ahead, and affluent whites had fewer concerns about these matters than the other students.

In April 2006, a few weeks before the second semester ended, students completed another on-line survey and then had their second face-to-face interview. With a few exceptions due to scheduling conflicts, participants were interviewed by the same person in the fall and the spring semesters. Spring interviews ranged from half an hour to close to two hours, with most interviews lasting over an hour. Students were paid $10 in the fall and $20 in the spring for their participation in the study. Readers interested in the details of the measures used on the on-line surveys will find them in Appendix A; the interview questions appear in Appendix B.

The results of this study were based heavily on material from the structured interviews. The interview method is particularly useful in a study whose goal is to generate themes that describe students' experiences, to "form explanations and theories that are grounded in the details, evidence, and examples of the interviews."[3] The interviews also provided a context for understanding the quantitative findings derived from the on-line surveys.

Analysis of the Interview Data

The fall and spring interviews were all recorded and transcribed. I began the data analysis by reading transcripts, statement by statement, with the goal of identifying categories (e.g., "Have desired to hide my class background," "Have felt pressure to be with people of my race," "Have been accused of not being black enough," "Have felt excluded based on my social class") that captured the major idea being described in each statement.[4] As more transcripts were read, the categories were redesigned, refined, and collapsed. By the time half the transcripts had been read, few modifications of categories were taking place, and most of the content was being captured in the categories that had been constructed. At that point, I began reading the transcripts again from the beginning and re-coded them so that the new categories that had developed as the coding had proceeded would be used for all transcripts.

Once statements were classified according to the different thematic categories, a second reader went over my classifications, and any differences of opinion were discussed and statements reclassified where appropriate. Where student responses to themes took the form of a few easily identifiable categories (e.g., have/have not desired to hide my class background), frequency counts were done so that the percentage of students in each group giving a particular response could be determined.[5]

As an affluent, middle-aged white woman, I of course had concerns about whether I could accurately capture and understand the experience of black and/or lower-income students whose backgrounds and experiences were dissimilar to my own. I wanted to make certain that my compilation and interpretation of student responses were accurate, that there had been no major omissions, and that incorrect meanings had not been ascribed to statements or behavior. To address these concerns, I invited two participants from each of my groups to read initial drafts of chapters and comment on them critically and in detail. I used their feedback to test the validity of my claims and to make additions and alterations to what I had written. Their willingness to open themselves up to me in sharing their perceptions about race and class at

Amherst gave me greater insight into their perspectives and experiences, which I was able to use in telling the story of their first year. They pointed out some omissions and inaccuracies, and helped me understand many of the issues more fully.

In presenting the results of the study, I draw heavily on the voices of the students who took part. Students were responding to questions without prior preparation, and spontaneous speech is not as polished as the statements students could have made had they been given more time to reflect and the chance to respond to questions in writing. To make the quotations easier to read, repetitions, false starts, and repetitive use of terms such as "like," "sort of," "kind of," "you know," "I mean," have been removed. Those students who were particularly articulate spokespersons of their group's concerns are represented by longer quotations. Where possible, the percentage of students in each group who gave a particular response is presented to indicate the extent to which individual students' voices are representative of other students' experiences in their respective groups.[6]

The presentation of the results would be enriched if background information could be provided on each student being quoted. However, given the very small number of potential participants for all but the affluent white group in the first-year class at Amherst, this could not be done without breaching confidentiality. Thus, identifying information about students was not used, and all were given pseudonyms.[7]

The reader will find descriptive statistics in the text: percentages of students in each group who gave a particular response or average scores for each group. Further statistical information is provided in the endnotes.[8]

Social Class

Determining social class is a complex matter. It has traditionally been defined by such indicators as educational attainment, occupational status and supervisory capacity (how many people a person takes orders from or gives orders to), income and wealth.[9] These indicators are not always consistent with one another: for example, some students in the study had parents who had graduate degrees but held low-prestige, lower-paying jobs, who were highly trained and educated abroad but after immigrating held lower-wage jobs, who were in high-prestige professions but were identified by the college as having high financial need. Several indicators were used to determine the social class of students in each group: size of financial aid awards (based on the college's determination of need for scholarship and grant aid), Pell grant eligibility, parental education, and parental occupation. Later chapters will present further information derived from the interviews regarding differences in students' material possessions, cultural and social capital, and understanding of their social class position. Here then is a closer look at the indicators used to determine social class.

Size of Financial Aid Awards and Pell Grants

Students were not asked to disclose the size of their financial aid awards. A list of the participants in the study was given to the Financial Aid Office, which determined the average size of the financial aid award granted by the college to students in the two lower-income groups. The average award was $34,203, with a total of $1,026,102 given by the college to students in these two groups to cover the costs of their first year in college. Seven white students and five black students in the study were recipients of federal Pell Grants.

Parental Education

The four groups differed considerably in the level of education their parents had attained. All the affluent students, black and white, had at least one parent who had completed a BA or BS, and 89% of the students in these two groups had at least one parent who had completed a graduate degree as well.[10] However, 43% of affluent blacks also reported that one of their parents had not completed a BA, whereas that was the case for only a single affluent white student.

As would be expected, the parents of students in the two lower-income groups had much more limited education than the parents of the affluent students. For 63% of lower-income whites, neither parent had finished college; for 19% the highest level of education attained by a parent was a college degree, and for 19% it was a graduate or professional degree. For half of the lower-income white students with a parent who had completed a college degree or beyond, their other parent had not gone beyond high school. Overall, 56% of the lower-income whites had one parent whose highest level of education was a high school diploma, and one student had a parent who had no high school education.

Parents of the lower-income black students showed considerable variability in their educational attainment. For 14% the highest level of education attained by either parent was high school; for 21% it was some college; for 21% it was a bachelor's degree; and 43% had a parent who had received a graduate or professional degree. One lower-income black student had a parent with no high school education; two black students had a parent who had completed only some high school. Of those students with a parent who had completed a college degree or beyond (64%), in half the families the other parent had not gone beyond high school.

Parents of affluent and lower-income students who had graduated from college attended very different types of institutions. Among the affluent whites, all but one student had a parent who had attended one of the nation's top 50 colleges or universities, according to rankings done by *U.S. News & World Report*.[11] This was true for three students in each of the black groups, and one lower-income white student.

Parental Occupation

Doctor and lawyer were the most frequent parental occupations listed by affluent students (57% of whites, 64% of blacks). These are occupations with high prestige and substantial managerial authority. Among the remaining affluent students, all had a parent employed in a position with managerial authority or one that drew on complex, educationally certified skills: for example, college administrator, investment banker, editor, producer, restaurant owner, career counselor, physical therapist, speech pathologist.[12]

Parents of students in the two lower-income groups had a wide variety of occupations. At one end of the spectrum were two black students who had a parent who was a lawyer. At the other end of the spectrum were four students (two white, two black) who lived in households in which parents did not hold down steady employment. Some students came from working-class households with parents holding blue-collar or service jobs. The remaining students had parents whose occupations fell in between: paraprofessional, secretary, police officer, technician, farmer, sailor, woodworker, pipe-fitter.

Prior Experiences with Race and Class

In order to understand students' experiences on campus with regard to race and class, it is useful to look at their prior exposure to people from races and classes different from their own.

Home Communities

Given the pattern of segregated housing in America, it should not be surprising that many students in this study entered college from communities with little racial diversity.[13] The two groups of white students came from predominantly white communities. On average 88% of the households in the home neighborhoods of lower-income whites were estimated to be white, and 4% black. Results for affluent whites were similar; on average 82% of the households in their home communities were described as white, 9% as black.

The affluent black students also came from predominantly white communities: on average 66% of the households in their home neighborhoods were judged to be white, 19% to be black. But averages do not tell the complete story. At one extreme was a student in the affluent black group who came from a neighborhood that was 95% black, while at the other extreme were six affluent blacks from neighborhoods in which 5% or less of the families were black. Other students' neighborhoods fell in between.

The lower-income blacks in this study came from more racially mixed neighborhoods than their affluent black classmates. On average 42% of households in their neighborhoods were reported to be white, 49% to be black. Again, averages can be misleading, since students' neighborhoods varied greatly. Four students in this group estimated that their neighborhoods were 90% or more black. By contrast, five students came from neighborhoods that were 10% or less black.

Schooling

Lower-income whites were much more likely than students in the other three groups to have attended public high schools.[14] Eighty-eight percent of the lower-income white students in this study attended public high schools versus 36% of affluent whites.[15] Students in both of the black groups primarily attended private or parochial schools: 64% of lower-income blacks and 86% of affluent blacks attended these schools.[16]

Prior Cross-Race and Cross-Class Interactions

Students from the four groups entered college with different degrees of exposure to peers who were very different from themselves. Ninety-three percent of lower-income blacks and 80% of affluent blacks talked about having had prior experience interacting with people from different racial groups versus 27% of lower-income whites and 64% of affluent whites. While the majority of affluent whites had attended private schools, on average 20% of students at these private schools were reported to be nonwhite. The data mirror findings of other researchers that most minority students come to college having had significant interracial exposure, while many whites have not.[17]

Many blacks who had attended private schools or boarding schools spoke of Amherst as being "surprisingly similar" to their high school experiences, "the same environment," or "the same worlds." They found nothing "shocking." They had gone to school with very rich students for many years, and felt that they had "already sort of acclimated to it." Some had grown up with "mostly white friends" as well. Because lower-income blacks were much more likely to have attended private high schools than lower-income whites, they came to college with more exposure to highly affluent classmates. Many lower-income whites described their communities as having little class variability and this would be their first encounter with wealthy classmates.

Test Scores and Academic Confidence

The students in this study, like those in the college as a whole, had high scores compared with other test-takers nationally. All but 5 of the students in the study agreed to release their Scholastic Aptitude Test (SAT) scores;[18] 2 had taken the ACT rather than the SAT, so the SAT data are based on scores from 51 of the 58 students. The average combined SAT score for whites in the study was 1488.[19] Their SAT scores ranged from the 90.9th percentile to the 99.9th percentile of white test-takers nationally in 2005; their group average placed them at the 98.8th percentile of white test-takers. Blacks in the study had average combined SAT scores of 1284.[20] While black students' scores were considerably lower than those of white students,[21] their scores ranged from the 92.1st percentile to the 99.8th percentile of black test-takers nationally in 2005; their group average placed them in the 98.1st percentile of black test-takers.[22] Thus the black students in the study were among the most outstanding black test-takers in the nation. The racial differences in SAT scores for students in the study were consistent with data from the entire entering class of first-year students at Amherst,[23] with findings from other highly selective institutions,[24] and with national data that show white students scoring higher on the SAT than blacks.[25]

SAT scores nationally are also strongly related to social class. Nationally, lower-income students have been found to score lower on the SAT than their more affluent peers.[26] But the college is able to attract and enroll some of the most academically outstanding students from families with high financial need and/or limited family education. The lower-income students in the study, black and white, scored somewhat lower on the SAT than the affluent students. Affluent students, black and white, had an average combined SAT score of 1408, and lower-income students had an average combined SAT score of 1371.[27]

Despite differences between groups in the types of schools students had attended and SAT scores, the four groups reported similar degrees of academic confidence in their fall on-line surveys—confidence in their academic preparation, writing skills, general academic knowledge, and intelligence.[28] In their fall interviews, only a few lower-income students expressed worries that social class would make a difference academically because the quality of their high school preparation was not as strong as that of peers coming out of private and preparatory schools. Those students expressed concerns not about their intelligence or innate abilities, but about the gap in their academic preparation, as they faced considerably more academic work, more challenging assignments, more classroom discussions, and expectations to think at a deeper level than they had faced in their high schools.

Discussion

In many ways the students in this study were unusual. They had undergone a highly selective admission process and won a place at a top liberal arts college: a total of 6,284 students had applied to Amherst for a place in the Class of 2009, and only 1,175 (19%) were admitted. The affluent white students were a highly select group. As the college has purposefully sought to build a class with more students of color and lower-income students, affluent whites were competing for a small number of places in the entering class.

The odds of very low-income students making it to Amherst are very small.[29] Many students in the bottom income quartile do not even take the SAT, and if they do, they are less likely to do well on it than students from the top income quartile.[30] Most students with high financial need and limited family education, black and white, cannot overcome the multiple obstacles they face to excelling at the level necessary for acceptance to Amherst. Those who do excel are unlikely to find their way to the applicant pool of a small liberal arts college in New England that is physically far from home and foreign to their home communities, a college whose reputation as an "elitist, Northeastern, all-white, preppy school for rich kids," as Marissa, an affluent black student heard it described, is only slowly changing, a college with a sticker price that is greater than their family's annual income.[31] Most very low income students, black and white, lack the savvy to understand that they could graduate from Amherst with no debt. And finally, those who do make their way into the applicant pool and are accepted to the college may well choose to go elsewhere, as they are highly sought after by other elite colleges and universities, many with larger numbers of black and lower-income students, many in more familiar urban settings. But some very low income students did make their way into the entering class and into the study, and they make up a portion of the lower-income groups.

While the students in this study were different in many ways from the average college student, the race and class issues that they encountered on campus during their first year were not unlike those being played out in society at large. Students, black and white, affluent and lower-income, had to decide whether to self-segregate into groups with people similar to themselves or negotiate ways to get along with a diverse group of students and take advantage of opportunities to learn from one another. They represented a microcosm of our society, and thus their experiences generalize beyond the specific students involved.

This study cannot answer every question. The sample size was small—too small, for example, to determine with clarity the role that gender may have played in interaction with race and class in determining students' experiences. The focus of the study was students' experiences with race and class over the year. Although the interviews covered much ground, all aspects of students' experiences were not probed. Further, the data were based on self-reports, whether in face-to-face interviews or on-line surveys. Many aspects of students' experiences can *only* be assessed through self-report, but pressure exists in an interview setting to present oneself in a socially desirable manner, and these biases may be present. With these cautions in mind, we turn to the findings of the study.

3

First Encounters with Race
and Class

perspective? beginning of frosh year.

Students came to campus with differing experiences, attitudes, hopes, and fears based on their race and class backgrounds. Students who were black, lower-income, or both were joining a predominantly white affluent community and had different concerns from affluent white students, who were joining a community where the majority of students would be similar to themselves. To what extent were differences in social class and race on the minds of students in the first weeks? What role did students think class and race would play in the journey ahead?

Social Class

Students' Possessions

Students first gained awareness of the class differences among them not through knowledge of the educational attainment, occupation, or income of their classmates' parents, which were not known or visible to them, but through differences in the material possessions students brought with them to campus. Amherst College has made great strides in being attentive to students with high financial need as they move to campus. Students with the greatest financial need received a $400 start-up grant the first week of classes to help with purchases like winter clothing and room furnishings.[1] At first glance this is an extremely generous amount of money, but for students who did not have much to begin with, it buys only the essentials. These efforts have gone a long way toward helping students according to their need, but considerable variance is still apparent in what students bought for or brought to campus.

Matthew, an affluent white student, had this to say about what he purchased for college:

> I bought a whole room worth of stuff. Bedding. I already had a computer. I bought a TV, clothes. . . . I already bought a lot of that because [I went to prep school]. A laptop. I think a lot of kids don't have laptops because when you're home, what do you need it for? What else? An iPod. I don't know, not freshmen here, but some kids buy a car. I already had one. That's all I can think of.

Here's what Robert, a lower-income white student, had to say:

> I only had two bags in the airplane. All I brought was a bag with as much clothes as I could bring and a bag of my [athletic] gear with my shoes and random stuff like that. When I got down here, I dropped about $400 at Wal-Mart. I had to buy bedding and lamps and rugs and things that I didn't even really think about until I got down here. My first night I was sleeping on the mattress with one little sheet, and it was so hot and I was really uncomfortable, and that first night was actually pretty tough. I was just like, this sucks. I felt like I was almost in a jail cell, just plain white walls, empty shelves. And it was money that I hadn't really budgeted for going out and spending. But you know, I'm going to be here four years, so I went out and made it more homey. I bought a TV. I shouldn't have bought a TV, but I did.

The families of students in this study varied greatly in economic capital, which was reflected in students' possessions, in what they already had and what they needed to purchase for college, and in the strain the new purchases placed on families. The physical possessions that the 58 students in this study reported bringing to campus ranged widely in quantity and quality, from sofas and flat-screen TVs to dental floss and pens, from Ralph Lauren polo shirts to Wal-Mart tees. Possessions are indicators, sometimes inaccurate, of socioeconomic class; as such, for some students they came with layers of feelings attached, and for others, especially those for whom a budget was never an issue, with little thought at all.

Personal computers today are considered by students to be a necessity, and on the high end of outlays. All the participants in this study, with the exception of one lower-income white female, brought a computer with them.

For 70% of students the computer was newly purchased.[2] All but one of the affluent students brought laptops, the more expensive and preferred option, while a quarter of the lower-income students brought a desktop computer.

As indicated by the lower-income student quoted above, the costs incurred for purchases necessary for moving to campus were more extensive than many lower-income students had anticipated. Hiking and camping in the woods during an orientation trip, a new experience for some, gave two students a reason to invest in hiking boots. For Amy, a lower-income white, winter clothing was a new expense. "I had to buy a lot because I didn't have any. I had never bought a coat before and sweaters and stuff like that." She was not alone—a number of lower-income students from southern regions spoke of that expense. Extra-long mattresses are standard at the college, and that meant new bedding for four out of five students.[3] The family-shared hair dryer, the curling iron or printer that could not be wrested from other family members, had to be substituted for. More clothes were needed because at home the family's laundry was done several times a week, while at the college doing laundry entailed time and money that could not be spared. Many items that went unnoted by more affluent peers were listed by lower-income students among the things they purchased or brought to college: normal school supplies (pens, paper, and binders), towels, toothbrushes, mouthwash, deodorant, floss, a shoe rack, hangers, lamps, storage bins. Most of the lower-income students spoke of bringing "only the necessities," "just simple things to make it feel a little more like home," "nothing too fancy."

From winter clothing to bedding to storage bins, the price tags can add up, as can the financial strain on families. One theme that ran through the comments made by students with high financial need was their expense and the sacrifice that went into buying them: "it was money that I hadn't really budgeted for going out and spending"; "I know I bought so many things and some were so expensive." Students drew on personal and family savings, and some students got help from more affluent relatives and/or additional grants and support from the college for start-up expenses.

Most affluent students described their purchases or things they brought to campus in a matter-of-fact manner, as nothing out of the ordinary, without reference to the expense. Some spoke of not buying or bringing "that much stuff" or not "too much." Their lists, however, included more electronics than those of lower-income peers—TVs, iPods,[4] VCRs, DVD and CD players, refrigerators, alarm clock CD players, as well as headphones and dorm furniture (stuffed chairs, folding chairs). Their lists also included lamps, rugs, a feather mattress, and floor pillows, things that made their rooms more homey and comfortable. Such items were, for lower-income students, unnecessary expenses, things that they could do without. Many of the affluent students already owned things they might need for college, so no further expense was incurred. They already had plenty of clothes, although some purchased new shoes and clothing as well, or brought lamps and furniture that could be spared from home.

One affluent white, Ashley, felt that she had indulged herself on her bedding, but she did not see her other purchases, items missing from the lists of most lower-income students, as anything out of the ordinary:

> I bought a portable computer, a laptop. I had a printer already. My bedding, I did splurge on my bedding. That is the one thing I need to have be really nice. I don't even know what it is. The softest sheets ever, and then a duvet and down comforter. It's lovely to sleep on. It's one place where I can definitely relax. What else did I buy? I did go shopping. I got a couple of pairs of jeans. I went to the outlet mall and bought some polo shirts and sweaters and socks, but nothing huge other than clothes. I didn't really bring that much. . . . I got those speakers you can put your iPod in so then you have noise so you don't have to put the headphones on all the time. I had the iPod already. I bought a pair of running shoes for college so I could exercise a lot. I went shopping a lot.

A few affluent students were self-conscious about what they had purchased, and were quick to point out that they bought the laptop "on sale" or got a printer "free" with the computer, or that the mini-fridge was bought "used for maybe $30," and a few pointed out that they had used savings from summer employment for some purchases like the fridge and TV, or to help pay for their new computers. In only one case did an affluent student see her purchases and what she brought to campus as something out of the ordinary. "I would say that I got a lot more stuff than other people got to come here. We kind of just went crazy. But it doesn't matter. Part of it was just being excited about coming to school, really excited. People kept bringing stuff for me" (Marissa, an affluent black student). The tendency to minimize money spent on purchases for college may come from different sources. Some affluent students were conscious of their privilege and wanted to downplay their differences from students who had less. While the parents of some affluent students paid for all their start-up expenses and were eager to set their children up in comfort at college, the parents of other affluent students expected their children to contribute to their living expenses, and these students, like their less affluent peers, knew how to cut corners and get desired items on sale or at a discount on-line.

Lower-income students did not fail to notice the extensive and expensive possessions of their more affluent classmates. Moving in was one of the moments when the enormous disparities in wealth between students were the most salient. Robert, a lower-income white, commented on seeing "people here with more money than I've ever imagined." Moving into the dorms, lower-income students were very attentive to "everybody's stuff and the way they put their rooms [together], and their parents and their parents' cars, and they have everything from before Amherst" (Linda, lower-income white). Lower-income students spoke of things large and small that their affluent counterparts possessed. Alisa, a lower-income black, noticed

> the type of things they have in their room, how it's accessorized, like flat-screen TVs, or really nice radios, and stuff like that. I have a friend who has this roommate who's sort of rich and she has all this stuff, maybe it's a laptop and this really big makeup case and all these fluffy things, all this furniture and stuff, and pillows. You can notice because they'll have a TV and a VCR and all that kind of stuff.

Nicole, a lower-income white, commented: "Everyone here has an iPod. I definitely don't have one of those." Other students had "just little things that would be nice to have but you can definitely live well without."

Other Markers of Social Class

Clothes and Appearance

Social class was made salient for many students not only by the possessions students had in their rooms, but also through their clothing, jewelry, and accessories. Affluent students readily identified clothes, either in their own wardrobes or those of affluent peers, that would mark them as affluent or "preppy." Colored polo shirts and khaki shorts and pants were the preppy attire for males. Name brands were a sign of affluence. For affluent females, Tiffany jewelry, pearl necklaces, designer labels, and coordinated outfits signaled wealth.

From another class perspective, over half the lower-income whites, female and male, were aware that their clothes marked them as different from their wealthier peers. "When you're meeting people for the first time, the first input is what someone's wearing, and where they bought it, and is it recent," said Larry, a lower-income white. Lower-income students were aware, as they put it, that they didn't own "$180 jeans," name-brand clothing, "$50 polo shirts," the "coordinating outfits," or "different accessories." They spoke of buying clothes on sale. Lower-income females were also aware that they did not have the same *amount* of clothes. "You go into another girl's room and you see the piles of shoes and clothes. And everything I own [fits] in a trash bag" (Emily, lower-income white). Kayla, another lower-income white, talked of "seeing people that came with more clothes than I've ever owned in my lifetime. And OK, one closet's enough for me, and someone on our floor has their closet and their roommate's closet."

Cultural Capital

Beyond the differences in economic capital manifested in possessions, some of the white students with high financial need, particularly those from public schools and with limited family education, became aware of their class difference through their lack of cultural capital compared with other students. "Cultural capital," a term originally developed by Pierre Bourdieu and Jean-Claude Passeron,[5] has come to assume many meanings: knowledge of highbrow aesthetic culture (e.g., the opera, classical music); educational attainment and credentials; personal style (e.g., ease, distinction, confidence), tastes, preferences, and linguistic aptitude.[6] Groups with higher social status unconsciously send signals that distinguish them from those of lower social status. Heather, a lower-income white, worried about her speech: "I'm not the most eloquent person. I just trail off." Another lower-income white, Emily, noted that she hadn't had the same kinds of experiences as more affluent peers:

> I've noticed a lot of people here are very well-traveled, you know, "When I was in Europe last summer, we did this." I'm just like, wow! . . . I haven't really done very much, and so it kind of makes me feel very uncultured because I haven't gone to see Broadway plays, or gone to this or that, or traveled around or anything. . . . I think in my interactions with people, I'm always very conscious of how am I fitting into this, and what do they think of me? I always wonder if people know that I differ from them.

A third lower-income white, Nicole, reflected on the cultural chasm:

> The first week we were here, I was sitting around and talking to a bunch of people I'd met, becoming friends, and we were just discussing things, and none of them could believe I'd never been out of the United States. Traveling-wise, they were talking about going to Europe and here and there, and it's one of those things that my family and I would have loved to do, but can never actually afford.

Initial Expectations

One might imagine that the lower-income students would be much more concerned than the affluent students, who made up the majority, about the role class would play in the year ahead. Indeed, the numbers bear out the assumption for the affluent students: most thought class would not make a difference socially (57% of blacks, 64% of whites). But for the lower-income students, the situation turned out to be less straightforward. The vast majority (80%) of lower-income whites *did* have some worries that class would make a difference, but *many* fewer lower-income blacks (only a third) showed this concern.[7] Most of the lower-income whites had never been around wealthy people, whereas the majority of lower-income blacks had attended private schools with very affluent peers. Close to a third of the lower-income whites reported having thought about social class "a lot" in the early weeks, twice the percentage of any other group.[8]

Many lower-income whites worried about whether they would be able to form friendships with their more affluent peers, though they struggled to minimize these feelings. Heather, a lower-income white, felt that sometimes "it's harder to connect with people where there's this gigantic social gap and different worlds. Sometimes it's a learning experience but sometimes it's so hard to relate and talk to them, where you don't know how to feel." Another lower-income white, Kayla, felt a distance from wealthy students whom she perceived as having values, attitudes, and outlooks different from her own. "I find that I'm not really friends with people that wear really expensive polo shirts, but our ideals are generally different." A third lower-income white, Emily, also sought out friends more like herself:

> You tend to relate to people and can instantly connect with people who have had similar difficulties, or can understand where you're coming from. You tend to gravitate toward people who feel the same way about things as you. And so I think it will play out that way. But it doesn't mean that that's always going to be the case. My roommate and I are very different, economically speaking. And we get along great. I generally don't think it's going to be a drawing a line in the sand, I'm standing here and I'm only going to associate with other people who are on this side. But I just think it naturally figures itself out that way.

A few lower-income whites worried that they might be excluded from activities because they lacked the funds to buy a ticket to a concert or a movie or go out to eat. They were concerned that more affluent peers might not understand that they were totally self-reliant and did not have unlimited spending money. "If somebody's saying, 'Hey, let's go on a cruise to the Bahamas!' I would be, 'You know, I can't afford a cruise to the Bahamas'" (Marie, lower-income white).

Many of the concerns raised by lower-income whites were shared by lower-income blacks, but by a much smaller percentage of that group. Like their white lower-income counterparts, some lower-income blacks felt that it would be hard not to be able to go out to eat or go on trips during spring break with affluent peers. Angela, a lower-income black, expected that she would primarily form friendships with "people who are more similar to myself in some respects." Another lower-income black, Brandon, wished it were easier to identify others of the same social class: "If there was some sort of meeting or something with people on a lot of financial aid or something like that, I would welcome it. 'Cause [there are] other people who are in the same situation as I am."

A few lower-income students, black and white, thought that social class would affect their choice of romantic partners, and that they would probably choose to date people of the same social class. "I'm not sure if I would be as comfortable going home to visit parents or whatever of someone who was really wealthy or if they would be comfortable coming home to my area" (Marie, lower-income white). Corey, a lower-income black, said, "Maybe if I were from a higher class, then maybe it would make girls more willing to date me." No affluent students thought social class would make a difference in choosing romantic partners.

Optimism about Class Differences

In the first weeks on campus, class differences were not highly salient for the majority of the affluent students, white or black, in the way that they were for lower-income students. Most affluent students were optimistic that social class would not make a difference socially. In interview after interview these students reported: "I don't think [social class] should make a difference"; "I don't think that social class has had any effect on the people I know or am friends with or the people I've met." They spoke of all students being "in same boat," taking the same classes, being members of the same teams. "For the most part people are either oblivious enough of their peers' background so that doesn't make a difference, or they're sensitive enough to any disparity that it won't make a difference. So I can't imagine that it will affect much" (Benjamin, affluent white). Class differences were seen as "not really a big deal. I don't really pay attention to it. Everybody's here, so [we're all] on level ground. Nobody's better than another person here . . . we're all starting off fresh" (Julian, affluent black). Affluent students who saw everyone as being "in the same boat," who saw class as "not a big deal," or who were "oblivious" of peers' backgrounds showed little cognizance that many of their peers did not share their advantages.[9]

The majority of lower-income blacks shared this sense of optimism as well. Marc, a lower-income black, did not sense "a divide," and Alicia, another lower-income black, reported that "people pretty much just mingle." The majority of students in this group had attended private high schools. They found that some of the cues about social class present in their high schools were missing at college. "You don't have to buy anything here. Your meal plans are taken care of. . . . I don't think it's noticeable compared to when I was back home and someone invites me over to their house and I'm just like, wow! We all live in dorms. You don't really know" (Brandi, lower-income black). Just a few weeks into the semester, a few lower-income black students commented that social class was already less on their minds.

Some lower-income black students who had felt marginalized by their classmates at private high schools were optimistic that they might now become part of the group. Trina, a lower-income black who had attended an elite private school for four years, thought she knew what Amherst was going to be like. She expected some people to be self-absorbed and rich, but was taken aback at Amherst when students

> made fun of students whose parents came back to buy all their books with credit cards. . . . It's weird that they're making fun of the rich people 'cause at my high school, there were people making fun of the poor people. So I think that having to go and buy my own books made me [feel] included in complaining about how much it cost.

Trina was struck by the comment of the dean of admission during orientation that over 50% of the students in the first-year class were on financial aid:

> That was so surprising to me. I thought it was like in my private school [where] everybody could pay the whole tuition, which is $27,000 a year, and then there were like four black kids who couldn't, so it made you stand out, especially because socioeconomics was sort of coupled with racial distinctions.

Hearing that welcoming address by the dean, this student finally "felt like a part of the group."

For a few lower-income white students, as well, their initial experience on campus brought a sense of relief because it was better than their expectation. Marie, a lower-income white, expressed surprise at "how much [social class] doesn't matter." Rebecca, another lower-income white, found: "Everyone here is open-minded. Maybe you could tell that somebody has more expensive things than another person, but nobody discriminates on that basis." In fact, the very few students who actually felt put down, dismissed, or discriminated against based on social class or judged by class stereotypes were more likely to be affluent, a topic that will be discussed in later chapters.[10]

Jeremy, a lower-income white, had worried about meeting so many students who had attended private schools. But he discovered:

> So far it hasn't been bad at all. It's been nice, being around people like that. . . . Everyone here is on equal footing. I don't think there are

kids who are flying out on the weekends to go to exotic islands or anything like that. I'm not going to be able to do that. Everyone here just hangs out. I feel like I have enough money where it's not a big deal if I want to order a pizza or something like that. I'm not really limited in that way. I don't think socially it's going to be an issue.

After the initial salience of social class while moving in and settling in, many students were finding class to play less of a role on campus than they had feared.

An additional reason for optimism that class would not play a large role on campus was that many students actually found it difficult to discern what social class a peer belonged to. Students used possessions, discretionary income, and clothes as markers of social class, but many realized that these markers were imperfect. Brianna, a lower-income black, had an affluent relative who spent a lot of money buying her "clothing, shoes, new bed sheets, bedspreads, towels. She pretty much bought everything I have in my dorm. A lot of people saw that I had all this new stuff, and they were like, 'Oh, you must have a lot of money.'" Similarly, the room furnishings of Carl, a lower-income black, included his laptop, new bedding, fridge, TV, and leather chair, giving the appearance of greater wealth.

Brianna said she had received "scholarships in excess so I don't have to work." This gave other students the impression that she must have money. She felt that her speech also disguised her class background. "I've actually been told that I speak really properly, and usually African Americans of lower class don't speak that way, so, yeah, that's why [my social class is] also not apparent at times." Students assumed that she must be middle class because she didn't use slang. She went on to say, "I decide which class I'm going to be in rather than where my parents came from."

The parents of some affluent students were not putting money into their bank accounts; their spending money was money they had earned, and they did not have a great deal to spend. These students were often assumed to come from families with less wealth than they actually had. They could not spend $30 a week on food, eating out or ordering in as some students did. On the other hand, some lower-income students were spending more money on food than a number of their more affluent peers.

Students could readily identify the clothes and accessories worn by preppy or wealthy students, but four out of seven students in the study felt that class could be disguised and was not necessarily expressed in self-presentation by clothes, accessories, speech, or behavior.[11] Ashley, an affluent white, was struck "that over half of our class is on financial aid, which I think is really cool, but it's really interesting because I have no idea who is who. I can't tell. . . . It's kind of disguised."

Some affluent students owned designer clothes or expensive jewelry, but many did not, or rarely wore them. When affluent students dressed down, their social class position was often not apparent. Devon, an affluent black, commented, "I don't really wear a lot of expensive things. Somebody would assume that I'm not upper class, but you can't really tell from the way I dress because it's just average." Sarah, an affluent white, reported, "I shop a lot in thrift stores, and a lot of my friends give me their Goodwill donations. They are like, 'Here, you would like this.'" She considered her dress *not* to be "normal" for her social class. Similarly, Geoffrey, an affluent white, said:

My parents always yell at me because I don't own any clothes. My hairstyle is messy. My clothes are mostly are just t-shirt, and shorts, and jeans, and most of my t-shirts are things that I've gotten from playing basketball in high school or from sports teams or whatnot. I'm not someone who's like, "I better go to, like, Polo and buy $50 shirts." I only have four pairs of pants.

Many lower-income students also felt class could be hard to determine based on their clothing. Two lower-income black males spoke of dressing in different styles on different days, so, as Anthony put it, "One day you might think I have a lot of money, and one day you might think I had no money." Robert, a lower-income white, noted:

You see some kids wearing little things that you can tell are pretty expensive, but . . . you really can't tell, especially how people dress because some people make a little money and all they spend it on is how they look and their appearance.

Indeed, Rebecca, a lower-income white, spoke of loving to shop, "to dress nice and have nice things. . . . I like to buy things that are on sale or at outlet stores, and knock-offs and things like that." She bought "fairly inexpensive pieces" of Tiffany jewelry, which might lead some to think she was from a higher social class.

Class was also difficult to discern for some lower-income students who had no previous exposure to wealth and were unable to recognize designer labels that might be cues. It came as a total surprise when it was pointed out to one lower-income white, Emily, that another girl was wearing a $300 pair of Prada shoes. She had assumed the shoes must have cost $20. From the perspective of Angela, a lower-income black, "People kind of look the same. Even though [another student] might be wearing a pair of Abercrombie and Fitch jeans and I'm wearing JC Penney, it looks the same, so I don't think we're looking at each other like, 'I bet those jeans cost $10.'" Some students were attuned to differences in the quality of jeans, t-shirts, or sweatshirts; others were not.

Race

Just as social class was more on the minds of lower-income students in the early weeks on campus, race was much more salient to incoming black students, a small minority on campus, than to their white peers who made up the vast majority.[12] Blacks and whites grow up with very different experiences with race. It is not unusual in our society for whites to grow up with little awareness of themselves in racial terms and to feel that race has little personal psychological significance for them.[13] Only half the white students in the study had thought about race or racial issues before coming to college.[14] Many seemed unaware of the advantages that had accrued to them because of their race.[15] By contrast, race was something almost every black student in the study had thought about before college. Blacks in the study were twice as likely as whites to feel that race had an impact on their lives (86% versus 42%).[16]

Blacks in our society face negative stereotyping, prejudice, and discrimination, either as major life events, minor events, or the "daily hassles" that occur most frequently, and black students in the study were no exception.[17] Some black students spoke of having been the victims of racial stereotyping, racial profiling, and racial prejudice. Other blacks, however, reported that race had had little impact on their lives and things they had done, that they had not faced racial struggles. For blacks whose previous interactions with whites had been positive, making their way in this predominantly white college world was not a major concern. But blacks who brought past histories of discrimination and marginalization by whites were more apprehensive about the kind of reception they might get.

Social Advantages

In the first weeks on campus, the majority of black students found their race to have advantages socially. Over 80% of blacks felt that race had opened up social opportunities for them or allowed them to be included.[18] In stark contrast, only 4% of whites perceived their race as providing any social advantages. While race conferred distinct advantages on whites in terms of social integration on campus, they showed little awareness of this privilege. Some black students, who had made up a small minority in their high school classes, were keenly interested in determining how many black students would be entering the class with them and were eager to make an initial connection with other black students. Over the summer they checked out their classmates on Facebook, a popular on-line directory on which students can create profiles with photos and personal information, exchange messages, and join groups of friends:

> I was on Facebook every day to see how many brown people joined. But not because I'm not open to meeting people who aren't brown. I think that sometimes you want to meet people that you have a cultural affinity with, not only black people but Caribbean people. I was afraid that I was going to be the only person who was brown who wasn't from these 50 states. (Trina, lower-income black)

Once on campus, blacks easily recognized each other. This put them in a very different position from lower-income whites, who could not easily recognize other students who might be in the same position as themselves. The majority of lower-income black students spoke with enthusiasm about their experiences in the first weeks on campus, forming connections with other black students.[19] Brandon, a lower-income black, said in the fall, "It's just like a magnet, when you see [other black students], you just assume a friendship 'cause they're in the same boat." "Whenever I'm walking around campus or anything, it always seems like some of the other black students will say 'Hi' or whatever" (Marc, lower-income black). As Brandi, a lower-income black, put it:

> I feel like black people seek out each other. You get here and you're like, "Oh look, there's another black person." I've had juniors come up to me and they were like, "We were so disappointed last year because there were only 10 black people that checked the box, but this year 50 of you guys checked the box and we're so happy to have you here, 'cause we need more diversity. . . . Before I even came here I contacted some people and they were just like, "Yeah, all the black people know each other. That's just the way it is."

Many blacks, both lower-income and affluent, felt an identification and ease of connection and communication with other blacks. "I always felt that it was kind of easier to initiate a conversation with other black students because there are so few of us. We're all looking for each other or are aware that each other is out there" (Greg, lower-income black). Dana, a lower-income black, felt more comfortable approaching students with whom "I might have something in common, and I guess that starts toward black people. It's pretty more obvious that oh, we're both black, maybe she's also nervous about coming to a mostly white school." Corey, a lower-income black, felt, "Other African Americans, it sounds bad, but they're probably more willing to accept me in their little clique or whatever than another student." An affluent black, Devon, said, "Certain people from the minority tend to just gravitate toward each other, especially if you're from the same part of the country or wherever you're from. You just want to be able to relate to somebody." Another affluent black, Whitney, spoke of the greater ease of communication she felt with blacks: "Honestly I've had more time with black people, so you can just sit down and talk to them about more." William, an affluent black, noted, too: "Black people try to be more friendly with black people. So I've met friends just based on my race." While this immediate connection was the experience for many black students, not all black students on campus were reaching out to one another in this manner. Some black students felt a greater affinity with students who were white or members of other racial groups, as will be discussed below and in chapters ahead.

Some blacks talked of an advantage in meeting juniors and seniors, since a group of black upperclassmen reached out in the early weeks to incoming black students and looked out for them. "Some of the black upperclassmen want to make sure we feel comfortable here, so they say 'Hi' or whatever when we pass them, and we're like, 'Come visit me' or whatever, and we talk" (Devon, affluent black). Trina, a lower-income black, also found black upperclassmen to be "very open to including. They're very excited that there are a lot of new black kids at Amherst. A lot of the kids on my floor don't know upperclassmen, but I know [black] upperclassmen 'cause they Facebook me and they talk to me in the hallways and stuff like that because they're like, 'Oh, she's black and she's at Amherst!'"

Some black students came to campus with social connections to other blacks on campus, making their entry to college much easier. One lower-income black in the study arrived on campus with a group of friends she had known ever since they were 10 years old. They had been participants in Prep for Prep, a program that gives scholarships to New York City students identified as having strong academic ability, enabling them to attend day schools and boarding schools.

Concerns about Race

Blacks' Concerns

Blacks were much more likely than whites to think race might make a difference to the year ahead. Over 70% of blacks felt that race would make a difference for them socially on campus, almost twice the percentage found for whites.[20] Four black students (two affluent, two lower-income) worried about encountering racism. One lower-income black, Corey, said, "There might be an instance where I get stereotyped there. I mean someone might have the wrong perception of black people, and they might take that out on me for some reason." Kevin, an affluent black, thought, "Some people might be turned away from making friends of a different color. I don't know how people think, but I would hope it is not a factor, but life shows that there are people that still think that." Another affluent black, Christopher, worried: "There are kids up here who are WASPy or a little racist, but I haven't experienced that at all. . . . But it's still freshman year, and true colors don't come out until second semester."

Just over a quarter of black students (three lower-income, five affluent) raised concerns about expectations to hang out with other black students: "I think there is pressure to join the ethnic group for whatever category you're in for minority students" (Kimberly, affluent black). Although she self-identified as an African American, Brianna, a lower-income black, reported, "I'm supposed to represent my whole race. If you represent your whole race, you should be affiliated with the black group on campus. But I'm more interested in Hispanic culture than black culture, so I think [joining a cultural group] should be based on my interests, not my race. . . . There's an expectation for me to join the BSU [Black Student Union] simply because I'm black." Andrea, an affluent black, expressed similar feelings: "I'm still probably going to encounter people who think that just because I'm black I have to be part of a specific group." William, also affluent, was "not really striving" to be part of the black group but felt "self-conscious that they're potentially wondering why I'm not."

A quarter of the black students (four lower-income, three affluent) felt that race would affect their choice of romantic partners, either because of the norms of the communities they came from or the expectations of family members. Some felt expectations or pressures to date other blacks, but were now freer to explore other choices. Angela, a lower-income black from the South, said that at home "dating someone outside of your race was really obvious and you'd get stared at and it was really awkward and uncomfortable. Here it might be different, but I don't know." Trina, also lower-income, said, "I can't see myself dating somebody who wasn't black, not necessarily because there's something inherently wrong with dating somebody who's white. It's just that I can't see myself doing it." Some black females talked of family pressures. "It'd probably just be easier for me to date someone from my race than someone not from my race, because that's just the way family is" (Talia, affluent black). Another affluent student, Megan, reported, "A lot of it for me is just that my parents are so hardcore 'Find a nice black guy,' like the same way Jewish mothers are 'Find a nice Jewish boy.'" However, she was not interested in restricting herself to dating blacks.

Whites' Concerns
Unlike blacks, who had considerable contact with whites before arriving on campus, many whites, particularly lower-income ones, had little if any previous interaction with blacks. Inter-group anxiety is heightened when

members of two groups have had minimal contact with one another, as they have no established norms by which to conduct inter-group relations and lack knowledge about the values or norms of the other group.[21] Psychologists Walter Stephan and Cookie Stephan write that in such situations people "may fear making mistakes, being misunderstood, or being rejected. They may also experience uncertainty, confusion, and stress during interaction."[22]

Many lower-income white students who had little exposure to blacks in their high schools and home communities felt initial difficulties making connections to black students on campus. A particularly poignant statement came from Emily, a lower-income white from a rural area of a conservative state. She was not used to socializing with students "who are different just because I'm from an area where no one is different. I do feel like everyone is equal, but it's hard for me to not treat people differently." She veered away from situations that made her uncomfortable, avoiding the integrated tables in the dining hall. She had to be on guard to make sure she didn't say something inappropriate:

> I'd say socially I kind of feel like I've been dropped on Mars or something. It's so different and people from my area are very behind in the times. I've grown up with things that probably are very politically incorrect. Just the way people refer to other people, like "nigger" and those things are very prominent. When you're not around other people, you don't have to accept them. When you're in an area where it's all white and everyone has grown up the same way, the only way you see other cultures is on TV or what other people say. So I think people tend to pick that up and use it negatively, even though they don't necessarily feel that way. It's just that they don't know anyone else to counteract the stereotype. And so for me, it's kind of like I have that in my head, and yet I really don't want to interact with people that way. To combat that is really difficult.

[handwritten margin note: what students come to campus with.]

However, she added:

> I definitely want to be very open. I want to meet people who are of different races. I mean, that's why I'm here. I want to see the diversity in action. I want to be a part of that. And I want to go out of my way to make friends who are different than me.

Whether interest in and valuation of diversity would lead Emily and other students to cross-race contact and the reduction of prejudice would be seen as the year unfolded.

Two in five whites were concerned that minority students would self-segregate, twice the percentage of black students.[23] When blacks hang out together with blacks in the dining hall, in activities or ethnic organizations, or in friendship groups, they are highly visible, creating the impression that blacks are exclusionary, which concerned whites. But no one comments or raises concerns when whites interact in all-white groups.[24] Jeremy, a lower-income white, found it "kind of disappointing" to see tables with blacks sitting together in the dining hall. He realized that he had not hung out yet with the two African American guys on his hallway, yet he was uncomfortable about approaching them "just because I'm not sure how they would feel if I did that." He went on to say:

I feel like I'm less likely to meet an African American student in a social setting because in certain ways I feel like they're kind of excluding themselves and by being in groups I don't know if it's intimidating to me as a white person to go approach a group of like African Americans.

Another lower-income white, Larry, also noticed:

The groups that I've hung out with in the dorms haven't included a lot of black people. Except with [my black friend] as the exception. That's the thing, self-exclusion and forced exclusion, I'm not sure where the line is. With Asian students and Hispanic students, I spend a lot of time with them in my own dorm and in other dorms. It just seems that the black students, they're even more separate for some reason. I'm not sure where that comes from.

Psychological research has found that when members of a stigmatized group, such as blacks, affiliate primarily or exclusively with each other, members of nonstigmatized groups (whites) may interpret these actions as exclusionary, even if that was not their intention.[25] In some cases a group of black friends sitting or hanging out together may not be open to including whites, but in other cases such a group may be totally permeable. The assumption of many whites that black groups wished to exclude them made it more difficult for them to reach out to blacks.

Despite the fact that many white students noticed blacks hanging out together on campus, whites still held that they would form friendships across race. In the first weeks on campus, only one in seven students in the study felt that race would affect their choice of friends.[26] It is striking that the numbers are so low, and this question may have elicited a socially desirable response (i.e., that race would make no difference). Many whites felt that blacks were more accessible to them when hanging out in mixed race groups, or one-on-one, than when hanging out in all-black groups. "If there was a mixed group of people, like a white kid, a black kid, and an Asian kid, I would be more likely to go hang out with that group than if it was a group of all African American kids or all Asian kids," said Jeremy, a lower-income student. Despite the existence on campus of ethnic/cultural groups such as the Black Student Union (BSU), Benjamin, an affluent white, still said, "I'm sure that I'll have many minority friends, and I do already." Others agreed: "It appears as though certain people of different races tend to come together, but the group I've been hanging out with is pretty diverse—I don't think [race] will have a huge impact" (Kaitlin, affluent white).

While most affluent whites expected to form friendships across race, a few expected that their relationships would be primarily with whites.

> Socially probably I will hang out with mostly white people. I won't be joining any black gospel choirs, not that I can sing. Most of my friends will probably end up being white, and if I was any other race, I'd probably have more friends of that race than I would now. I think people are most comfortable with other people of their own race. They don't feel like they have to think about what race they are, or how that's affecting their situation or their relationship, and that's awkward, if you want to have people of other races as your friends. Not that I don't want to have any, because I do, but that's just how it happens most easily. (Alexander, affluent white)

Whether white students reached outside their comfort zones and formed cross-race friendships over the year will be examined in Chapter 5.

Discussion

We live in a society with great race and class divides. Most people live in *Campus neighborhoods* neighborhoods surrounded by individuals of the same race and social class as themselves. A residential college is an unusual setting in that it is one of the few places in our society where people from different races and such different class backgrounds live together in the same room or as neighbors on the same dormitory hallway. Students are expected to make their way in this unusual setting and to navigate divides that many in our society never cross.

Disparities in wealth between students were particularly salient in the fall, when students arrived and moved their possessions into their rooms. Concerns about differences in possessions or cultural capital and about fitting in were heightened for lower-income whites, for whom this was the first encounter with people from a much higher social class. But all students were eager to make friends and find a place for themselves at the college, and students overall were optimistic that class need not play an important role on campus. Most felt that social class could be disguised, and that students' dress and possessions were not always accurate indicators of class. Some lower-income students found that things were better than they had feared.

We live, too, in a society with considerable tensions between blacks and whites. Blacks were coming to a college where they would be a minority, and race was much more on their minds than on the minds of white students. Some had concerns about encountering racism, about expectations to hang out with other black students, and about finding romantic partners. Being black also turned out to have social advantages at the start, as a group of black upperclassmen reached out to incoming black students, and many entering blacks reached out to one another and formed immediate connections. Many whites, particularly those who had never interacted with blacks, expressed anxiety about how to make connections, but they were eager to do so and hoped that blacks would not self-segregate.

The orientation program for these entering students did not have extensive programming that addressed issues of race and social class. Much was expected from students, yet relatively little guidance was provided to facilitate their connections. It was clear from the fall interviews that students were eager to discuss their concerns about race and class but found no forums where they could safely share their perceptions, feelings, and difficulties, and gain new perspectives to help them bridge race and class differences.

Despite the concerns some students raised about the role that race and class might play in the year ahead, race and class were not good predictors of how students were doing socially and psychologically in the first weeks of the fall semester. Data from the on-line surveys, not covered earlier in this chapter, show that students in the four groups gave similar assessments of their feelings of comfort, inclusion, and confidence in relation to peers,[27] of their social lives, and of their psychological health in the first weeks.[28] While some students were feeling more comfortable socially than others, race and class were not predictive of these differences.

Regardless of their differences, students had considerable optimism about the role social class and race would play in the year ahead. One explanation for students' ability to work around differences in race and class comes from the work of psychologists John Dovidio, Samuel Gaertner, and their colleagues. Their research has shown that when members of different groups are able to envisage themselves as members of one superordinate group, rather than as members of separate groups, they have more positive attitudes toward one another.[29] In other words, if incoming students come to see themselves less as affluent or lower-income, black or white, and more as students on a journey together at Amherst College, then attention to race and class distinctions between them may well diminish.

4

Negotiating Class Differences

S tudents came to campus from very different places on the class spectrum, and, as a consequence, faced different challenges in living and interacting on a daily basis. How did students, both affluent and lower-income, view their position on that spectrum and make sense of the differing privileges or obstacles they had faced in getting to this point? Did students with high financial need feel envy or jealousy toward peers who had been dealt a different hand than they had? Did affluent students feel guilt about their privilege? Did lower-income students see advantages to their social position? How did students handle the discrepancies in their class backgrounds in daily life on campus?

Affluent Students' Perceptions

In the fall interviews most affluent students, both black and white, were well aware of their class privilege, spoke frankly without guilt about it, were happy with what they had, and did not really want more.[1] As Julian, an affluent black, put it, "I like where I am. I don't really have any complaints in my life. Everything that I've needed I have gotten, and some things that I haven't needed I've still gotten." Almost 80% of both affluent blacks and whites referred to themselves as "fortunate" or "privileged."[2] No affluent whites—if they and their families could be born again— would choose to be born into a higher social class, and only two affluent blacks would. Some affluent students spoke of not wanting to be super-rich because they held negative stereotypes about the very wealthy, characterizing them as people who have everything, "don't really work very hard," "take everything for granted," are "wasting time and opportunity," and are "isolated from a lot of other people."

When affluent students, both black and white, talked of the benefits of their class position, they referred to the varied opportunities and experiences they had been given. One of the most universally recognized benefits was access to a superior education at a private school or a public school in a wealthy school district.[3] Some described the public schools they might have attended as being "in horrible shape"; they realized that such schools would have provided them "a much inferior education." The affluent students were used to "college level courses and writing extensively," and students who attended prep schools acquired additional skills at networking and socializing in situations such as formal dinners, as well as interacting with faculty members.

Affluent students recognized the advantages they had in the college admission process. Not needing financial aid, they did not have to limit themselves to state schools or schools offering them scholarships. Some spoke of personal SAT tutors for $150 an hour giving them "a leg up," and of taking the SAT more than once, advantages unaffordable to lower-income students. Some noted that they had received plenty of college counseling and that college admissions directors knew their high schools, thus putting them on an inside track to elite colleges.

Both blacks and whites realized that the expensive vacations their families had taken to destinations around the world were atypical, that they were "very well traveled compared to the average person," and had gone to "places that people don't go very often." Some affluent students had accompanied parents on trips for work or on vacations to South America, Africa, Europe, Asia, and Australia. Some spoke of these travels as having helped them to develop their academic interests. Marissa, an affluent black, said her trips abroad "helped me decide what I'm going to study, and it's affected even what I want to do later in life." An affluent white, Alexander, spoke of a summer trip studying subtropical ecology that "really determined what I wanted to major in [in] college. So without that experience I would be a different person."

For most affluent students, acknowledged class advantages included numerous extracurricular activities and lessons:[4] for example, sleep-away camps and summer programs, music lessons on a $5,000 instrument that "someone who came from a different class wouldn't be able to afford" (Alexander, affluent white). For one affluent black, Devon, extracurricular activities had included "figure skating, gymnastics, dance. I always got tutors if I needed it and stuff like that." "The first thing that comes to mind is the word 'training,'" noted Christopher, an affluent black, when talking about his class privilege. "You know, violin lessons, tennis lessons, tutoring, SAT tutoring—all that stuff." Many affluent students were able to work at unpaid internships during high school because they didn't have to make money over the summer. Their parents could afford to take them to plays and other cultural events, "which is all pretty lucky for me," said Benjamin, a white student.

Social capital—that is, important connections that they could call upon to better their lives—was another benefit that affluent students attributed to their social position, and they realized that their less privileged peers lacked those connections. Parents and grandparents who were in professions such as law, business, or medicine had connections students could draw upon for summer internships: "People are much more likely to take their friend's son than just some other person who has the same qualifications" (Alexander, affluent white). For Talia, an affluent black, a grandparent's prominent position in a hospital helped when her sister faced a medical emergency. "We were able to get the best doctors to work on her."

Over 90% of both affluent blacks and affluent whites spoke of themselves as positioned at the privileged end of the social class spectrum, seeing themselves in relation to those who had less.[5] But over a third of these same students also described themselves as less privileged than those at the very top of the social hierarchy, the wealthiest and most advantaged.[6] For some, thinking about themselves in relation to those who had much more than their own families had minimized the guilt they felt about their own class privilege. Students recognized objectively that they came from "an upper-class society," from the "upper middle class for most of the country." However, some lived in communities in which they saw themselves as "not particularly rich" because they were at "the lower end of the spectrum." Sarah, an affluent white, compared herself with friends whose families "had four houses around the country for every season," leaving her feeling "kind of poor." "I always thought that there were so many things I couldn't do in high school and I was always like, 'Oh, wow, everyone else can do all these things and spend all this money and I can't do that." Sarah was not alone. Julian, an affluent black from "a very good private school," felt "especially coming into the school I went to, I was just a poor kid, kind of."

Lower-Income Students' Perceptions

Feelings about Class Status

Most of the lower-income students, both black and white, saw their social class position in relation to those above *and* below them in the social class structure. Three-quarters of these students talked about what they lacked in comparison with those above them in the class structure, and just under half talked about the advantages they had compared with those below them.[7]

Lower-income blacks and whites had somewhat different feelings about their perceived social class positions. If given the chance to be born again, at the beginning of the year *twice* as many lower-income blacks as whites would wish that they and their families could be members of a higher social class (57% of blacks versus 27% of whites).[8] This may be because most of the lower-income blacks had attended private schools, where they were exposed to highly affluent peers, unlike most of the lower-income whites. The advantages of attending private schools came with a cost: heightened awareness of their class position in relation to those who had more, and a desire that they and their families could have more.[9] Martin, a lower-income black who had attended an elite private school, reflected on "having to see things that I couldn't have. That kind of angered me a little bit, just the privileges that my classmates have." Lower-income blacks saw their high school classmates' nicer cars, nicer houses, new computers, nice couches, new CDs. They were aware of things their economic position prevented them from doing: they couldn't afford to "go out to the movies every weekend" or to "take some of the trips that some of the kids took." They came to desire for themselves and their families things that their peers had. They wished they could "travel more and have a richer experience," avoid taking out student loans, make life easier for a single parent, enable a parent to "buy the house that she always wanted."

Many of the lower-income whites came from communities where "most people have the same economic status." Coming from a small farming community, Nicole, a lower-income white, said, "Most families are working middle-class families. And so I was never really exposed to people that had a great deal more money than we did." Having never been exposed to people with great wealth before coming to college, these students had not gone through high school seeing themselves as disadvantaged relative to their peers. When no one had wealth, no relative disadvantage existed: "Nobody really felt deprived or anything" (Marie, lower-income white).

Most of the lower-income white students realized that they might have had more, but expressed contentment or had made peace with what they had. When Jeremy's family moved to a new community, this lower-income white student at first was reluctant to have kids over "because all my friends had really nice houses and we didn't have as much money." But Jeremy "got over it." Once he got to high school, he reported, he "stopped caring about that kind of stuff." He realized, "It didn't matter. Kids were going to like me whether I had a huge house, or a normal kind of [house]." Jeremy went on to say that if there is an experience he wants to have or his parents want for him, that "we usually find a way to be able to do it. . . . So I don't feel like not being really rich has limited me." "Maybe things would have been a bit easier if we had a bit more money," said Heather, a lower-income white, but "everything has worked out okay so far. I don't see how it could possibly be too much better if we were in a different social class."

Most of the lower-income white students who would like to have been born into a higher social class associated affluence with better educational opportunities, private schools, or even a parent's opportunity to attend college when younger. One white student, Rebecca, spoke of "luxuries" she might have liked: "little electronic gadgets, like an iPod, or a nice car for the family and maybe me also having one, being able to pay for college without difficulty, maybe even more traveling and shopping." These were things she could see that her affluent peers at Amherst had. Students were not asked again at the end of the year if they would like to be born into a higher social class. But with their exposure to very wealthy students, it is possible that some lower-income whites, like their lower-income black peers, might by then have answered yes.

Given the great disparities in economic, cultural, and social capital among students, one might have expected lower-income students to voice more resentment, jealousy, or anger about the inequalities that surrounded them. While some of these feelings were expressed, the preponderance of lower-income students, both black and white, expressed positive feelings about who they were and what they had.[10] Contentment with class position must be understood, however, in the context of the fact that these students had much reason to feel satisfied with the way their lives had turned out. They had been given the opportunity of an Amherst education, which put them on a trajectory of upward social mobility, and a chance to move into positions of power and wealth. Many would graduate with relatively little debt, thanks to the generous financial aid policy of the college. They were the exemplars of the notion that if you work hard, you can rise in society.

Kayla, a lower-income white, voiced acceptance of her social class position, knowing that she was positioned to move up, an acceptance and understanding shared by others. "There are things I'd want, but I think even if I were the richest person I'd still want other things, so I think I have enough. I have the means to go to a really good school, so I can get a really good job, so I can get the money to travel when I want to. So I like where I am. I think it's fine." Many lower-income students liked where they were *because* they were on a trajectory that would enable them to have more in the future.

Class Advantages

Affluent students spoke of the advantages of their class positions in terms of the experiences and opportunities wealth had given them, but lower-income students spoke of advantages in terms of character traits they had acquired from their class upbringing, traits they took pride in and felt that many of their affluent peers lacked.[11] Affluent students, too, may have developed qualities they valued as part of their upbringing, but no affluent students brought them up when describing the advantages of their class position. Some lower-income students claimed a superiority in character based on their class values and spoke critically of affluent peers who took things for granted, who did not have to work for what they had, who were dependent on parents and lacked self-reliance. This is in keeping with the findings of social psychologists that people feel better about their social position if they believe one group does not have it all, that "poverty has its rewards and affluence its drawbacks."[12]

Working Hard for Things

Working hard for long hours was not the exclusive purview of the parents of lower-income students. But most of the parents of the lower-income students were employed at lower-status, lower-paying jobs that did not provide the same financial rewards for the labor put in and the hours worked as those attained by parents of the affluent. Many lower-income students identified with their parents' strong work ethic and valued the importance of hard work as the basis of getting things they wanted. It is not that affluent students on campus lacked a strong work ethic. Most affluent students were working very hard, and their outstanding academic and extracurricular accomplishments were the product of their hard work. But when comparing themselves to more affluent peers, many lower-income students saw themselves as working hard at low-paying jobs to acquire things that were simply given to more affluent students: opportunities to go on school trips, computers, cars, spending money.

Alicia, a lower-income black, contrasted her experience with that of some wealthy students around her. She described her family as "first-generation middle class, so we have a lot of working-class values like work hard." Growing up, Alicia learned that "you have to work hard for money." She had friends whose parents "give them money every week. My parents don't do that for me. They're like, 'You need to work. You need to learn that we're not just going to give you money.'" She learned "not to have to ask somebody for something." Anthony, a lower-income black, echoed similar sentiments. "I've had to work for things. I've never had everything given to me. And so I value hard work to get things that you want." He thought he might not have valued hard work as much if he "never had to have a job to get money." Seeing where her parents had come from and gotten to through hard work had inspired Brandi, a lower-income black, to believe that "hard work definitely pays off." Brandon, a lower-income black, felt that his class background helped him "learn to work harder for things, and I wouldn't want to change that."

Appreciation

Many lower-income students believed that they were more appreciative of what they had than were their affluent classmates. Some lower-income students spoke with appreciation of having the basics, things that the affluent students never mentioned and felt <u>entitled</u> to. Justin, a lower-income white, was taught "to be grateful for the things other people have done for me. I know how much better it could be and what's out there, but I also know how much worse it could be. Because I can put things in perspective, I can be grateful for what I have." He was appreciative of having "food on my table. I'm eating a meal." "We make enough, and I have all the food and all the clothes I need, so we're lucky in that regard," reported Kayla, a lower-income white. Another lower-income white, Emily, felt that many affluent peers

> don't even think about the things that they own, don't even think about how that compares with other people in the world and how they're living. And I think about that. Even though I don't have a lot, I still feel very lucky to have what I have because I know the worth of it.

Their gratitude extended beyond having "things" to include appreciation for the opportunities they had been given. Carl, a lower-income black, did not take his private school education "for granted" as he felt many of his peers did. He was "thankful" and felt "blessed" to have had that opportunity. Linda, a lower-income white, valued her Amherst education "as a gift and an opportunity," which she contrasted with the upper-class students who she felt regarded education "as something which you always get automatically." Another lower-income white, Nicole, similarly treasured the opportunity to be at Amherst because it was unexpected. "I feel it's such a big deal, me being here, because it's not the normal for where I come from and my family." Many lower-income students, black and white, spoke of their greater appreciation of the opportunity to be at Amherst College and all the benefits that came with it: the chance to study abroad, great professors, remarkable speakers coming to campus, good financial aid, a wide variety of food in the dining hall and all the food they wanted, which some students had not always had. Unlike a big state school or community college, Amherst was "a whole community as opposed to just four classes that are working towards a degree," said Angela, a lower-income black student.

Lower-income students appreciated the amount the college had invested in them, and the fact that Amherst had "taken a chance" on them. Consequently, some were determined to "do really well academically." Robert, a lower-income white, felt that if he had more money, "maybe I wouldn't take [college] as seriously." Others shared these sentiments: "This is an opportunity that a lot of people with my economic status would not have, and so it makes me want to work harder" (Emily, lower-income white). "I'm motivated to do my best, because people are investing in me" (Alisa, lower-income black).

Students from all class backgrounds had appreciation for their parents, but a separate dimension arose for the lower-income students, who expressed gratitude for the sacrifices their parents had made in their own lives to get their children to this place. They recognized how hard their parents had worked to raise them and the fact that the opportunities their parents had given them had come at a cost. Danny, a lower-income white, spoke of "some pretty serious sacrifices" his parents were making to put him through school. The contribution the college expected parents to make toward a student's tuition and fees could weigh heavily on students from middle-class families.[13] Such families find it virtually impossible to pay the full contribution, particularly if they do not have extensive savings to draw upon. These parents must cut back on expenditures or rely heavily on loans to pay their contribution. "Being here, it's just made me appreciate all that [my parents have] given me and what they've had to sacrifice to provide me with this opportunity, so I think in that way I just really have come to appreciate my parents even more than I did before" (Nicole, lower-income white). "Knowing how difficult it is for my parents to pay and knowing the sacrifice they're making, I'm going to work that much harder to make it pay off for them sending me here" (Rebecca, lower-income white). Paying for college required sacrifices for some of the affluent students as well, and these students too appreciated what their parents had given them.

This appreciation was in one respect a double-edged sword. Whereas many affluent students approached situations with a sense of entitlement, many lower-income students did not share that attitude. For some lower-income students, gratitude for all they had been given at times constrained them from feeling entitled to ask for more, be it help from professors or additional financial resources when in need.

Self-Reliance and Independence

Many lower-income students placed great value on their self-reliance and independence, traits they felt their affluent peers lacked. These character traits developed from necessity and, for some, had come at a cost. While most affluent peers had protected childhoods during which many things had been done for or given to them, some lower-income students had had to grow up more quickly and learn to rely more on themselves.

Marie, a lower-income white, felt that her class background made her "more independent, and I think that that's important. Whenever I want to take a vacation or something, I save my money to do it, and it's not just given to me. I think that's better." She was incredulous that a student would ask,

"What do I do?" when something broke: "Everybody's smart of course, but a lot of people have very little practical knowledge." Brandi, a lower-income black, was used to "handling my own money and going to the bank and balancing my books." She reported, "I'm very self-sufficient here. I don't ask my parents to send me money if they don't have to." She contrasted herself with a friend who "has the type of family where they're, 'Pick up what you want, and we'll just pay for it.'"

Lower-income students met classmates on campus who were used to being waited on and expected people to clean up after them, do their laundry, and make their beds. Martin, a lower-income black, spoke of a girl on his floor

> who is so used to having a maid who cleans up after her that she leaves her stuff everywhere on the floor. She's been known to leave stuff in our common room for weeks at a time. Her room is a mess because she just expects somebody to clean it up for her. It usually doesn't get cleaned until her parents come to campus. . . . . She's so spoiled.

Kayla, a lower-income white who was used to making her own bed and doing her own laundry, offered a similar perspective:

> There is a larger level of responsibility that I feel I have. There are people who grew up with nannies and housekeepers and had everything done for them. It surprises me when they leave stuff all over and just expect that there is going to be someone there to pick it up after them.

Some lower-income students expressed discomfort at being dependent on others for money: "I'd rather have to work all summer and then know that I have money and I can go spend money. I have been saving up so I can go abroad, and so I can travel when I'm abroad. I'd rather have to work for it than be given it" (Kayla, lower-income white). Along these same lines, accepting financial aid from the college was complicated for some students because it weakened their sense of independence:

> I just got a start-up grant from the college, and it's very nice to be just handed money. But it's something that at home, if you don't need it, if you're not starving to death, you don't take money from anybody. I mean, you don't. It's sort of hard to take that help, to take that and not see it as a handout, that is. It has a negative connotation to it. That to me is something that is hard, because it makes me feel sort of inadequate, [that] I'm not able to provide for myself. But it's also [something] that you just have to deal with and say, "OK, it's great that they

do have these programs out there and in place, and I'll take the help and hopefully some day I can return the favor to somebody else." (Emily, lower-income white)

Frugality

Because their families did not have a great deal of money, lower-income students had learned to be frugal, a value often reinforced by parents. "You don't spend money if you don't need to," said Kayla, a lower-income white. "My dad insists that I don't buy things unless I really need them," said Rebecca, also a lower-income white. "He always tells me that no matter what background we come from, even if we were extremely rich, he would still have raised me the same, to know the value of money and not to be extravagant with it."

Realizing the financial constraints their families had faced, lower-income students learned to live within their means. "My family [has] never spent money freely, so I guess I have a good sense of budgeting, and I don't feel like I need a whole lot of material things" (Peter, lower-income white). Two lower-income students spoke of learning to rein in their desires. Larry, a lower-income white, recalled his older brother approaching him when he was a child of eight or nine and telling him that money was tight and "you really shouldn't be asking Mom and Dad for this stuff." Although Larry didn't fully understand the situation at the time, and "didn't see those burdens at all and those responsibilities," he understood as he got older not to "let on that I wanted things." The experience gave him "awareness and a sensibility of living within means and being thankful for opportunities that are there." Alisa, a lower-income black, also talked about wanting things that were too expensive for her family to afford, but learning to budget and realizing that she could pass up doing things or buying things when her parents were out of work.

Comparing themselves with some of their peers at Amherst, several lower-income students spoke of their relative frugality. "I'm a lot more careful about how I spend [money]. I know a lot of people who go out to eat a lot on the weekends, and then they go to see movies, and I don't do that as much" (Dana, lower-income black). Kayla, a lower-income white student, was "dumbfounded" by what seemed to her the excessive amount of clothing some students owned. "I do see something, not wrong, but strange, spending so much money on clothing. I do laundry once a week. . . . It amazes me the number of people who can go a month or more with a completely new outfit every day, and instead of doing laundry sometimes they go and buy more clothing." Another lower-income white student, Robert, was struck by the profligacy of some students. "'Waste not, want not.' In the cafeteria, for instance, I can't imagine how much food is wasted. I see kids loading up their trays, eating a few bites, and just throw the rest out. [I'm] tighter with the things that I have."

Cross-Class Understanding

Though their relative standing at Amherst classified them as lower-income, only a small group of students in this group were poor; most were lower middle to middle class. Situated at neither end of the class spectrum, some lower-income students felt that their class background had given them the ability to connect to people above and below them in social class. Many lower-income students had parents who had worked low-wage jobs, as had they, and they believed that they had a greater identification than the affluent students did with workers on campus, with the low-income children and adolescents they tutored off campus, and, in general, with people who had less than they did. Marie, a lower-income white, thought that her class position made her "identify more with people that have problems, and worry about human rights issues." Another lower-income white, Emily, felt that she could be "compassionate" and "more understanding" of those who have less "because I've had similar instances of wanting something and not being able to have it." Brandon, a lower-income black, thought that his class position made him more sympathetic to workers on campus, like the custodians; he was upset by students who were not doing the little things the custodians asked for. Instead he saw an attitude "of just eh, whatever, just like blowing it off."

Some lower-income students felt that their class position enabled them to "relate to people all across the board" and gave them "a more balanced perspective." They had "more opportunities to see aspects of both extremes and to be able to identify with both extremes." One lower-income black, Anthony, felt that being middle class:

> I've been able to relate to a lot of different people above and below me. And so I've been able to make friends with a lot of different people because this is a pretty diverse college. . . . Kids who are of poorer backgrounds, we can talk about stuff that they would talk about and be interested in and that I would know about because of being in both situations. I can also talk to richer kids or kids of higher class because I'm in the middle. Basically I feel like I can talk to everybody and, like, relate to them.

Extended Family and Community

Some lower-income students had a strong sense of family and community growing up that they associated with their social class. Sociologist Annette Lareau, in her study of families from different class backgrounds, described children in working-class and poor families as having ready access to extended family.[14] By contrast, she found that more affluent children missed out on close kin relationships as their lives were organized around after-school activities (lessons, sports leagues, summer camps) and their parents' jobs. One lower-income white on campus, Amy, valued the fact that she had been raised by family members. "Maybe I have a higher importance placed on my family than a lot of other people do that I've met who have had nannies that raised them, and I didn't."

Limited resources can also contribute to reciprocity between members of lower-income communities, who rely more often on one another for help, in contrast to affluent families, who regularly purchase needed services. Some students from lower-income rural communities spoke of this reciprocity:

> Everybody where I'm from is pretty low-income. And it's made for more of a sense of community; neighbors will help each other out. One of my neighbors is older. And after her husband died, her house had a lot of problems and just a lot of issues. And everybody got together and helped rebuild her house and fix everything up. And then just little things. Coming home from school, there was a tree down in the middle of the road. And one of my neighbors just came up and cut it out for me. (Marie, lower-income white)

Alisa, a lower-income black, spoke of families in her community who exchanged wood or fruit from their property. This sort of reciprocity between community members was not mentioned by lower-income students from urban neighborhoods.

Hiding Class Differences

Having examined students' perceptions of their own social class positions, and some of the advantages they saw in their class upbringings, our focus shifts now to ways in which they handled the discrepancies in their class backgrounds in day-to-day interactions on campus. At times social class became salient and evoked in some students awkwardness, jealousy, shame, or guilt. But students were motivated by a desire to find common ground, which meant, on occasion, trying to downplay class differences. Three in seven students in the lower-income black and white groups spoke of times when they had desired to hide their class origins. Affluent whites were somewhat less likely to report such feelings, and affluent blacks somewhat more likely.[15] The percentages may be higher for affluent blacks than affluent whites because black students were drawn together based on racial commonalities as members of a minority on campus, and downplaying class differences facilitated affluent blacks' relationships with lower-income blacks. Many affluent whites hung out primarily with members of the same social class and thus may have felt less need to hide class backgrounds.

Affluent Students

Many negative stereotypes about the very wealthy were expressed on campus. David, an affluent white, felt that the wealthy students tried to dissociate themselves from stereotypes about the upper class and the "stigma" associated with being a wealthy white Anglo-Saxon Protestant. Marissa, an affluent black, felt that students "don't want to be known as someone whose family has a lot of money. I'm just not comfortable taking on that role. I would rather be known for something much more important and more defining." Almost 20% of affluent students, black and white, reported that they had been teased about their family's wealth.[16] Joking or teasing was used to express feelings about the privileges of the wealthy, such as access to private high schools. Such teasing about private schooling extended to lower-income students who were thought to be wealthy because they had attended these schools. "My floor-mates make jokes about crew and stuff, how I probably was rowing in high school and stuff like that, with my butler, things like that, and that I was paying full tuition to go, which is just not true," said Martin, a lower-income black.

In order to appear less wealthy and to avoid negative stereotypes of the rich, some affluent students, both black and white, chose to be indirect about their financial status. When asked by other students about class origins, "instead of saying maybe upper middle class, you just say, 'Oh, I'm middle class'" (David, affluent white). Kimberly, an affluent black, was inclined not to talk about her class position: "I don't really talk about my experience at boarding school." Julian, an affluent black, commented on his evasiveness: "There are times when I do *not* say, 'Oh, my family can do this.'" Whitney, another affluent black, would not "speak about certain issues with some people," so students would not "think that we're billionaires . . . because we're not." She felt uncomfortable talking about her family's spur-of-the-moment decision to attend her sports team family weekend, which entailed expenditures many students' families would find prohibitive.

Some affluent students who came from communities known to be highly affluent chose not to reveal the name of their home communities. Andrea, an affluent black, had a country home in an exclusive location, but started avoiding its name because students would assume, "Oh, she has a pool, and a mansion, and she lives next to some movie stars," or would label her a "big shot." Their assumption that she was "super-wealthy" was "definitely not true." Andrea had many friends on financial aid, but if asked whether she received it, she would "definitely play down the fact that I'm not on financial aid" and would say, "Not now." When asked about bringing a car to campus for sophomore year, Geoffrey, an affluent white, told his friend he was bringing "an old sedan." He did not want to reveal that the "old sedan" was his mom's old BMW, a much nicer car than his friend had.

One of the affluent black students had grown up as a member of a highly exclusive, by-invitation-only social group for affluent black parents and children, an experience that had a "positive influence" on her life. She had enjoyed the group, and it enabled her to meet people "I wouldn't have met elsewhere" and "do things I wouldn't have done." Yet this was something she wanted initially to hide because "some people have very negative associations with it and feel it's exclusive and elitist."

Some affluent students expressed feelings of "guilt" and "unfairness" in talking about the advantages that they and their families had. "Maybe sometimes I feel guilty for not having to really worry about money," reported Lauren, an affluent white. She remained quiet "when people are talking about how desperately they need money to pay for something." Hearing close friends talk about going through the financial aid procedures made Jason, an affluent black, feel "uncomfortable" and "somewhat guilty about the resources my family does have." Geoffrey, an affluent white from "a pretty wealthy background," felt "required to not be extravagant and to hide it because I feel like it is unfair that I'm more wealthy than many people I know. And I don't feel like I should have that advantage. . . . I feel bad about being more wealthy than other people."

Lower-Income Students

In contrast to the affluent students, some lower-income students wanted to hide their class origins to avoid negative stereotypes about the poor and a sense of not fitting a "perceived set of standards" based on wealth.[17] Some had feelings of inadequacy or inferiority based on their social class and worried about being judged in a negative way because of what they did not have, in contrast to affluent students who were concerned about revealing what their families did have. Emily, a lower-income white, said, "I don't feel comfortable necessarily putting my life out there to be examined. It's just different difficulties and things. If you haven't had those difficulties, maybe it's easier to present [your life]."

Some students spoke of wanting to hide class origins to avoid negative assumptions. Justin, a lower-income white on "a lot of financial aid," didn't want to share that because he didn't want people to label him as someone who "wants to pull himself up by the bootstraps, because that's not a character type that [gets] included. I feel that person can be respected, but that person is the outsider trying to come in." Alisa, a lower-income black, consciously tried to "downplay" her southern accent and stopped carrying a bag with her state's name on it facing out because another student had said that her state seemed "third world."

Lower-income students hid aspects of their class backgrounds to avoid feelings of inferiority or humiliation. Marc, a lower-income black, felt that his peers would "think of me differently if I say my family doesn't have three cars and a huge house or whatever or second house." Another lower-income black, Carl, had some very rich friends: "Inviting them to your house and you're not as rich, it can sort of be intimidating." "Sometimes I'm not ashamed of my social class," said Rebecca, a lower-income white, "but I don't say certain things that might make me feel inferior, like the fact that I don't live in a big house, I live in a townhouse, and that I don't drive expensive cars and stuff."

Some lower-income students felt embarrassed about their parents' occupations. Rebecca, a lower-income white, said, "My mom works in retail and my dad works for [a government office]." She admired them for coming to this country and being "able to set up a family and everything here." She wasn't "ashamed" of her class origins, but when she heard about "people whose parents are doctors and lawyers and investment bankers," she didn't want to say what her father's job was. Heather, a lower-income white, spoke of her father, who held a blue-collar job, and her mother, who moved between working at a low-paying retail job and unemployment:

> I don't like to share that often with people just because I'm a little ashamed of it, even though I probably shouldn't be. I've shared it sometimes with people whom I'm comfortable with mostly. And it's fine because these are my friends, and I'm close to them and I'm comfortable with them, and they're not going to judge me 'cause they've already accepted me.

In contrast to the affluent students who struggled with feelings of guilt, lower-income students struggled with "shame," a word that has appeared in several quotations above, and a feeling that many took pains to minimize or deny: "I'm a little ashamed of it even though I probably shouldn't be." "It's not about being ashamed of who I am." "It's not that I'm ashamed [of my class origins]." Feelings of shame were not restricted to lower-income students, but were evoked in Katelyn, an affluent white, when she was around much wealthier peers. Katelyn was "used to being one of the wealthier ones," but feared that very wealthy students would look down on her "because I'm not as wealthy or as well groomed."

Resentment over differences in the financial aid awards granted by the college left at least one student with a desire to hide aspects of her class background. Financial aid awards were based on estimated family resources and included "self-help" (i.e., students were required to work *or* borrow to pay for part of their educational expenses) and "gift aid" (scholarships and grants that did not require repayment). "Low-income" students received sufficient grants to graduate without any loans to repay, while "middle-income" students would graduate with debt because they received grants as well as loans, an arrangement that inspired bitterness in some students. Kayla, a white student with high financial need, felt "some amount of resentment" from other students, "like you're not struggling enough. I'm really lucky that I don't have to be in debt, and I know that." At the beginning of the year, "certain people were like, 'Wow, I'm going to be in debt for the rest of my life and you're going to graduate from college with a minimal amount if any.' I would choose not to tell everybody about [my financial situation]. It's not something they need to be aware of." In the summer of 2007 the Amherst trustees voted, beginning in 2008–2009, to eliminate loans for all students and replace them with scholarships, thus reducing the financial strain on middle-income families.

Over the course of the year, as groups of friends from different backgrounds developed deeper relationships and students established themselves as individuals, they moved toward greater openness and comfort in revealing information about their lives. Julian, an affluent black, reported, "With my closer friends, even if we're from different backgrounds, I'm definitely open with everything." Students in some friendship groups were curious about and eager to learn about the experiences of friends whose social class was very different from their own. They became close enough friends that they were able to talk openly about their varied experiences; social class no longer felt like "a big deal." Class differences were often the source of friendly joking in these relationships. Humor was a sign of affection and helped manage what might have been difficult feelings about class inequalities.

Attending to Social Class

Clearly situations arose when social class differences became salient and affected students' experiences, but by the end of the academic year, when asked, close to 60% of lower-income students and over three-quarters of affluent students reported that they rarely thought about the differences in wealth between them.[18] While class remained salient for some students, most of the time the majority of students, affluent and lower-income, reported that they did not attend to class differences. The results are particularly striking for lower-income students, as class was an issue that had greater salience for them as the year began. Jeremy, a lower-income white, thought when he arrived that class would be "a big issue" and would "play a part daily," but he discovered at the end of the year that "I never really think about it. . . . Except for the people who clearly try to show off their wealth, I don't think that people attempt to make any sign of what social class they are." Another lower-income white, Peter, thought about social class "more at first when I got here" but found that "I don't really think about it much anymore." He felt that "college is somewhat of an equalizing force" because everyone lived in a dorm room, and without seeing students' homes, class was not obvious. Class mattered less than expected to Brandi, a lower-income black:

> Here I can't tell what people's social classes are because you never have to spend money on anything. If you go to a party it's free. If you want to do something it's just free, or Amherst will just pay for you. It's never been an issue. It's very hard for me to tell who, I mean other than the way they dress or stuff they have in their room, it's hard to tell what people's social classes are. I've never felt I couldn't do something because of my social class. So I don't really think it's had an effect. To be honest, I really don't notice it at all.

Angela, a lower-income black, observed that class almost doesn't matter "because we live together and we have the same friends. You don't always know [what social class people are] unless people want you to know." If a student wore a sweatshirt and jeans, "I don't know where he's from. I feel comfortable." While some students simply saw sweatshirts and jeans, others were aware that sweatshirts and jeans could differ greatly in quality and price, and that some brands were markers of greater wealth.

Several explanations can be put forth for why social class was not salient to most students on a daily basis by the end of the year. In some cases this happened because differences were acknowledged and accepted, and students had gotten past them. In other cases social class was not salient because primary markers of class such as homes or cars were not present on campus, and most students dressed in "regular casual clothes." This made it difficult to identify the social class of a peer. Finally, concerns about social class were not prominent for some students because they had formed friendships predominantly with students of the same social class as themselves.

Same-Class Friendships

Just as many black students derived benefits from relationships with other students of the same race, many lower-income students, both white and black, derived support and understanding from relationships with students from a similar class background. They reported experiencing shared perspectives and values that put them at ease. Having a larger number of lower-income students on campus than in the past gave them the opportunity to form friendships with peers in a similar financial position. Rather than being on a solitary journey of class mobility, they had companions along the way who understood where they were coming from, the obstacles they had had to overcome and the ones that remained before them, and who also looked to affluent students as a reminder of where they were headed. While many lower-income students developed close friendships with students who were affluent, some lower-income students formed a core group of friends from a class background similar to their own.[19]

Lower-income students had shared similar experiences growing up. Corey, a lower-income black, expressed pleasure at discovering that he and his lower-income friend both had the same old inexpensive model of car. "Things like that come up. It's random too. Something will come up like we have this brand of something, like soda in my house, just something like a cheap generic brand that we both really just related to." Mutual understandings existed between lower-income students. They talked about sharing "a similar outlook on life" and similar "ways of communicating"; they felt that they were readily able to "come to a meeting of the minds." Justin, a lower-income white, said, "With my friends, I can say, 'I don't have any money,' or 'I can't spend money on this, I'm wasting too much money,' or things like that. . . . Somebody that comes from a lot of wealth wouldn't necessarily say something like that."

Friends of the same social class provided support to one another. Alisa, a lower-income black, reported that at times she turned to friends of the same class background when feeling frustrated. "You have those days, you can just go to each other and like, 'Oh my gosh, rich people. They just don't take care of anything.' We'll just complain. It's really comforting. It's not like we really feel that way the entire time. It's just sometimes you just got to get it out."

Discussion

Despite the great disparities in wealth on campus, most students from both ends of the class spectrum expressed acceptance of their class positions and felt good about what they had and who they were. The results are consistent with social science findings that people develop self-protective strategies to navigate a route to a positive identity and to provide self-worth and self-respect.[20] Lower-income students expressed relatively little resentment or jealousy about not having had benefits afforded to their more affluent peers. Rather, many spoke of advantages derived from their own class backgrounds, which they framed in terms of the character traits they had acquired through the economic struggles of their families, traits they felt that their affluent peers lacked. Many lower-income students believed that they had much to feel good about. They had made it to an elite college, which will likely bring significant upward mobility.

Situations arose in which social class became salient, but most students were able to relate to diverse peers without having class play a prominent role on a day-to-day basis. Some students tried to downplay or hide their social class to minimize their differences. Over time they became used to the exposure to class differences, and class inequalities became less of a divide. For lower-income students, downplaying class differences protected them from the injuries of class,[21] while for affluent students it avoided feelings of discomfort or guilt about their relative privilege. Some of the lower-income students were curious about and intrigued by the rich, but did not feel belittled by the differences because they did not share the same values, saw advantages to what they had, and felt that they had status on campus. Over the course of the study, students grew more comfortable and trusting of one another and were willing to be more revealing of their class backgrounds. Without this type of exposure of identity, cross-class relationships cannot lead to learning from differences.

The data speak to the importance of having a critical number of lower-income students on campus. People tend to form friendships with others similar to themselves,[22] and just as blacks derived support, comfort, and understanding from relationships with other blacks, many lower-income students developed a core group of friends from class backgrounds like their own and derived similar benefits from those relationships, a topic to be discussed in the following chapter. With a greater number of lower-income students on campus, students with high financial need were more able, should they choose, to find other students who shared their class backgrounds.

Lacking in students' reports on this first-year experience was an understanding of how the class differences between them came about and were sustained in society.[23] In comparing his parents' occupations to those of his wealthy peers, Corey, a lower-income black, struggled to make sense of the inequality but lacked a framework for analysis to help him understand the reproduction of social class.[24] He felt that people of his own social class were:

> harder workers, but at the same time, they're not really hard workers, because the people that have a lot of money have worked hard most likely somewhere along the way. [Those people] just seem to have hit it big, and then the people of my same class are working the same jobs. They don't make that huge step to gain a lot of wealth. I guess if you looked at it in terms of a company, they would be just the regular desk workers. The people with a lot of money would be the people that move up in the ranks. I just feel the people in my class don't reach that next level. They just stay at the same salary or at the same pay.

When he looked at the parents of some of the other students at the college, he saw that they were not "working at the same job, the same pay, the same rate as people of my class. I see them as accomplished." While the parents of wealthy peers had "hit the pinnacle of their job," he felt that his parents could never get there. "I think it's just too late." When asked whether he had any sense of why that might be, he said, "I don't know. I guess education might be a part of it, your family, what kind of wealth you inherit."

Other students were likely struggling with similar questions. As a group, the students in this study tended to believe in the notion that people's life outcomes rested in their own hands and that with hard work, effort, and determination they could be socially mobile. Without finding their way to academic classes or speakers that can provide them with analyses of class in America, without talks with students who had taken such courses or who had been exposed to such analyses, it will be difficult for them to develop a more sophisticated understanding of how social class differences are maintained from one generation to the next. In forming cross-class relationships, students may get to know more about the lives and experiences of students from very different backgrounds than their own, but these relationships alone will not afford them a more analytic framework for understanding social class.

5

Relationships across Race and Class

assessed at the end of frosh year.

S tudents at the college have the opportunity in the dorms, in extra-
    curricular activities, and at social events, to get to know students
    from a broad range of races and class backgrounds. But do they?
Are students able to overcome apprehensions they might have about how
to act with members of another race or social class, anxieties about how
they might be viewed and whether they might be accepted or rejected?[1]
Or do students stay within their comfort zones and self-segregate with
friends of their own race and class? The first half of this chapter will examine these questions with regard to cross-race relationships. The focus
then shifts to cross-class relationships.

Cross-Race Relationships

As part of their study of the long-term consequences of race-conscious
admissions policies at selective colleges and universities, William Bowen
and Derek Bok asked a sample of students from their study to look back
on whether they had formed cross-race friendships over their four years
of college. For purposes of comparison, students in the present study
were asked the same question, but were looking back on only a single year
of college. In Bowen and Bok's 1998 study, 56% of whites reported that
they had gotten to know well two or more black students; at Amherst
75% of white students made this claim. In Bowen and Bok's study 88% of

blacks reported that they had gotten to know well two or more white students; at Amherst 96% made this report.[2] Clearly the majority of blacks and whites were engaged in cross-race interaction.

Let's take a closer look at the data. Although most of the white students at Amherst reported getting to know two or more blacks well, the social class differences are striking. Considerably more of the lower-income whites reported getting to know two or more blacks well than affluent whites did (93% versus 54%).[3] Research has shown that adolescents most commonly form friendships with people similar to themselves in race and social class, and thus, given the preponderance of students on campus who were affluent and white, affluent white students might be expected to form friendships with others like themselves.[4] By contrast, the small number of lower-income whites on campus made it difficult for lower-income whites to surround themselves with people of the same race and class, and thus they had to reach outside of their comfort zones in connecting to classmates. Some lower-income whites reported that they more readily found similarities across race lines with students who were lower-income and who understood their struggles than they did across class lines with affluent whites. Given the small number of affluent blacks on campus, affluent whites would find it more difficult than lower-income whites to find black peers from the same social class.

Cross-Race Friendships

Another way to look at the data on cross-race connections formed by first-year students is by examining the percentage of students' close friends who were members of their own race. Cultural anthropologist Rebekah Nathan enrolled as a freshman at the university where she taught and spent a year "underground" studying undergraduate life.[5] She found that when students were asked whether they had close friends of another ethnicity, the majority said yes. The friends they named were usually from shared activities. But when Nathan asked students *first* to name their closest friends and *later* to identify the ethnicity of those friends, the findings were quite different. Five of six white students in the sample she interviewed reported that *no* members of a different race or ethnic group were among their close friends. By contrast, five of six minority students reported having one or more white friends.

In the on-line surveys, students were asked to report the number of close friends they had, and then were asked how many of those friends were of the same race. The results are similar to those reported by Nathan. Two-thirds of whites reported that their friends were of the same race, while only a third of blacks reported that their friends were the same race.[6] Social class again made an important difference in these percentages. The percentage of same-race

TABLE 5.1   PERCENTAGE OF CLOSE FRIENDS OF THE SAME RACE

LOWER-INCOME		AFFLUENT	
White	Black	White	Black
52%	43%	80%	25%

friends for affluent blacks and affluent whites was strikingly different.[7] For affluent blacks the average percentage of same-race friends was 25%, while for affluent whites it was 80%. (Friends of a different race included not only blacks and whites, but also Latinos and Asians.) For lower-income students, both black and white, on average half of their friends were of the same race (see Table 5.1).

Group averages, however, mask differences between students within the same group. For lower-income students at Amherst, both black and white, no consistent pattern applied to the percentage of same-race friends. The percentage of same-race friends for lower-income blacks ran from 0% to 100% (14% had no black friends);[8] for lower-income whites, percentages ranged from 13% to 90%. Thus, while some lower-income students surrounded themselves primarily with friends of their own race, others surrounded themselves with friends of other races.

The two affluent groups presented contrasts not only to the lower-income groups, but also to one another. Affluent whites had primarily same-race friends. Almost a third of this group had exclusively white friends.[9] Affluent blacks, on the other hand, made friends primarily with students who were *not* black, but varied greatly from one another. Close to 40% of affluent blacks reported that none of their close friends were black.[10] A third stated that over half of their close friends were black. Unlike affluent whites, who were surrounded on campus by students of the same race and class, affluent blacks were few in number. This meant that their primary friendship choices were lower-income blacks or students of other races. Some affluent blacks found it difficult to bridge class differences with lower-income blacks, as will be discussed in Chapter 8, and experienced a greater ease of connection with nonblack students.

What do these numbers tell us? Despite white students' initial fears that blacks would self-segregate, blacks could certainly not be interpreted as doing so. Only two blacks, both in the lower-income group, reported close friendships exclusively with other blacks, and two-thirds of black students had a majority of cross-race friends. In an entering class in which only 9% of the students were black, it would be relatively easy for white students not to get to know any black students well, yet the vast majority of lower-income white students and half the affluent whites did get to know black students well. If any group might be seen to be restricting their close friendships to members of the same race, it was a subgroup of affluent whites who had only white friends. Previous research has also found that self-segregation by students of color may be less typical than that by white students.[11]

It is important to note that the existence of black-white relationships does not say anything about their depth. For some students these relationships had clearly achieved depth. For example, Alisa, a lower-income black, spoke of her white friend this way: "I can tell her everything, and she pretty much tells me everything." At the other end of the spectrum, many black-white interactions were comfortable and friendly, but not deep and meaningful. As Benjamin, an affluent white, said, "There are plenty of [black] kids who I'm friendly with, but nobody who's in my inner circle."

Reaching across Racial Lines

Some black students found Amherst to be less segregated than their private high schools. They found it easier to form relationships with whites than they had expected, and were pleased not to feel excluded. A lower-income black, Carl, reported that the college was "not like other schools where black kids sit at this side and you have an Asian table on this side. . . . I think here things are a lot more blended. And you find yourself interacting with kids that are on a team with you, in a class with you, more so than you find yourself interacting with kids that are of a particular race that you share."

Many blacks spoke of being welcomed by students who were white. Julian, an affluent black, said, "I think I've always been pretty much included in whatever I've wanted to be a part of [here]. . . . I think everything is mixed very well at this school and I've never felt excluded from anything." He went on to say:

> If I was coming to lunch by myself on any given day, the people I probably sit with will be all white, and I never really feel excluded if I'm the only black person coming and sitting with them. I think everyone is pretty open, pretty nice and welcoming and everything like that, and it's not intimidating and it's not overwhelming at all, at least to me. I'm used to this from high school, being around a whole bunch of white people.

Brandi, a lower-income black, felt that race did not influence the relationships that she had formed:

> I don't go into a relationship with certain expectations [that] because I'm black [a friend is] going to treat me a certain way or because she's

white I'm going to treat her differently, or I'm going to censor myself and not say certain things. I make it a point not to make [race] influence the decisions and the relationships that I have with people.

Many whites, both affluent and lower-income, felt that blacks were accessible to them as friends. Some talked of blacks looking past race when it comes to choosing their friends, and believed that "it's really possible to interact with anyone that you want." Geoffrey, an affluent white, found it easier to connect to black students at Amherst than he had in his high school, where blacks were bussed in from a different community and kept to themselves. "They very rarely interacted with other people significantly. So I never really had real friendships with people of the black race when I was in high school. And now that I'm in college they're more around and they're actually more open, so I have more relationships."

Breaking into Black Groups

Many blacks, however, found it easier to join groups of white students than whites found it to include themselves in groups of black students. Having attended predominantly white high schools, many blacks on campus had faced the potentially uncomfortable situation of breaking into groups of white students many times. By contrast, few whites had ever been in the racial minority. Many whites felt that they could interact with blacks one-on-one, but as one affluent white, Sarah, put it: "When they're in their clique I don't know if I can really approach them." Andrew, an affluent white, said he would not feel comfortable joining a group of blacks: "I'd be concerned that somehow I was doing something that I shouldn't be." Likewise, Kayla, a lower-income white, felt that groups of blacks were perceived to "have this tie and this bond and this friendship thing going on that I wouldn't be able to intrude on." It might be hard to break into any group of friends, she said, "but when race is an added factor, it makes it even more awkward to interact with them. Individually, I have no issues." Other whites who had close friends who were black agreed that if a black friend was with a group of blacks, they wouldn't join that group because they would feel "uncomfortable," "out of place," "unwanted." Nathaniel, an affluent white, spoke about a black friend from his prep school who always sat with blacks in the dining hall. Nathaniel would stop by and say hello to his black friend but wouldn't join that all-black group for dinner. Most black students, upon seeing whites together, did not assume any special "tie" or "bond" in operation because of race, or perceive a racial agenda behind the interaction. Nor did many blacks assume that if they joined a group of whites, they were doing something they "shouldn't." But whites often assumed when groups of blacks were together that blacks did have a racial agenda and wanted to exclude them. In some situations whites' assumptions may have been correct; in other situations blacks might have been welcoming had whites taken the risk of reaching out and approaching them to find out. Thus a barrier to greater black-white interaction may come from whites' perception that blacks want to be exclusively with blacks and harbor hostility toward whites, and from the social discomfort these whites feel about reaching out to blacks to find out, and possibly facing rejection. Many whites placed the burden on blacks to explicitly invite them in, expecting black students to make the overtures rather than themselves.

Julian, an affluent black, spoke of his conscious efforts to promote integration. He would invite whites to hang out with his black friends. If close white friends had nothing to do, he would say:

> "Come over here." And they'll say, "Well, is it all black kids?" "Yes, come up anyway." I'm kind of helping my white friends know more black kids and my black friends know more white kids. I think it's because, as a black person, we always have this, like, "Go meet the white kids." White kids never have to go meet the black kids, because it's a white school, so they never really have to interact with the blacks, whereas the black person always has to interact with the white kids. So when I bring my white friends to interact with my black friends, I think that is good for them and good for me, so, therefore, life too. A lot of my white friends don't know black girls. Black girls are completely different from black men in every way.

When Larry, a lower-income white, accepted an invitation to the birthday party of a black friend where the guests were primarily black, he discovered that "it was really fun."

Valuing Diversity

Psychologists Linda Tropp and Rebecca Bianchi have found that members of minority groups are more likely to feel welcomed and accepted if they perceive that diversity is valued.[12] Indeed, diversity was valued by the majority of whites. Two-thirds of white students, regardless of social class, felt that it was important to make a close friend who was black.[13] Forming close relationships with blacks "really is important to me," said Larry, a lower-income white, "because I feel it's such a big chunk of the American population that I very admittedly don't know much about." Julian, an affluent black, sensed that whites who "haven't been around black people want to get to be around black people, and those that have been understand that we're the same as everybody else, so, I think it'll work out well." The value placed on forming cross-race relationships has important implications for the potential reduction of prejudice, which will be discussed in the following chapter, since prejudice is more likely to be reduced by inter-group contact when partici-pants place value on contact.[14]

Nearly half of black students, too, felt that it was important to form a close friendship with a student who was white.[15] Many blacks, both affluent and lower-income, talked about not wanting to hang out exclusively with black students, but rather wanting to "branch out to students of other races," to "broaden their horizons," to open themselves up to everyone and to "meet all different kinds of people." An affluent black, Marissa, said, "I don't like just hanging out with people all of any race 'cause I just don't think that's fun. I like to meet all different people, and I think sticking to your race is normally close-minded about making friends." Some black students formed their primary friendship group around other black students but were inter-ested in connecting to students of other races. They spoke of trying to "make sure I have friends of every race, because I want them to get to know about other cultures" (Alisa, lower-income black), and of "actively trying not to self-segregate" (Trina, lower-income black).

Students were not asked to describe the racial composition of their friend-ship groups, but the majority of students spontaneously described very ra-cially diverse groups of friends in the course of their interviews. These de-scriptions, however, were least likely to come from affluent white students, because many had formed friendships primarily with other whites. As some lower-income whites described their friendship groups: "My best friend is Haitian. . . . My friends are predominantly white, and one is half-Ecuadorian and one is half–Puerto Rican" (Kayla). "There's me and another white girl, a couple Hispanic girls, two Asian girls and a black guy" (Marie). "[My friends include] black kids, Asians, everybody" (Danny). This student went on to say that whereas in the past he had only interacted with blacks on sports teams, his friendships with blacks now went beyond the playing field.

Many blacks described similarly diverse groups as including, for exam-ple, "one Indian, there's two Latinos, two white, and two black" (Brianna, lower-income black); "two of us are black, one's white, and three are Asian" (Marissa, affluent black); "a white Jewish girl, a Jewish boy, African Ameri-can, Asian, Jamaican. [I] guess that's about it. Ah, Indian. So I like to be able to say that, instead of saying all my friends are all black. And these are all close friends, too" (William, affluent black).

Comfort with Blacks

For whites, many of whom had not had close relationships with blacks be-fore, their experience at college produced greater comfort with blacks. Over a quarter of the white students reported becoming more comfortable interact-ing with blacks over the course of the year.[16] Robert, a lower-income white, came to college with no previous exposure to blacks but lived on a hallway with a number of black students and grew "more comfortable over time" being around this group. "I think they know who I am a little bit more and where I'm coming from. I'm a little more accepted. . . . I feel more comfortable talking and joking around."

Emily, a lower-income white from an all-white community where stereotypes of blacks were prevalent, became "a lot more comfortable" with black students than she was at the beginning of the year. She found common ground across race and discovered:

> The blacks I have interacted with have not been that different from me. They haven't grown up in a very different culture than I have. So it's been really easy to interact with them. I think I was very open-minded when I came here, and I wanted to be open-minded about it, but I think it's broadened to the point now where I don't even think about it. I don't even think about I want to get to know people from different backgrounds. It just happens naturally.

Several affluent whites talked of having "come to appreciate black people more and be more comfortable" with them (Alexander), of feeling "more open and much less shy" around blacks (Geoffrey), and "more accepting of all the races" (Rachel).

Cross-Class Relationships

Most Americans grow up in communities with people from a similar social class background, and for some students Amherst provided the first opportunity to become well acquainted with people from a very different class background. Although the majority of the students on campus were affluent and few were poor, there were opportunities to meet students from diverse places on the class spectrum. For students like Benjamin, an affluent white, high school friends had been entirely of "a similar socioeconomic standing," yet he, like others, found that at Amherst he had "plenty of friends who come from all ranges of class backgrounds."

Many students valued the opportunity to get to know people from dissimilar class backgrounds. Almost half of the students said that they felt it was important to make a close friend of a different social class than their own, with whites valuing such relationships somewhat more than blacks (57% versus 37%).[17] While class inequalities can engender discomfort, jealousy, envy, resentment, shame, or guilt, the value placed on cross-class relationships helped some students overcome their social anxieties.

Marissa, an affluent black, found it intimidating to talk to people of a very different class background and worried that they might not want to talk

TABLE 5.2   CROSS-CLASS RELATIONSHIPS: TWO VIEWS

GOT TO KNOW WELL TWO OR MORE STUDENTS:	SAMPLE	BLACK	WHITE
From a much wealthier family	Bowen and Bok	70%	69%
	Amherst	85%	79%
From a much poorer family	Bowen and Bok	55%	53%
	Amherst	74%	66%

to her, but said that she wouldn't feel very good about herself if she limited her interactions to people of the same class. She found it "very important to reach outside of my comfort zone." From the other end of the class spectrum, Justin, a lower-income white, likewise said that in interacting with people from a very different class background: "There is discomfort, not to the extent that I would avoid it, but absolutely there is discomfort. Part of it has to do with the person and the way they deal with their background versus yours. . . . But my feeling is that you shouldn't flee from it." Another lower-income white, Emily, had felt "very apprehensive" about interacting with wealthy students and "wasn't sure if that was going to be possible. And granted, the people that I am closest to here are of a similar background. But there also are people that I've gotten close with here who are completely different. I have a friend from [a very affluent community], and [another] friend who's quite wealthy."

William Bowen and Derek Bok reported data not only on cross-race relationships, but also on whether students had gotten to know well two or more peers "from a much wealthier family" and "from a much poorer family" than their own over their four years of college.[18] Students at Amherst were asked the same questions at the end of their first year for comparison (Table 5.2). For blacks and whites in both samples, over 70% reported getting to know students from a much wealthier family than their own, but the averages were over 10% higher at Amherst. In the Bowen and Bok sample slightly over half of blacks and whites had gotten to know well two or more students from much poorer families than their own, whereas at Amherst 74% of blacks and 66% of whites had done so.

What happens to the findings when the data for black and white students are broken down by social class? Class differences were very small in the percentages of affluent and lower-income students who had gotten to know well two or more students from a much wealthier family (for affluent students, 85% of blacks and 71% of whites had; for lower-income students, 86% of blacks and 87% of whites had).[19] Because of the presence of many very wealthy students on campus, numerous students in the affluent groups got to know students from much wealthier families during the year, even though they themselves were from affluent families. The greater wealth of the affluent white group than the affluent black group decreased the likelihood that some of the affluent whites would get to know students from much wealthier families.

As might be expected, students from the affluent groups were twice as likely as students from the lower-income groups to become well acquainted with students from much poorer families than their own (96% versus 45%).[20] Few students come from poor families, and thus students in the lower-income groups had less opportunity to get to know students from much poorer families than their own, though many did. Thus, while the presence of a wide range of class backgrounds in the student body does not guarantee that students will form meaningful relationships across class lines, clearly that is happening. That it happened was a pleasant surprise for some. Dana, a lower-income black, had a friend who was "really, really rich, and it's a bit odd at times, but I was surprised we were able to become such close friends." Others shared her sentiment.

Cross-Class Friendships

By two other measures, students were crossing class boundaries in their friendships. Three-quarters of the students reported having made a close friend from a very different class background than their own, and this pattern was consistent across the four groups.[21] Further, the four groups were similar in their reports on the percentage of friends who were members of the same class as themselves, with, on average, just over half of students' friends coming from their own social class.[22]

Students within each of the four groups showed considerable variability from one another in the percentage of friendships they formed with students of the same social class. For a group of affluent students, both black and white, the majority of their friendships were primarily with students from similar class backgrounds. Two affluent blacks and two affluent whites reported that all of their friends were of the same social class as themselves, and for a quarter of the students in each of the affluent groups, three-quarters or more of their friends were from the same social class. Some affluent students found themselves gravitating toward students who had "the same freedom with spending money" (Kimberly, affluent black); students who shared "knowledge of a certain lifestyle" (Matthew, affluent white). Affluent blacks reported the highest concentration of friends of the same social class.[23]

By contrast, some students across the four groups described friendship groups as "very socioeconomically diverse," with students "from backgrounds different from mine, either far richer or far less wealthy," from "all over the class spectrum." As one lower-income white, Heather, put it, she had friends "from a much different class than I am, who've had different opportunities.

But they are still some of the best friends I've ever had and they're amazing people." A striking example was Matthew, the affluent white student who initially felt that it was important to form connections with affluent students who were more likely to be able to "help you later down the line." In his spring interview, Matthew spoke of having formed a group of friends who were very mixed in race and class; he felt that "your close friends you're friends with because you like them as people and not because you think they're going to be successful." He was still interested in meeting the students that you "just know" are "going to be real successful" but had tried "to meet as many people as I can."

Lower-income whites entered college with the least prior experience interacting with wealthy people and had initial apprehensions to overcome, but 60% of the lower-income whites reported growing more comfortable with affluent classmates over the course of the year.[24] Heather, a lower-income white, had attended a large urban public school where students were not affluent, and was uncertain whether she would be comfortable with affluent students from private schools. At the end of the year, she reported "definitely" feeling "a lot more comfortable." Jeremy, a lower-income white who said initially that he was less likely to approach students "if I saw that they were all decked out in expensive clothes," remarked in the spring, "I don't think I would feel that way anymore." Emily, a lower-income white, felt that it had taken time "just letting go of the stereotype that [affluent students were] not going to understand," but she had been able to overcome her apprehensions and get close to students who were "completely different" in social class.

Exclusion Based on Social Class

Economic and Cultural Capital

Moments arose when differences in the economic and cultural capital of students became salient and evoked feelings in lower-income students of being outside a culture shared by wealthy peers.[25] Social class was prominent, particularly for lower-income whites, when students first arrived on campus, but once the year was underway, it receded in importance in day-to-day life. Class was brought back to consciousness on particular occasions, discussed below. Many lower-income students could recount incidents in which they felt excluded based on social class, but in general they reported that these experiences were infrequent and did not define their overall experience on campus. Further, they did not feel alone on the margins, but rather part of a larger group of students who were unable to afford the activities of some students.

Many but not all students from affluent backgrounds, black and white, had more income at their disposal than their lower-income peers. From the perspective of one affluent black, William, having spending money played an important role in social life, enabling him to do group activities, go to movies, go out to dinner, order food, buy alcohol: "You need money to be able to fit in socially here." When William's funds were diminished at the end of the year, he had the experience of having to "sit out" a few things. Many lower-income students would disagree that you need money to fit in socially. The policy of the Association of Amherst Students (AAS), the student government, is to make all events it funds on campus free to students. Lower-income students considered this to be a strong equalizing force in ongoing campus life, since they could thus easily take part in campus activities. In addition, the college's financial aid package enabled lower-income students to participate in many of the opportunities other students had. Brandi, a lower-income black, spoke of a weekend religious retreat she was going to attend; although, because of work, she ended up not going, she felt she would have been included because she did not have to "come up with $30 out of pocket to register."

School breaks. Social class became prominent, and disparities in wealth manifested themselves, when many students left campus during January intersession and spring break in March. During these breaks some students with financial means took the opportunity to travel abroad with friends or family, a continuation of the lifestyle they led before coming to college. Robert, a lower-income white, spoke of a trip to the Bahamas that some students took over spring break:

> A lot of guys were like, "Yeah, my parents gave me their credit card number and I'm going to the Bahamas for a week," which would have been nice, but, again, I don't have a couple thousand dollars sitting in the bank to go to those places. That's where you notice the "have" and the "have nots" a little bit.

Lower-income students were bolstered at these moments by knowing other students who likewise could not afford these trips. As Peter, a lower-income white, put it, "Some people talk about their trips to Europe over spring break but it's not like I'm excluded from that because it's not like other people are going." Kayla, a lower-income white, spoke of a student on her floor who lived in India and had "invited everyone to come see him, and so a lot of people went and others didn't." Students had asked why she was not going, failing to consider the fact that some students "don't have thousands of dollars to go to India." She was "just going to go home" over spring break, but noted, "Me and my closest friends all feel the same way. None of us are going to India."

Exclusion from trips around breaks was not limited to lower-income students. Some affluent students could not keep up with the lifestyles of very wealthy peers. Katelyn, an affluent white, had "a couple friends who traveled around Europe over interterm," and while she would have loved to go, she knew "there's no way my parents would pay for that and I would never have considered that an option."

Travels abroad highlighted class differences and put affluent students in a difficult position. They were uncertain whether it was better not to talk about their trips, which some found to be a highlight of the year, or whether to be more open in sharing these experiences with peers who could not afford them. Sarah, an affluent white, "felt bad" about having been to Europe for spring break; it was not a big deal for her, but she realized that it probably made a lower-income friend "feel shitty." Another affluent white, Ashley, found it hard to bring up: "'Oh, where did you go over winter break?' 'Oh, I went home.' 'Where'd you go?' 'I went to like France,' or something. It's uncomfortable sometimes." A third, Benjamin, echoed these sentiments. He found it awkward when "one girl goes to her house in France and another can't afford a plane ticket [home] and winds up spending the entire break with her aunt and uncle [locally], because she can't go home." Benjamin didn't feel that affluent students were trying to "make a big deal about their circumstances," but it came up "just naturally."

Summer plans. Lacking economic capital in some cases meant that lower-income students were excluded from trips planned by affluent students for the summer. Nor could lower-income students afford to take unpaid internships that would provide not only important intellectual experiences to those that could afford them, but credentials and connections for the future. At the time this study was conducted, the college had not yet opened its Center for Community Engagement, which would provide lower-income students with funds so that they could take advantage of unpaid public service internships.

Ashley, an affluent white, noted the tensions that arose in conversations about summer plans: "Are you working or are you sitting on the beach somewhere?" Amy, a lower-income white, had wanted to join a group of friends who were doing a summer project abroad for three weeks. She couldn't afford the airfare, and "everybody else could. It ended up not happening anyway. If it had happened, I would have felt left out."

Lower-income students needed paying jobs over the summer to help pay for college and could not afford to use that money toward travel. Nicole, a lower-income white, had formed a very close group of friends. "Even over break, we'll call each other a few times because we're gone for a week. So the thought of three months at summer is killing us." Nicole found it "really hard" because her friends were planning

> to get together here and there and it's something I can't do. I'm like,
> "I'm working this summer, and so if you'd want to do it at the end, I

could probably, depending on how much I've made." But [these are] plans that I just can't work in, so it's really hard because they're all going to be together.

Such constraints were not restricted to lower-income students. Katelyn, an affluent white, felt excluded from summer plans as well because her family did not have the resources that some of her very wealthy peers had. "In conversations it will come up, things that they're planning to do this summer that I can't do. . . . There are people talking about traveling and taking fun internships, and I have to work and get paying jobs this summer."

Food and off-campus activities. Although students had already paid for a full meal plan, some chose to eat off campus or to order food into the dorms on a fairly regular basis. Kayla, a lower-income white, was amazed by students spending "so much money on the Val meal plan" and then going out "constantly":

> I can go out to eat with people sometimes, and I know there are people on campus that can't do that ever or very rarely. We go out or order food like once or twice a week, which is more than a lot of other people do, and it's significantly less than other people do.

Martin, a lower-income black, similarly felt that he was able to "go out to dinner with somebody once a month" but couldn't be "going out and ordering in every night." Another lower-income black, Greg, spoke of "a couple of times not going into town to get food, having to go to Valentine [the college dining hall] just because I didn't have extra money to spend elsewhere, where I had already paid for meals at Valentine."

In addition, a lack of economic capital at times excluded students from wealthier friends' off-campus activities. When friends said, "Let's go visit New York and go to a play," Kayla, a lower-income white, found the $70 cost of a round-trip bus ticket to New York "amazingly expensive" and chose not to go. Rebecca also noted, "If I had a friend who was gonna go out to, let's say, a concert, where a ticket costs a lot of money, I wouldn't go because it's too much. . . . There are some things that I might hold back on doing because I think they're expensive."

For lower-income students expenditures represented a choice and had to be carefully weighed. Money spent for food meant having less money to do something else. Going on a Freshman Outdoor Orientation Trip, for example, had to be "evaluated in depth" by Emily, a lower-income white:

> A lot of people would just think, "OK, a hundred dollars, that's what I'm going to do." I had to think, "OK, that hundred dollars, that's

coming from this fund which means I can't do this, and how much is that worth to me to do this."

Some very low-income students had financial aid packages that did not require them to work, but they took jobs on campus to earn spending money for food and off-campus activities. Alicia, a lower-income black, worked two jobs on campus but found it hard:

> I really don't have the money to go to the movies and go shopping and do all this stuff or go to Boston for the weekend. But sometimes I have to be, well OK, in my own head figure out, "Do I want to go to the movies or do I want to go out to eat later in the week?" blah, blah, blah, and just having to reconcile that with the fact that I'm working really hard at two jobs.

Conversations. On occasion lower-income students felt excluded from conversations because of their lack of exposure to and knowledge of the world of the wealthy. Larry, a lower-income white, spoke of being left out of conversations

> when people are sitting around a table talking about summer trips, or the private schools they went to, and talking about some of the lifestyle things like going to Cape Cod or something—that sort of stereo-typical thing. Or spending a lot of summers abroad when they were younger and things like that, or sailing or yachting or something.

Robert, a lower-income white, also felt left out of friends' conversations about yachts and summers in the Hamptons. His knowledge of the Hamptons and associated lifestyle was derived entirely from the media. But Robert went on to say, "I don't feel uncomfortable hanging out with those students at all."

Some affluent students, too, felt excluded from conversations among lower-income peers, but their exclusion was not from a world of social privilege to which they had no access. It was from a world of economic difficulties. Matthew, an affluent white, had nothing to contribute to a conversation among friends who were "talking about how, when they were young, they had to really cut corners and stuff like that, because they didn't have a lot of money. I don't really have that. I can't really participate in that conversation, and so maybe it sort of magnifies the fact or draws attention to the fact that that's my difference." Class-based conversations could lead to feelings of exclusion, but they also provided an opportunity for students to learn about aspects of another class experience that was unknown to them.

Prep school activities. Some lower-income students lacked any knowledge of prep schools or elite private schools, and had no exposure to activities that are prevalent there. Angela, a lower-income black who had attended public school, felt "a lot more isolated from the mainstream than I thought I would be . . . because I don't do a cappella, all the mainstream stuff." Some lower-income students felt excluded from sports teams, which required prior training and resources that they did not possess. Alisa, a lower-income black, had "never heard about lacrosse or a lot of sports." Justin, a lower-income white, felt that "exclusive aspects" of Amherst existed that he didn't have access to because he didn't play a sport, had not attended an east coast private school, and was not from a wealthy background; he didn't "really have the door open" to a lot of groups.

Social Capital

Unlike their lower-income counterparts, many affluent students came to college with social capital, pre-existing networks and connections to other students and their parents from schools, sports leagues, and camps that immediately inducted them into friendship circles.[26] In the first weeks on campus, Justin, a lower-income white, recalled walking around with kids who had gone to private schools. He was amazed that "they just knew all these other kids who went to similar private schools or schools in their area." Justin had a friend on the soccer team who knew "all the kids are that are coming to play soccer next year" because of sports camps and sports leagues. Justin didn't know "a single person" when he arrived and felt that not being part of the "pre-existing networks definitely dominated by east coast wealth [and] students that went to private schools . . . definitely affects your experience here." To Justin "it was weird. Who knows someone before they go to college?"

It is important to note, however, that some of the entering black students also began the year with social connections to other students. Two black students in the study had taken part in Prep for Prep and arrived on campus with a social network of friends from this program. In addition, the college runs a summer science program for students who express interest in the sciences but who the college feels are underprepared for the rigors of Amherst's curriculum. The program included a cohort of black students who, beyond the academics, had the opportunity to get to know one another and form friendships before the academic year began. In contrast to the majority of lower-income whites, who knew no one when they arrived on campus for orientation, black students who participated in the summer science program returned to campus for the beginning of the year with a pre-existing set of friends.

Lower-income students' lack of social capital relative to their affluent peers manifested itself when students began seeking summer jobs and internships, evoking feelings of envy. Jeremy, a lower-income white, reported, "One of my friends that I know—she is very well off—was able to find an internship through her dad at a really good law firm in a day, and I was so jealous of that." Some lower-income students were aware of the *importance* of connections before coming to college, but their families lacked the kinds of connections that would help them find jobs in the professional world. Other lower-income students were just learning the value of social capital as they observed their affluent peers draw upon connections through parents and parents' friends for professional internships or preprofessional summer jobs. They came to see that having connections was "crucial" and could "definitely help you out" and give you "a leg up," and that "if you don't have them, you need to make them." Many lower-income students, both black and white, reported that their class position made it more difficult for them to make contacts for the future, while many affluent students felt that their class position made it much easier for them to make such contacts.[27]

Although lower-income students lacked connections to attractive job prospects through family and family friends, they were learning from sports teams or programs run by the college that being an Amherst student could provide connections to peers and alumni who might help them ultimately get desired jobs. Dana, a lower-income black, reported:

> Every time I talk to someone, they're like, "It's all in your connections." We had Black Alumni Weekend, and we were all told, "Make sure you do some serious networking because this is going to help you after college, and this will help you get your internships." I feel like there is such a stress on making connections, but I don't have any particular experience on how well it works.

Rebecca, a lower-income white, spoke of events on campus "where they bring back alumni," or they bring in speakers from various professions to "give students the opportunity to make connections with people who might be able to help them later on."

Recognizing the importance of connections was a first step. Beginning to make use of the connections that friends' families, faculty, or alumni would provide was not as ingrained in lower-income students as it was in the affluent, and would take time to develop.

Social Influence

In the first weeks on campus, some forms of social life were dominated by the wealthier students. These students were visible because they had the money to entertain, purchase alcohol, and throw parties.[28] Lower-income students might be invited to these parties, but did not have the resources to host the events. From the perspective of an affluent black, William, at the beginning of the year a group of students seemed to be the "most social" and to form "an elite class." William did not see these students as the most "popular," but they were highly visible. Other students seemed "more in the background" and weren't "always at every party, like the elite are," but they appeared not to want to "gravitate" toward the elite. However, the social situation changed after the early weeks. Sports teams organized, pooled money to give group parties, and played a large role in organizing social life. Other extracurricular groups on campus also began sponsoring social events. Thus, being wealthy was not the only way to have an influence on social life.

Social life at Amherst College was once dominated by fraternities that had large houses and hosted large parties where alcohol was prevalent. In 1984 the Board of Trustees formally abolished on-campus fraternities, but a few fraternities continued to exist *off* campus; they went "underground." Administrators prohibit fraternities from using campus resources and provide no support for the groups, but a few underground fraternities continue to play a role in the social lives of some students. What is the connection today between fraternities and social class? Students were not asked directly about fraternities, so this study yields little information about them and the role they play on campus. One fraternity is reputed to consist primarily of wealthy white students, while another is diverse in race and class and does not expect any student to pay dues who does not have the means. Indeed, the underground fraternities today continue the tradition of buying alcohol and throwing parties, but they are not running social life. What is clear is that for many students, fraternities were not a desired center of social life from which they feel excluded. Some students were hardly aware of off-campus fraternities' existence, and many did not desire to be part of these groups. Amy, a lower-income white, reported at the end of the year: "I just recently found out that there are fraternities here that I didn't know about. Last week I was like, 'What do you mean, DKE Champagne?'"

Self-Exclusion

The majority of students, both affluent and lower-income, perceived cliques of very wealthy students to exist on campus. These groups were described by one lower-income white, Kayla, as "upper-class sort of stereotypically polo [shirt] wearing." But when asked whether they felt excluded from any cliques on campus that were based on social class, only about a quarter (27%) of lower-income whites and 15% of lower-income blacks said yes.[29] It appears that rather than feeling excluded, many lower-income students chose alternative groups. Given the range of peer choices on campus, they found friends who shared their interests and pursued the same extracurricular activities and a lifestyle in which social class background did not matter. In some cases, lower-income students *did* get to know some of these very wealthy students individually, but tended not to feel comfortable hanging out with groups of wealthy students. This pattern mirrors the experience of many white students in relation to blacks: whites felt more comfortable in one-on-one relationships with blacks than they did with groups of blacks.

In speaking about groups of very wealthy students, many lower-income students, both black and white, spoke of not wanting "to be in their group anyway" (Jeremy, lower-income white), or of not wishing "I was one of them" (Trina, lower-income black). Comments such as these were typical of lower-income students' sentiments: "It's a two-way exclusion because they don't want to associate with me any more than I want to associate with them almost" (Angela, black). "I wouldn't feel comfortable around them. . . . I don't know if we could connect on the same things" (Alisa, black). Or as one lower-income white, Kayla, recounted:

> I feel excluded, but I also wouldn't want to feel included. It's not who I'm friends with, and it's not like I feel the need to be involved with that group of people. If I did feel the need, I wouldn't be included. I really don't care about it. I have my own friends, and I'm not really worried about spending exorbitant amounts of money on things that I don't find necessary. . . . People whose outlook is *that* different, and more materialistic or more money-based, I just don't have any desire to interact with them on a significant level.

Few lower-income students expressed feelings of being marginalized by wealthy peers. While Heather, a lower-income white, felt "kind of left out of the social hierarchy," although "part of something too," other lower-income students did not feel that a social hierarchy existed on campus, perceiving, instead, multiple social groups on campus without certain ones being more desirable or having higher status than others. In the eyes of Jeremy, a lower-income white, the tables have turned:

> I feel like it hasn't hurt me in any way to be from the class that I'm in. I feel that people who are clearly from an upper class, who show off their wealth, they might have even more trouble fitting in. I feel like it's really interesting because people come here expecting that if you're not from that wealthy group, then you are going to have trouble fitting in. But I feel like it's the opposite because people who have a similar background to me kind of peg [very wealthy students] unfairly and are less likely to hang out with them. So I feel like they might have more trouble than someone who is from more of an average background.

Megan, a lower-income white, too, did not attach any stigma to being poor, but rather saw some stigma attached to being wealthy. She recounted an incident when some Smith College students came to campus to do a survey about financial aid. She was accompanied by her roommate and friends, and they were asked about their family backgrounds:

> My roommate goes, "I'm poor." And I said, "Me too." And a couple of our friends who walked with us who aren't poor didn't really say anything. It's interesting because in some situations where there's more than one financially disadvantaged person, like it sounds kind of cheesy, but it's cool to be the really poor one. Like yes, I have no money! I win! It sometimes makes others feel a little uncomfortable.

It is interesting to note that some affluent students, white and black, also felt estranged from the cliques of very wealthy students on campus and did not desire to be part of them. They spoke of not wanting to be friends with "the richest people." They were critical of these students for their "stuck up, sort of arrogant, 'I-can-do-what-I-want' attitude," for bringing up "their social class whenever you talk to them," for their "way of life."

Inclusion

Faced with disparities in wealth within friendship groups, many still found ways to do activities together. In order to include lower-income students, affluent students were often willing to alter plans or to pay for those who had less, although this latter arrangement was not always comfortable for the recipients of continued generosity.

For spring break, some groups of students reworked their plans to be inclusive of friends with less disposable income. Regarding a trip to a southern state, Brandon, a lower-income black, said of his friends that "the majority could have just flown down," but because some students weren't in "the same position financially," he was appreciative that his friends decided to drive instead and "did some budgeting and twisted some things around," which made it possible for him to be included. Some affluent families simply paid the costs for students who couldn't afford to join them on trips to popular vacation spots.

On campus, cross-class groups of friends adjusted what they were doing to meet everyone's needs, or to offer support to friends who lacked money for the group's activities. Matthew, an affluent white, reported, "When I want to go out or some mutual friends are going out to eat, [a nonwealthy friend] might say, 'I don't want to go, because I can't afford it.' And so you think about it a lot, and you feel terrible about it. We value him so much as a friend that we'll all chip in, or we won't go out to eat or whatever. We're very accom-modating." Some affluent students spoke of themselves as "flexible and con-scious of what other people can afford and can't afford." Likewise Brandi, a lower-income black, spoke of occasions when friends were going out to din-ner and a more affluent student said, "Don't worry about it. I'll pay for it." Marc, a lower-income black, had a girlfriend who was much more affluent than he was. If they went out to dinner and he was "low on cash, she'll be more than willing to cover it." He reported:

> We've talked about these things before and it's not a really big deal or anything. But it's just kind of humbling. She has this money to spend, and she's not thinking any less of me just because I don't have. I can't do these flourishing things and buy her tons of crap or whatever. I think she does appreciate whatever I can do, when I can do it. And I appreciate a lot her being able to cover things and not necessarily making a big deal out of it.

Difficulty accepting the generosity of others was shared by a number of lower-income students. It was not easy to always be the recipient of other students' kindness and not be able to reciprocate. Emily, a lower-income white, spoke of friends offering to pay for her when going to a movie, and of her roommate's generosity in stocking the fridge and offering, "'Oh, you can have anything you want of mine.' And I feel like I can't repay her for that, so I'm very careful of what I use and taking care of myself." Alisa, a lower-income black, was uncomfortable accepting things offered by her roommate; it placed restraints on their relationship. Her roommate's parents had bought the re-frigerator they both use, and things for their room:

> It was really nice, but then I just started to see things that I didn't like about her. It was kind of like, well, do I say something or do I not? Because her parents were really nice, and I just didn't want to be like ungrateful or obnoxious about it. Maybe had that not happened, I may have like expressed myself but I didn't want to.

Some affluent students also experienced this discomfort when they did not have sufficient discretionary money to keep up with the activities of much wealthier peers who offered to pay for them. They, too, found it diffi-cult to be the recipients of more affluent friends' generosity.

Some lower-income students reported ways to adapt to lifestyles that they could not easily afford. Not having as much money had not kept Marc, a lower-income black, from going out to dinner with friends. He would go but "get something less or spend less." Some students felt comfortable turning down invitations they could not afford. Dana, a lower-income black, said, "A lot of my friends acknowledge that I don't have as much as they do, but it doesn't get in the way of my social interactions with other students, and a lot of time if I can't afford something, I'm like, 'I'll sit this one out. I'll see you guys later.'"

Discussion

Given the diversity in the student body and the residential setting of the college, students had many opportunities to socialize with peers from different races and social classes, and, indeed, the majority of students in the study formed relationships across both race and class. These findings are hopeful. Research has shown that positive cross-group contact can lead to reduced anxiety about future cross-group interactions,[30] which sets the stage for continued growth in cross-group interaction over the next three years,[31] and that emotional ties to cross-group members can encourage generalization of positive feelings toward the entire group.[32]

Simply bringing blacks and whites together on campus, however, was clearly not sufficient to guarantee that students would cross racial lines in their close friendships. Lower-income whites were much more likely than affluent white peers to get to know blacks well and to form racially diverse groups of friends, despite the fact that many of these students had no previous contact with blacks and had many apprehensions to overcome. As the majority, affluent whites could more easily surround themselves with close friends similar to themselves, and many affluent whites did not look further for possible friends.

Many whites assumed that blacks were interested in self-segregating, which led them to wait for blacks to take the first step in reaching out to them. Tables of blacks eating together in the dining hall may give the impression of a unified group of blacks who wish primarily to be with one another, but this assumption was erroneous.[33] Only a third of the blacks in the study had a majority of close friends who were black, and among the affluent blacks approximately 40% had no close black friends. These data clearly show that black students were not self-segregating. Rather, it was a subset of the affluent whites who were more likely to socialize exclusively with same-race classmates on campus.

One question that remains is whether additional growth will occur in the future. Will students reach further out of their comfort zones in forming or deepening black-white relationships? Assertions that they are "relatively race blind" in forming friendships suggest that students, black or white, were able to look past race to see commonalities. But this "color blindness" also suggests that students in some relationships may have closed their eyes to race, overlooking racial differences rather than acknowledging and learning from them, a topic to be discussed in Chapter 6.

If we turn to the data on cross-class relationships, we see that three-quarters of the students reported forming a close friendship with a student from a very different class background than their own. The students most likely to make friends of the same social class were the affluent students, particularly affluent blacks, and thus affluent students remained least likely to have their notions of class challenged and to learn from the experiences of those from other classes. As is the case with race, being in the majority made it easier for students to simply surround themselves with people from their own class background.

Times have changed on this campus in that wealthy students used to be at the very center of the social geography. Lower-income students lacked the economic, cultural, and social capital of their affluent peers, which led *at times* to feelings of exclusion on campus. But most of the lower-income students did not report feeling marginalized.[34] By affiliating with students who shared their interests, activities, and values, they were able to find social support and self-validation. Further, some lower-income students felt that being poor now has cachet. It was the very wealthy who were now viewed critically, a topic to be discussed in Chapter 7.

6

Learning from Racial Diversity

The college offered optimal conditions for students' racial stereotypes to be challenged and replaced by more accurate views of members of other races, for students' racial understanding to be broadened and deepened. But did such learning actually occur? The majority of blacks had gotten to know two or more whites well, and the majority of whites had gotten to know two or more blacks well. Did such cross-race interaction lead to learning about race? Did being in the classroom with students of other races contribute to students' racial learning? This chapter begins with an examination of students' racial stereotypes and then moves to a consideration of the extent to which racial stereotypes were broken down and students' notions about race changed over the course of their first year of college.

In addressing students' racial stereotypes, it is useful to take a step back and look at the forces that have shaped their conceptions of race. Psychologists have found that the tendency to categorize people into in-groups (e.g., white) and out-groups (e.g., black) is rapid and automatic, and that stereotyping can easily become activated following racial categorization.[1] Racial stereotypes are ubiquitous and strongly socialized in our culture,[2] and the faulty attribution of negative stereotypic characteristics to members of a racial group leads to prejudiced perceptions of and responses to individuals.[3]

Whites have tended to characterize blacks as "lazy, ignorant, loud, musical, rhythmic, poor, stupid, dirty, and physically skilled (e.g., athletic)" and, more recently as "militant, violent, criminal, and hostile."[4] While the breadth of negative characterizations of blacks has increased, whites have shown an actual decrease in the attribution of the negative traits stereotypically associated with African Americans over the past 50 years.[5] But racial stereotypes persist. They have simply become more subtle and complex, and less overt.[6]

Psychologists such as Samuel Gaertner and John Dovidio have found that whites, having grown up in a racist society, "almost unavoidably possess negative feelings and beliefs about blacks."[7] But it is important to their self-concepts to endorse egalitarian, nonprejudiced principles, so their aversive racism may be unconscious. Indeed, many researchers have found that whites hold implicit stereotypes of blacks that are outside of *conscious control* but can be spontaneously activated and have the potential, unbeknownst to the perceiver, to affect judgments.[8]

Racist beliefs are internalized not only by whites but by blacks as well. Many blacks tend to accept and incorporate the dominant society's negative images of them and prejudices against them, just as whites tend to accept or be unwilling or unknowing participants in a system of racial oppression.[9] In addition, in some studies blacks have been found to hold antiwhite attitudes and to consider whites to be racist.[10]

Given the pervasiveness of racial stereotyping in our society, it should not be surprising that racial stereotyping surfaced in students' interactions on campus. When asked, approximately half the black students and half the lower-income white students in the study readily provided an example of an incorrect stereotypic assumption that had been made about them or members of their race, versus only 7% of affluent white students.[11] The presence of these assumptions reflects the passive acceptance of dominant beliefs that are so much a part of everyday life in America. Many white students lacked contact with or education about blacks before college, making them more prone to stereotyping. For the most part the stereotypes that arose were about blacks, but some pertained to whites as well.

Racial Stereotypes on Campus

Intelligence

A prominent societal stereotype of blacks is that they are less intelligent than whites; a corollary is the belief that black students at the college are less academically talented than whites. Black students' comments suggest that some perceived themselves at times to be in an environment in which their intelligence, and that of members of their race, was under question. Both affluent and lower-income black students spoke of times when they felt that assumptions were made about their intelligence or that of black classmates. Jason, an affluent black, said, "There are definitely times when people just assume when you're in a classroom setting you don't know what's going on. They sort of feel the need to dumb down the class for you." Christopher, another affluent black, felt "a lot of people" will think that because a student is a minority, "he probably wasn't that smart" and probably got a lower academic rating in the admissions process. "I'm sure people [assume] the reason I got in here was because I'm black." Christopher expressed dismay at his own acceptance of this stereotype about his racial group. He had some black friends whose grades he knew:

> I almost feel like judging them the same way. How did you get in here? It must have been because you're black. It sounds [like a] really, really terrible thing to say, but I mean I think it's interesting that even if, as an African American myself, if I'm able to judge someone like that, I can only imagine what other kids say.

Trina, a lower-income student, said, "I don't think people are ever going to stop thinking that my SAT scores are lower than theirs, or they're ever going to stop thinking that my GPA in high school is lower." She spoke of feeling that white students had "preconceived notions" about what she knew, and sensed a racial bias when a girl in her class "tried to cut me off by saying, 'Well, historically . . .' And I was able to say, 'Actually, no, in the Franco-Prussian War, that didn't happen.'" Angela, another lower-income student, received a lot of encouragement from a professor but felt that the professor might have been "trying to encourage me because I'm a black student and you think I need that."[12] Kevin, an affluent black, initially believed that one of his professors assumed he was less intelligent than other students in the class based on his race: "I just had to prove myself, that I was able to handle the material and the class." Devon, also affluent, spoke of a classroom discussion about an article that included Pushkin, the great Russian poet and writer, in a list of "Negroes." A white student claimed that Pushkin and others on the list were not black people, expressing the assumption that such great writers could not have been black.

From these examples, one thing that is clear is that the stereotype of blacks as less intelligent than whites causes blacks to perceive whites as questioning their intelligence in many situations. In many cases, not necessarily all, this may indeed be happening. There is no way for blacks to know for sure and avoid the pain that comes with the perception that whites may view them in this demeaning way.

Athletic Talent

A widely held societal stereotype is that blacks are athletically skilled. A number of blacks felt that other students assumed they were athletically skilled or had been admitted to college because of their athletic talent. Jason, an affluent black who was quite tall, reported that "a scary amount of people assume that I'm good at basketball. I'm just about the worst basketball player ever. I can't dribble. I can't shoot." Similarly Marc, a lower-income student, was told, "You're black so you jump higher or farther or faster." Steven, who was affluent, said, "When people know that I'm black they'll go, 'You're black so you're fast.'" Brandon, a lower-income black, felt that some students assumed "black people are in general faster than the other races." Implicit in the assumption that blacks got into college because of their athletic talent was the belief, discussed above, that they could not have gotten in because of their academic talent, an assumption several blacks had heard voiced: "Sometimes people feel that I'm here just for athletics" (Carl, lower-income). "[People] just assume that 'Oh, you're here, you're black, and you're here because you play football,' or 'You're black and you're here because you play basketball'" (Trina, lower-income).

Urban Culture and Dangerous Neighborhoods

Stereotypic images of blacks commonly portrayed in the media are based on urban black cultural forms. To Alicia, a lower-income black, the assumptions included

> wearing certain clothes and being interested in hip hop and driving certain cars and living in certain areas and blah, blah, blah. I mean if you watch BET [Black Entertainment Television], you'll know what you're supposed to be to be black, to fit into this group. . . . There's metal in your mouth and there's all this jewelry and the guys are all wearing really baggy clothes and the girls are all wearing bikinis. And you're all supposed to be able to dance. . . . I think people assume certain things like I'll act a certain way and then I don't. And then it throws them off, like not all black people act a certain way. . . . I don't wear certain clothes and I don't shop at certain black, urban areas or black urban shops that you're supposed to shop at.

Julian, an affluent black, felt that "people expect me to wear baggy clothes and all that, and when I don't, that's a change-up and they realize not all black people are doing this." Megan, also an affluent student, said that because she was black and hung out with a lot of students who belonged to Dancing and Stepping at Amherst College, students assumed, incorrectly, that she could dance. Another affluent black, Kimberly, said students assumed that "a black person likes rap music or something like that, but it's not necessarily true."

A number of affluent blacks had encountered the stereotype that all blacks live in dangerous, crime-ridden neighborhoods in the inner city. Some students associated the large city Marissa came from with violence and crime, and incorrectly assumed that the area where she lived must be dangerous, with "gangs everywhere." Talia spoke of a student who had commented in the classroom about "feeling unsafe in certain all-black neighborhoods in New York." From Talia's perspective, that assumption was "just stupid. There are dangerous areas all over the U.S. It's not just because there are black people there." Dana, a lower-income student, said friends of hers who had little previous contact with blacks would ask about her inner-city black community: "'Is it really hard? Are there gunfights every day?' They think it's the ghetto and people get shot every five minutes, and it's not."

Family, Intimidation, and Ethnicity

Certain other misconceptions were mentioned by only a few black students, but it is likely that they were more widely held on campus. Brandi, a lower-income black, had heard that "black people must raise their children differently, and maybe that's why they're not doing well in life." Such ideas trace back to the controversial Moynihan Report of 1965, which depicted lower-income black families as unstable, disorganized, and inadequate for the socialization of future generations.[13]

Other assumptions were that black males were threatening, and that blacks with an "Afrocentric" appearance were vehement about racial issues and prone to question the blackness of others.[14] Students told William, an affluent black, that they were "scared" and "intimidated" by him initially, which he attributed to the combination of his height and race. Devon, an affluent black, had an Afrocentric appearance because of her hair style. Upon meeting her, another black told her, "'I thought you were going to have an attitude or something because you looked all Afrocentric.' Or [she thought] I looked like I was not going to think she was 'black enough.' . . . They said I looked intimidating."

Finally, it is not uncommon for Americans of Caribbean descent to be assumed to be African Americans, and for stereotypes of African Americans to be applied to them.[15] Trina, a Caribbean American, said, "People just assume that I'm African American, and not just that I'm African American, they just see all black people as being the same culturally. And actually I'm a first-generation immigrant." Incongruously, Caribbean blacks might be looked to in the classroom to present the "inside" perspective on things African American.

Race and Wealth

Another stereotype that manifested itself with some frequency derived from the fact that a disproportionate number of the nation's poor are people of color, while most of the wealthiest Americans are white. Blacks are assumed to be poor, whites to be rich.[16] On campus, Anthony, a lower-income black, had heard "a black person say something about 'rich white kids,' and vice versa, a white person say something like 'poor black kids.'" Several affluent blacks reported that some students had assumed they must "live in run-down neighborhoods," "live around a lot of violence and poverty," and be "on financial aid." Andrea, who was affluent, said students "feel that I shouldn't live in the neighborhood that I do, I shouldn't be in the social class that I am." Students assumed Devon, an affluent black from the east coast, must come from the inner city in New York: "They don't associate affluence [with being black]." Trina, a lower-income black, recognized the importance of the presence on campus of "students of color here that aren't extremely poor and aren't living in the ghettos that you see on *20/20* that are on public assistance. I think it changes people's perspectives on what it means to be a student of color."

The other side of the coin was that all white students were assumed to be affluent, as the following reports from lower-income whites make clear. Emily stated, "People assume that you've come from the same background as a lot of people here, which is the private school, boarding school, whatever. . . . They often assume that I come from a wealthier background." She recounted talking with a wealthy minority friend about wanting to buy something but deciding to hold off for a while. Emily's friend remarked, "'But you're rich, aren't you?' And I'm like, 'No.' And she's like, 'Oh, I thought all white people were rich.' That's a general stereotype." Similarly, Justin commented: "I'm white and that's why people would think I'm wealthy. Maybe if I was Latino, people wouldn't think I'm wealthy. . . . I think most people who meet me would think I came from an upper-middle-class, suburban background." Kayla, another lower-income white, reported, "People assume that people just send me money when that's not how it is. I work all summer for my money. . . . I buy my own clothing and stuff like that. It's not handed to me as a lot of people seem to think it would be." "My friend assumed that I was richer than I really am for a while. Maybe it's because I'm white" (Amy, lower-income). Megan, who attended an excellent prep school thanks to financial aid, said:

People hearing that I was from a boarding school would often assume things about me, like a different social class background than I actually had. And so it was difficult for me, especially at the beginning of the year when I was getting to know people. If I tell them I went to [my prep school] or whatever, I had to be careful who I told that to because I didn't want to be unfairly or incorrectly judged by it.

Ignorance about Blacks

Another racial stereotype that emerged was felt to be held by blacks about whites. A number of whites believed that students of other races and cultures assumed that as members of the dominant group, whites were uninformed about, uninterested in, or indifferent to issues faced by people of other races and cultures. From the perspective of a lower-income black, Alicia, white students had "no idea of hardly anything that comes along with being black or knowing about black people by history, economic situation, education." David, an affluent white, found that minority students often assumed he fit the role of a "race-blind white kid who couldn't possibly care about racism or know anything about x, y, and z, or lives in a sheltered world." Amber, a lower-income student, reported being referred to as a "dumb white girl" when she didn't know something pertaining to a black cultural event.

Learning about Race

It is clear from the racial assumptions that students made about one another and about members of other races that young people come to campus with internalized racial stereotypes. Opportunities to have these stereotypes challenged were present in the classroom and in social interactions outside the classroom. Approximately three-quarters of black students felt that they had a contribution to make to students' learning based on their race.[17] Many black students believed that they could help counter stereotypes about blacks and educate whites about their experiences. Greg, a lower-income black, commented, "I think it's a great opportunity I would like to take on to destroy stereotypes, and that's basically my thing, and I think that's why I'm at Amherst." As Trina, a lower-income black, put it:

> You [whites] benefit from me being here. If Amherst was just homogeneous, everybody is blond-haired and blue-eyed, there are no Jewish people, there are no black people, there are no Hispanic people, then what do you learn from it? Yes, you're learning in the classrooms, but your social interactions are with people that are just like you. You don't learn about any other cultures firsthand. By being a community, a diverse community, it's not me benefiting from you because you're an almighty, all-knowing white guy. You benefit from me because I'm here and I'm culturally different from you and you're culturally different from me. And we exchange things. I think that

Amherst is a microcosm of American society. Every time there's a diverse group of people that get together and learn from each other, that helps to make greater America less racially polarized. . . . Nobody's going to call you out on your own racism if all you hang out with are people who think like you. So hanging out with somebody who's not the same race, you learn from their culture and all that good stuff. But they also call you out when you're being racist or when you're being racially prejudiced.

Let us begin by looking at classroom diversity, both learning about diverse groups through the curriculum and learning through interacting with diverse peers in the classroom.[18] Both have been found to play a critical role in the impact of diversity on students' learning.[19]

Classroom Diversity

Amherst has an open curriculum. With the exception of a required one-semester seminar for first-year students, students are given the freedom to make their own course selections. The transcripts of the students in the study revealed that black students were over three times more likely than whites (52% versus 14%) to have selected at least one course in the Black Studies Department or with "Black" or "Africa" in the title during the year.[20] In addition, 80% of blacks spoke in their interviews of having taken a course in which racial issues were covered as a subtopic at some point during the semester, compared with 46% of whites.[21] Thus black students were learning through the curriculum more than whites about race and racial issues pertaining to blacks.

Racial issues had personal relevance for blacks in making sense of their lives, and many found it fascinating to examine in courses issues they confronted in their daily lives. For example, Anthony, a lower-income black, had gotten to look at racial profiling from different perspectives in one of his courses. "Our professor would argue both sides. And first he would say 'No. You can't do that. That's stereotyping. That's violating all kinds of rights. That's not allowed.' And then [students would] say, 'OK. You can't.'" The professor would then make the argument for racially profiling as the best use of limited resources, "and students would reflect on that, and that just made me think about that a lot."

A diverse classroom allows for the possible sharing of a broader variety of responses, perspectives, and experiences than a homogeneous one, which in turn can help students examine their own perspectives and values. Close to half the students in the study provided an example of sharing by students of different races in the classroom that they felt had led them to change the way they understood race or racial issues.[22]

Students, black and white, talked about benefiting from hearing the perspectives of classmates of another race. Kevin, an affluent black, spoke of enjoying a debate about "how much racism is still around. Some people were more adamant that there is [racism], and some thought there isn't. . . . It was fairly interesting to get a bunch of different opinions on that." Marc, a lower-income black, particularly enjoyed a course "because you got to hear the Hispanic side, then the white side and African American side and stuff. I felt like I got different viewpoints and things that I may not have necessarily thought of on my own. . . . It definitely changed a lot of what I thought."

Lauren, an affluent white, gained a new perspective on herself and black students from a black student's statement about her difficulties handling her anger about the racism she perceived in *Heart of Darkness*. The black student entered the discussion by saying:

> "I've been quiet because I didn't want to be the angry black girl in this class." And then she went on and just explained why she hated the book so much. And I just thought that that was interesting that she would say before she spoke how she was afraid to voice her opinion because she didn't want to be typecast as the angry black girl. I have never had to deal with that because I would never have thought to hold back an opinion just because of what someone else would think of me.

Megan, a lower-income white, came to more fully understand the variability among blacks through a comment made by a black student whose parents immigrated to America from the Caribbean:

> She was talking about the different black communities [in New York] and how they have come from different places geographically and culturally. . . . I've known for a while that not all black people are from Africa; people come from different places. But I didn't understand the extent to which those different identities were still held onto here.

Kayla, a lower-income white, felt that she gained a "nonstereotypical outlook" from hearing the perspectives of wealthy black students in a course she took. She came to see that wealthy blacks identify with people based on their social class, but "still feel this tie to the minority plight," giving them a foot in two different worlds. Kayla saw that for wealthy blacks:

> Their life monetarily is easier and more stable than mine, but they just have a personal connection to this minority issue that I don't personally have. So it is interesting to see when social class can be put

aside to connect with race—and then there are those people who are of the upper class and choose to identify more with their social class than with their race so as to not be discriminated against, to take advantage of those things, play up the advantages they have as, say, a richer person and to lessen the disadvantages from the discrimination [they] might have as a minority member.

Andrew, an affluent white, spoke of a classroom comment by a black student about a personal experience:

I was just blown away. I forget what it was exactly. It was just, "Oh my God, that's awful, just horrible racism." . . . You always hear about things like that, of course I knew that was going on, but to hear someone talk about it, it was very sobering.

Cross-Race Friendships

The literature in psychology on the reduction of prejudice has shown that cross-race friendships can play an important role in generating identification with and empathy for members of another race, can contribute to learning about members of a different racial group, and can lead to more positive attitudes toward an entire out-group.[23] Sociologist Joe Feagin and his colleagues found that through friendships with white classmates, some blacks at a predominantly white university were able to see whites as individuals, and mutual learning about race occurred through these relationships.[24] Many of the students in my study had formed cross-race friendships, an important condition for this learning to take place. But did such change actually occur?

As the year began, Anthony, a lower-income black, was optimistic that, given the diversity on campus, such learning *would* take place: "There're so many different kinds of people and we're intelligent enough to not stereotype like that. I think everybody can get to know one another and figure out the truth about somebody and not stereotype them." Maybe not *everybody* can, but his optimism was not unfounded. At the end of the year, almost half of the lower-income whites believed that their experience living and interacting with students of different races at the college had changed the way they saw people of different races, their own race, or both. This group entered college with the least prior cross-race experience, yet they formed quite racially diverse groups of friends and learned from the differences.

Of the remaining three groups of students in the study, only about a third saw their campus experience living and interacting with classmates of different races as having changed their views of people of different races or their own race.[25] The group reporting the lowest percentage of change, the affluent whites, most easily found friends similar to themselves in race and class. By and large, they had less racially diverse groups of friends than their lower-income white peers and thus seem to have benefited less from the racial diversity on campus. Some reported having had few interactions with blacks. When asked if their views about members of other races had changed, many affluent whites simply said, "I don't think so," "not really," "not that much," or "no."

But many white students, both affluent and lower-income, who reported that their views of people of different races had *not* changed *had* formed close friendships with blacks. How can this lack of change be explained? In reporting on their interracial friendships, a number of whites, both lower-income and affluent, said race was not discussed in these relationships. Megan, a lower-income white, said, "I did notice this is the first relationship with someone who is not of my race. I didn't really think of the relationship in terms of that. He was him and I was me." Some whites had been taught that people should ignore racial differences. Nicole, a lower-income white, recognized that she "grew up color blind" and "knowing people as people, and that's still the way it is." She said race "never really came up as a factor in anything." In talking about relationships with black friends, one lower-income white, Amy, said race was "sort of invisible when we're just hanging out." Several affluent white females spoke of relationships with black students in similar ways: "Race doesn't usually come up in our conversations or how we interact really" (Lauren). "I've just interacted with [black friends] as I would anyone else" (Katherine). Alexander, an affluent white, reported:

> I don't really think about racial issues when I'm talking to people I know well. . . . I don't really see much of a difference in behavior between any different races at Amherst. I think the Amherst community molds everybody into almost the same sort of—not person—but people act very similar.

The lack of attention to race likely helped facilitate the development of these relationships.[26]

The friendships in which race was overlooked can be interpreted in different ways. From one perspective, students have been able to connect across racial lines and recognize commonalities across race. That students have formed close cross-race relationships bodes well for the future, because inter-group friendship increases the likelihood of further inter-group friendship.[27] Growing up in a racist society, however, most blacks have to think about race; it is a part of their self-definition. Almost every black student in the study reported having thought about racial identity before coming to college, compared with only half the white students.[28] Not "really think[ing] about racial issues" or finding "race is invisible" is a luxury few blacks share. As W. E. B. DuBois put it, blacks live with "this sense of always looking at one's self through the eyes of others,"[29] with a double consciousness both as blacks and members of the larger society, aware of how they see themselves and how others see them.

From another perspective, these "race-blind" relationships have not gone as deep as they potentially could. It could be that some whites avoided bringing up race for fear of saying the wrong thing and jeopardizing the relationship. It could be that some blacks did not wish to draw attention to race, and thus had not disclosed thoughts and feelings about the role race played in their lives. Based on the statements above, it appears that those white students remained unaware that an aspect of a black friend might not yet have been revealed to them.

Approximately two-thirds of the black students (the same percentage found for white students overall) felt that living and interacting with people of different races had *not* changed their views of race.[30] Most blacks in this study had had much previous contact with whites by the end of high school, if not their whole lives. Carl, a lower-income black, felt that he had learned little new about race in college because "I've had the same kind of exposure in high school." Corey, another lower-income black, said, "I live in a city, so I'm around a lot of black people, but I'm also around a lot of white people, and I've always just seen the differences and nothing new has really popped up since I've been here."

Perceptions of Out-Group Members

Stereotypes of out-groups persist in part because members of out-groups (in this case, people of a different race) remain unknown to members of in-groups and, as a result, are seen as homogeneous and undifferentiated.[31] But if in-group members have more interactions with out-group members, knowledge about them becomes more personalized and differences between out-group members become more apparent.[32] This new learning can correct negative views of an out-group.[33] At Amherst, much of the reported learning that was derived from interacting with people of different races involved students' coming to see members of another race as more heterogeneous and differentiated from one another, as will be described below.

Blacks' Stereotypes about Whites
In the process of informal interaction with whites, many black students came to recognize that all whites were not rich, "preppy," "snobbish," and racist, and that some whites were genuinely knowledgeable about black culture and interested in getting to know blacks. Whitney, an affluent black, had experienced whites at her private school as "snobbish" and having "this air to them . . . like I know I'm better than you just because. . . . And people here, I don't see that snobbiness. It doesn't mean I see friendliness. They don't have

this air to them." Whitney spoke with admiration about a white friend standing up to another white friend who had made a racial joke:

> A lot of [black] people think all white people are racist and that when they're behind closed doors they just say whatever they want to say about other races. And this experience shows how it's complex, it's not so black and white. It's always situational. I guess a lot of times I assume that white people make black jokes and laugh and no one ever stands up and says this is wrong. And there are people who do that.

Trina, a lower-income black, had attended a high school at which all the whites were extremely affluent and almost all the students of color were on financial aid. She reported that at Amherst, "I've seen that not all white people are rich, and not all black people are the poor ones." One day when financial aid forms were due, a number of students, both black and white, were in the common room filling out forms: "We're all like, 'You're all on financial aid too? There are white people on financial aid?'"

Angela, a lower-income black, had developed a close friendship with a white male "from a really poor family, *really* poor." Angela discovered that when this white student was growing up, he had to go to speech classes to learn Standard English. "It opened me up to a variety of [social] classes, because even though he's a white male Protestant, all those other things, that doesn't automatically equal privilege." Although being white still confers upon this white male a layer of privilege denied to blacks, whites were clearly a more heterogeneous group than Angela had assumed. Brandon, a lower-income black, too, came to see greater differences among whites, learning that they have "different styles, because there's some [whites] more into the preppy thing and there's some who're more into the punk rock thing and some more into just 'whatever.'"

Devon, an affluent black, reflected on the friendships she had formed with a lot of whites on her floor and realized that she was wrong to assume that race was a good criterion for who might be a good friend. She found white students to be

> just really friendly people as well, and they're open to new people from different backgrounds or whatever. It's just reaffirmed my belief that you shouldn't really judge people at first because you really can't tell what they're going to be like. [Students] can be black but are not necessarily automatically going to be friends with you. If they are white, they could be really friendly, real open people.

Trina, a lower-income black, became friends with an affluent white male who was very interested in issues of racism. "It made me see that there are white people that do care about issues of race." She also encountered a white male with a genuine interest in rap music. "It sort of let me see that some-body can enjoy hip hop, can enjoy rap music, can enjoy reggae, without hav-ing an artificial interest in black culture. . . . He knows a lot more than I do." She found people at college who "don't think that your whole personality is wrapped up in the fact that you're black," and who do not stereotype you as "'she's black, you basically know her now.'" Instead she met whites who "are interested in who you are."

Jason, an affluent black, became close friends with a white from the Deep South. Jason came to see that all southern whites were not overt racists. He reported that for "understandable reasons," he had been "kind of leery" at first of his southern white friend. The thought had crossed his mind, "Is there a fire hose in his room?" Jason went on to say, "I've had some bad expe-riences in the southern part of the country." He had visited his mother's rela-tives in the South every summer: "I consider it a pretty prejudiced place and not a place I'd prefer to spend any time [in]. So I guess I have over the years just developed a knee-jerk reaction of being leery of white southerners. And my friendship with this guy helped me get over that."

Whites' Stereotypes about Blacks

Only a few white students spoke directly of having their stereotypes about blacks changed through their experiences on campus. Larry, a lower-income white, came to recognize his own inadvertent stereotyping of blacks as lower class and lacking in social capital when, in speaking to his black friend about a course reading, the friend, referring to the author, said, "Oh, my parents know this guy." Larry's view of blacks was further called into question when he realized that his black friend's knowledge and interests were very different from the "hip-hop black culture" and "popular culture" presented in the me-dia. Hannah, an affluent white, came to see that people of the same class, but of a different race, may have more in common with her than people of the same race and a different class. Hannah had a "really, really rich black friend" and came to recognize that his experience was not "that much different from mine," whereas the experiences of a lower-income white student could be quite different.

Alexander, an affluent white, had his first personal opportunity to com-pletely dispel the stereotype that blacks are less intelligent than whites. Few blacks had been in his courses in high school, "so it was hard to tell if they were smart or not, but here at Amherst you can really tell that there are peo-ple from all races that are very smart. I didn't necessarily have the thought that they weren't smart before, but now I really have proof that they are."

Emily, a lower-income white, felt overall that she was now "definitely a lot more open-minded. . . . I come from an area that is very closed-minded and somewhat ignorant and somewhat racist at times, without even knowing it. I knew that I didn't believe in those stereotypes when I came here, but it's definitely brought me to the point where I don't even think about it."

Conversations

Beyond a direct change in stereotypic views, other changes in students' understandings of and perspectives on race occurred through conversations about racial issues. Those conversations occurred largely between blacks and whites, but some important conversations about race took place among students of the same race. Whites may fear exposing themselves by inadvertently saying something racist, or something that could be interpreted as racist. Yet 70% of students reported having had "meaningful, honest conversations" with other students about racial issues.[34] Students likely used different criteria in defining whether a conversation about race was "meaningful." Because students were starting at different places in their understanding of racial issues, the important point may be that, wherever they were, they were having conversations they considered to be important.

For some students, such conversations were frequent. Approximately a third of the students reported that they found themselves discussing racial issues at least once a week.[35] At one extreme was Kayla, a lower-income white, who discussed race daily with people in her friendship group. She spoke of a long conversation with a friend about the need for increased diversity at the college. "People do have these discussions—we have them a lot actually. And then the next day we went to friends and told them about our conversation, and it sparked a lot more conversations." Similarly David, an affluent white, reported having conversations with fellow students about race

> like 30 times a day. But I have friends that talk about race a lot. I talk about race a lot, like a million times a day, and it's not a bad thing. It's something I'm used to. . . . It's the way we have always done this, as part of my really diverse friendship group. . . . I hang out with my black friends. We talk about race all the time. Not just because sometimes we need to, to maintain our really good friendship. If one white person does something to my friend [who is black], I suffer from that. And our relationship suffers from that. So we have to talk about race all the time, in order to have a really good and healthy relationship. . . . What I've learned is just how important it is to be in that constant dialogue around race, because it's really hard to deal with a lot of these racial issues if we don't keep this dialogue going. One of my frustrations at Amherst is we don't really have a dialogue around race.

David described a friend who told a lot of racist jokes and didn't see "how that really affects all the other people he's friends with." David and his friends took the difficult step of approaching this student about his behavior. They told him:

> It's not about saying something politically incorrect. It's hurting the other people that you're friends with, but also not being able to claim that. It's like we all perpetuate racism, whether you're saying overtly racist things, or just, as a white person, living a certain way that sort of allows racism to go on. We're part of racism. We're all racist. And it's not necessarily our fault, but we need to understand how we can deal with that.

A third of the students participated in meaningful conversations about race a few times a month; a third of the students did so much less frequently, at most a few times a semester.[36] One in 10 students reported never having had meaningful conversations about race or racial issues. Affluent whites were nearly twice as likely as students in the other groups to report infrequent conversations about racial issues. For many students a close friendship may be a prerequisite for potentially charged conversations about racial issues. Hannah, an affluent white, felt that she could not talk about race with students she did not know or knew only casually "because I don't know how they'll react to it."

Some black students saw themselves as presenting a "black" perspective in conversations and felt that they had a unique point of view to offer whites. These students were able to present *one* person's perspective and could not, of course, speak for all blacks. It would only be from hearing the perspective of many blacks that whites would be able to see that blacks held multiple points of view. Both affluent and lower-income blacks talked about giving close white friends "a perspective on how black people feel about stuff" (Julian, affluent black), about always trying to "make sure different opinions are being heard" so that students might think about things from a "different angle" (Marc, lower-income black). Marc noted that he was "very attuned to my race and my blackness and so I will let my opinion be heard on certain issues." Hurricane Katrina hit just as students arrived on campus for orientation in the fall. Jason, an affluent black, believed that he offered a different perspective on the media coverage of Katrina, which he found "suspect."

> When there are black people breaking into supermarkets to get food they're "looting." But if they're not black, they're looking for sustenance. That certainly hit closer to home for me than it did for a lot of the other students. . . . I wasn't as quick as some of my classmates to just write off the people who got left behind in the evacuation.

Brandi, a lower-income student, said: "A lot of the time you're the first black person they'll meet. And in a way I feel like I have to inform them, give them a valid representation of who I am."

Both blacks and whites spoke of benefiting from hearing the differing perspectives of classmates. Julian, an affluent black, said that conversations with his white friends "give me a perspective on how white people feel about stuff, and we joke around and nobody gets offended by anything and it feels good." Amber, a lower-income white who did not have a racially diverse group of friends before college, found it "very interesting listening to all our different viewpoints," a sentiment expressed by several other lower-income whites from similar backgrounds.

Racial differences in perspectives, not always resolved, came into play in discussions of affirmative action. William, an affluent black, spoke of two male students in his dorm, one black and one working-class white, who "always kind of go at it. They were yelling about affirmative action." Martin, a lower-income black, reported on discussions about increasing the number of students of color on campus. In these discussions he and black friends would argue that there was no lack of "bright African American students out there" who might be brought to campus, a notion some classmates disagreed with.

A topic of particular interest and concern to some students was interracial dating, and that interest led them to seek the perspectives of other students, black and white. In the interviews, unfortunately, students were not asked specifically for their views on interracial dating, so the study yields little information on the topic. From the students who did comment on this topic, it was apparent that student views were mixed. Greg, a lower-income black, noted, "It's really interesting what my minority friends would say and then what my white friends would say. My minority friends were more against [interracial dating], and my white friends didn't really understand why it was so much of a problem."

Some black students were open to interracial dating and believed that students should be free to date whomever they want, "no matter social class or race." Other blacks disapproved, holding to the view that students should want to date people of their own race. Sociologists have reported that interracial dating is seen by some blacks as a betrayal of norms of racial solidarity, of family and community, and as an escape into white society.[37] No black men brought up dating whites, but two black women who had dated whites reported being made to feel "uncomfortable," or being "looked at a little weirdly" by other blacks when part of an interracial couple.

Black-white relationships in America are more likely to involve a black man and a white woman than the reverse,[38] and research has found that black women hold less favorable attitudes toward interracial dating than black men.[39] Demographically, black women face limited prospects for finding partners.

Along with the incarceration of black men, drug abuse, and homicide, black men dating white women reduces the number of available partners for black women.[40] Research has also shown that black women perceive it as a rejection of black womanhood.[41] In my study, a few lower-income black females wondered whether white men avoided dating black women because it would be perceived as "pulling [white men] down socially" if they did. Interracial dating is clearly a charged topic, and one that is worthy of future attention.

Awareness of Racial Issues

Many white students from predominantly white communities had not given a great deal of thought to race before coming to college, and had little consciousness about it. For Robert, a lower-income student from an all-white community, getting to know blacks on campus made blacks "more real," not just figures on television. Nicole, a lower-income white, felt that her experience at Amherst of living and interacting with students of different races had given her "a larger base of experience and knowledge to pull from in life." Another spoke of "learning about how much of an identity [race] is" through her relationship with a black friend. "Because when you're white, you don't really necessarily think, 'OK, this is my racial identity,' versus it's definitely something that [her black friend] would think about" (Emily, lower-income).

For some whites the opportunity to get to know black students played a very important role in increasing their understanding of some of the experiences blacks face in society. Blacks' experiences with racism were made more poignant and real and could not be denied when whites heard them firsthand from blacks. Such knowledge led to increased empathy for black students, a variable that has been found to be important in improving attitudes toward an out-group.[42]

Robert, a lower-income student from a town that is 99% white, talked about conversations with a "really good" black friend. On television Robert had heard blacks' claims of being apprehended or arrested because of their skin color, but it was quite different for him to hear his black friend say that downtown cops "would come up to him and had given him a hard time just because he's black." Robert's friend told him:

> "It's real, this does happen. I'm not a gang banger; I'm not living in Compton; I do the same things you do; I'm the same kind of kid you are. But Saturday night I'm downtown, the cops look at me a few seconds longer, and they've come up to me before." And that was just like, wow, those stereotypes do exist. Even though I knew they existed, they just became a little more real. . . . I've never really been close with a person who's been affected by that.

Two other lower-income white males spoke of gaining a new understanding of the reality and negative effects of racial profiling by hearing of the experiences of black friends. Danny was struck by the fact that despite his black friend's wealth, when walking down the street in his home city the friend was "treated differently by people who assume he's a gangster, or whatever, when he's not at all. Just seeing through his eyes, and his perspective, I'd just never really done that before." In a conversation about law enforcement, Marie, a lower-income white, was informed by a black friend that his father "gets pulled over all the time, not even for any particular reason. I had thought about it, and I knew it happened, but I guess it really doesn't connect so much until it's a direct thing."

Likewise, for Rebecca, a lower-income white, because the information came from a best friend who is black, the learning was so much more powerful because it was personal:

Some of the stories that [my friend] told me kind of opened my eyes. I think that people say that discrimination is still going on, and I think I just had never witnessed it. But when she was telling me stories about how her family is black, and things that have happened to them, I was shocked and really didn't know that these things were going on. . . . I had never known a personal example of something like that. What I did realize was that I was unaware that there were still certain prejudiced things going on.

An affluent black female who came from a wealthy community and had been largely protected from racism growing up because of her class standing learned from other blacks on campus "how racism has affected some people [although] it hadn't affected me, or how stereotyping has affected them that I hadn't experienced. I think it's important to know that these things are going on, 'cause I'm sheltered. I went to a private school and I've experienced various little things but not a lot" (Monica). Another affluent black, Jason, had learned about race relations in the Deep South from a black friend because "he has a ground's-eye perspective" that Jason lacked.

Getting to know students who had a black parent and a white parent added another dimension to students' understandings of the complexity of racial identity and finding one's place in society. In their interviews some students, both black and white, spoke of gaining greater knowledge through conversations with biracial classmates about the complexities they faced. Justin, a lower-income white, became aware of the struggle for racial identity of one of his friends of mixed race who told him a story about "a snowball fight when [the friend] was younger. And the kids said, 'Let's have the white kids versus the black kids.' And he didn't know where to stand." Black students who had not been exposed to many biracial individuals also learned about issues confronting their biracial peers. Whitney, an affluent black, had a conversation with a biracial friend who had grown up mostly with her white parent. Not spending much time with her black parent gave that friend little exposure to black culture: "This girl doesn't know who she is or how to identify herself. I think identity crisis has been an issue."

Students could easily draw conclusions based on conversations with a single biracial friend and fail to recognize the variability of experiences for biracial individuals. Only three black participants in the study described themselves in their interviews as biracial, much too small a sample to examine the distinctive issues faced by biracial students on campus. However, a growing research literature exists on biracial individuals. Sociologists Kerry Rockquemore and David Brunsma have found "no singular understanding among black/white mixed-race people as to what biracial identity means or how it translates into an individual self-understanding."[43] Today it is more common than in the past for biracial adolescents to identify themselves as biracial, mixed, or black *and* white, to affirm a blended identity, and to resist dichotomization.[44] Most black/white biracial young adults in Rockquemore and Brunsma's study thought of themselves as biracial. Some, however, defined their racial identity as exclusively white or exclusively black, some opted out of the racial categorization system and perceived themselves not to have a racial identity, and a few saw their racial identity as sometimes black and sometimes white, depending on the social context. While early research portrayed biracial individuals as suffering from identity confusion and other problems, that research was based primarily on small-scale clinical case studies of individuals who were experiencing personal conflict and had sought counseling.[45] In more recent research using nonclinical samples, biracial adolescents have generally not been found to show social dislocation and personal alienation.[46]

Discussion

As members of the larger society, it should not be surprising that many students in this study had internalized racial stereotypes and that students encountered stereotypic assumptions from classmates about themselves and members of other races. The diversity that exists at the college provides the opportunity for students to acquire further and more accurate information about members of other races, and to generate close ties across race (which can contribute to more positive attitudes toward members of another racial group). Students' accounts suggest that for *some* students, black and white, racial stereotypes were broken down, a new awareness and understanding of racial issues was developed, and new perspectives on people of different races were attained. Almost half the lower-income whites and a third of the students in the other groups reported that they had changed the way they saw people of different races or their own race through their social interactions.

Getting to know some blacks well was a necessary condition for white students to report that learning occurred from living and interacting in a diverse community: the white students who reported that they had gotten to know two or more black students well were the ones who reported that they had learned something from living in a diverse racial community. But getting to know some blacks well was not sufficient for that learning to occur: just over half of the white students who reported having gotten to know two or more black students well also felt that they had *not* changed the way they saw people of different races or their own race from living in a diverse community. White students who formed cross-race relationships where race never came up, however, had found common ground across racial lines, and their bonds of friendship held the promise for future cross-race relationships, and for greater learning to occur in the future. Three years of college were still ahead of them. Getting to know some whites well, which was the case for almost every black student in the study, was not sufficient for learning to occur. Most blacks in the study had considerable previous experience with whites, and only a third reported learning about race.

The classroom offered two other potential sources of learning. Nearly half the students in the study talked about personal sharing by students of another race in a course they took that caused them to change the way they understood race or racial issues, with lower-income whites again reporting the greatest learning. Half the students who gave examples of learning from students in the classroom did *not* report having learned about race from living and interacting in a diverse community. Given that the social realm was the main focus of the students' interviews, it is likely that students failed to take the classroom into consideration in assessing the overall impact on their learning from living in a diverse community. Learning also occurred through the curriculum. Blacks were much more likely than whites to select courses in black studies or that addressed blacks, and only one affluent white had taken such a course. These courses provided black students analytical frameworks for thinking about racism and enabled them to better understand the role race played in their own lives and families.[47] Whites, too, have much to learn about racial issues, but fewer chose to direct some of their attention to racial issues through the curriculum.

One way to understand the nature of students' learning about race is to view the data through the perspective of racial identity development models. Bailey Jackson created one of the first models of black identity development. He joined with his colleague, Rita Hardiman, creator of one of the first models of white identity development, to create a more general model of racial identity development pertinent to both blacks and whites.[48] They describe an initial

stage of *acceptance* by blacks and whites of racist stereotypes that are a byprod-
uct of growing up in a society where racist assumptions are pervasive. Whites
may not see themselves as racist or prejudiced at this stage, but they have unconsciously internalized racial assumptions and have become unknowing participants in a system of racial oppression. Whites consciously hold that they are
not racist and that they do not believe racial stereotypes, but unconsciously
they hold implicit stereotypes that can be activated and can impact their judgments. Hardiman and Jackson argue that blacks, too, have internalized the
larger society's racist assumptions about blacks. The data from the interviews
in this study provide examples of acceptance thinking in the stereotypic assumptions made about race on campus: for example, that blacks were natural
athletes, unintelligent, or poor, or that whites were wealthy.

Hardiman and Jackson's next stage, *resistance*, takes first a passive and
then an active form. In the passive phase people gain a critical consciousness
of racism, its multiple ramifications, and the ways in which it affects people
daily. The data from this study suggest that some students, both black and
white, either arrived on campus at this stage or moved into it over the year:
they encountered students on campus who challenged their stereotypes, they
came to see members of another race as more heterogeneous and differentiated from one another, and they became more conscious of racism. Whites'
stereotypes were challenged by encountering blacks who were rich and who
were academically talented, or they were questioned in the classroom, and
some white students became more sensitive to issues of racial prejudice and
discrimination. Blacks' stereotypes were challenged by encountering whites
who were not wealthy or who were not racist. Thus some students showed
movement toward resisting and questioning their racist assumptions, and
learned from hearing different perspectives presented by cross-race peers
inside and outside the classroom.

The attitudes and behavior of a smaller group of students might be characterized by the active form of resistance, in which people take an active role
in challenging racism and trying to reduce it. Those students, primarily but
not exclusively black, were eager to challenge racist statements wherever they
occurred and frequently engaged in dialogues about race. Some students arrived on campus at this stage, and it is unclear how many may have moved
into it after their arrival.[49]

There is potential for greater learning. With the opportunity to develop
new cross-race relationships, to deepen ongoing cross-race relationships, and
to learn from classroom diversity, much growth is still possible over the next
three years of college. One would hope that students will move closer to understanding, resisting, and challenging racist assumptions, but more active
steps may have to be taken for such learning to actually occur.

7

Learning from Class-Based Diversity

S
tudents entered college with different levels of prior exposure to class differences. "Social class wasn't really something I thought about for the most part. . . . All my friends growing up were on the same level as me," said Nicole, a lower-income white, and she was not alone. Many students came to campus having given little thought to social class and with little experience interacting with people of a different social class. Even students from high schools that brought together students from diverse class backgrounds had not necessarily interacted with people different from themselves or thought about the meaning and implications of those differences. By contrast, some students came to campus from communities or high schools that had given them exposure to great disparities in wealth, which made class highly salient to them and caused them to be highly attuned to class differences on campus.

What preconceived notions did students bring to campus about people of different social classes? Given the opportunities on campus for notions of social class to be challenged and understandings deepened, to what extent did students' experiences at Amherst, living and interacting with people from a range of social class backgrounds, alter some of their stereotypes and understandings of members of their own social class and other social classes?

As is the case with racial stereotypes, when individuals have little knowledge of members of a different social class, out-group members remain undifferentiated and homogeneous and are more easily subject to stereotypic judgments. Indeed, stereotypes of both the poor and the rich were espoused on occasion by students of different social classes on campus, though class stereotypes surfaced less frequently than racial ones. About one in five students spoke of having heard incorrect assumptions made about them or members of their social class, with slightly more affluent than lower-income students reporting having heard such class-based assumptions.[1]

Lower Social Classes

The poor are negatively stereotyped in our society; poverty is associated with pathology and inadequacy.[2] Members of lower social classes are stereotypically seen as uneducated, irresponsible, impulsive, and lazy, in contrast to members of the middle class, who are characterized as intelligent, educated, ambitious, skillful, competitive, hardworking, and sophisticated.[3] The competencies of the lower classes are devalued and seen as less desirable.[4]

A variety of research studies have found that the rich, too, can be subject to negative characterizations. The rich are described as having a sense of superiority and exclusivity, of wanting to share only the company of equals.[5] Compared with their lower-income counterparts, the affluent or wealthy are perceived as less considerate (e.g., less kind, likable, and caring),[6] more boastful, arrogant, and egotistical, and less honest, sympathetic, sensitive, and warm.[7] Affluent college students are seen as less serious about academics and more snobbish than low-income students.[8]

A number of lower-income students reported hearing overtly negative assumptions about members of lower social classes over the course of the year. For example, on the college's *Daily Jolt,* an on-line forum in which statements are made anonymously, offensive comments sometimes appear, seemingly without sensitivity to the feelings they might engender in their targets. Robert, a lower-income white, reported reading a *Daily Jolt* entry about students on full scholarships: "some rude comments toward people that have to work. . . . I wish I could know the person . . . and say, 'You go work for a living and see how hard it is not having Daddy pay your bills.' " Similarly, Trina, a lower-income black, spoke of a thread on the *Daily Jolt* suggesting that "Amherst 'lowers the standards' for students of color and low-income students. They just assume that low-income students are stupid."

Some overtly pejorative comments about members of lower social classes surfaced in response to a *Business Week* article that appeared in February 2006.[9] The article focused on the college president's initiatives to bring more lower-income students to campus. Concerns were raised by some alumni in the student newspaper and by some students on campus that if Amherst were to admit more lower-income students, the college's standards would be lowered and Amherst would no longer be an elite institution. David, an affluent white, was extremely concerned about the denigration of lower-income students, and worried that this placed stress on them: "We talk about people of lower socioeconomic class as not being able to do math, or not being able to write," as not being "ready for college" or able to succeed. A similar concern was raised by Julian, an affluent black, about wealthy students complaining that lower-income students would "bring down our standards," that the Office of Admission was going to "let in all these C and D students just because they have less money. I'm like, 'No, they're smart kids. . . . These are kids that are getting in, but they're just not able to pay for it, so we're helping them.'" Alums and current students who raised concerns about lower-income students "lowering" the standards at Amherst have often done so without sensitivity to the fact that they are not talking about an abstract group of potential students, but rather about students who are currently part of the Amherst community. Such disparaging comments put additional academic pressure on lower-income students, requiring them, as representatives of their group, to prove the inaccuracy of the stereotypes and defend their right to an Amherst education.

One affluent white, David, expressed concern that lower-income students were treated at times like outsiders: "We talk sometimes about people of lower socioeconomic classes as though they don't go here, when they do." Emily, a lower-income white, agreed. She felt that lower-income students were sometimes referred to as "they" or "those people," as if they "don't actually exist here." She believed that lower-income students "remained unseen by many on campus."

Stereotypic assumptions about the poor were sometimes evidenced on campus. Marie, a lower-income white, reported hearing the assumption that domestic violence against women was a "solely lower class thing," and she was offended to hear students describe poor people on welfare as "lazy" and "wanting a free ride." In a discussion of welfare she said:

> a lot of the students have a common perception that it's just lazy people who don't want to work. It was really difficult for most of the students to understand how a person could just not have anything growing up, no family resources, and then they're on their own and they have a kid.

Whitney, an affluent black, too, felt that some students believed "people who are poor don't work hard and they're not trying to better themselves."

Emily, a lower-income white from a farming community, spoke of a classmate who referred to someone as "white trash," which she found to be just as offensive as any other racial slur. When people heard where she was from, they assumed that people in her community were "very hick-like." Class-based stereotypes were applied to people who came from Appalachian states, the Midwest, and the South, areas of the country that themselves were stereotyped along class lines. Nicole, a lower-income white, noted that some classmates assumed that people from "more affluent, coastal regions are considered to be better educated." She took offense when students assumed that she was "obviously not as intelligent" because she was not from a coast. Marie, a lower-income white from an Appalachian state, recalled another student's assumption that she came from a poor community where people were "just kind of dumb low lifes. I remember one person in a class talking about [my home state] and saying, 'I mean, isn't it like a third world country? They don't even have hospitals.'" "One girl in the beginning of the year found out that I was from [a southern state]," reported Amy, a lower-income white, and "she immediately thought I was a 'hillbilly.' I don't know if that's social class or just geographic assumptions and stereotypes."

The Very Rich

The wealthy as well as the poor could carry the burden of negative stereotypes. During the interviews, most students, including students in the affluent groups, expressed some degree of negative feelings about a number of very wealthy students at Amherst who were perceived to be "upper-upper-class," "preppy," or "arrogant," and to "live in a world of their own." Many students described this subgroup's focus on clothing and accessories, but descriptions of the rich extended to interests, lifestyles, attitudes, and behavior. To some students, the exemplars of this subgroup were white females who "wear expensive clothing, jewelry," carry "the same Coach bag," have "the same Dooney and Bourke rain boots," spend money on alcohol or "stupid things like purses," "go on the expensive vacations and have the expensive cars," are "very into their own group," and "very isolated from the general Amherst community." They are "the snottier girls, who show off their wealth," girls who "would exclude people based on class issues" or be "all about keeping people out."

Other descriptions of the subgroup of very wealthy students were not sex-specific. The very wealthy were described as having "really arrogant, off-putting personalities," as "very snobby" with "loud, obnoxious manners." "There's a certain attitude associated with it. Just the way you walk around, sort of feeling like you own the world and that you can get what you want no matter what it is, that they haven't had to work for where they are or what they have today," said Amy, a lower-income white. The very wealthy were thought to dress "Polo-kind-of-stylish," wear "their collars up" (referred to as "popped collars"), wear "some outrageous bright colors" or "brightly colored polo shirts." Students reported that the very wealthy were "more active socially," go out frequently to bars or parties, and throw parties "more often than the general student." They "constantly assert that they're upper class," "bring up their social class whenever you talk to them," are "constantly complimenting each other and talking about how much they have. They brag a lot." They were the students who were "constantly going off campus and traveling to places like Boston or going golfing or skiing or going to New York City, just trips on the weekends and things like that." This group of wealthy students was seen as not "focused on school," as students who would say, "Oh, I'm just not going to go to class tomorrow," who were seen as not working as hard academically "because their futures were assured." "They'll be taken care of." "They just inherit money." They "just want to have a good time while they're here."

These depictions of the very wealthy represent a stereotype, and like all stereotypes, are overgeneralizations and exaggerations. The term "preppy" was readily applied to the very wealthy, but expensive designer clothing and accessories are not associated with the "preppy" style of dressing, which typically includes polo shirts, bright colors, a put-together, coordinated look. While some very wealthy students may not have been focused on academics, many were working extremely hard academically as they, too, were in competition for desired jobs after college.

So, in a reversal of old values and stereotypes on campus, a stigma is now attached by some lower-income and affluent students to a subgroup of very rich students because of their privilege, their perceived arrogance, and their sense of entitlement. It is striking that on a campus where it is unacceptable to disparage people based on their race, religion, or sexuality, and where such comments would bring censure, students felt quite free to make pejorative comments about very wealthy students. Many more negative stereotypes existed on campus about the very rich than the poor. As Amy, a lower-income white, put it, "It's just not politically correct here to be like, 'I'm rich and I am better.'" Others agreed that the very wealthy are "made out sometimes to be the villain," that "going to private school is a little bit stigmatized." Larry, a lower-income white, felt: "It's also easier to demonize really wealthy people with criticism. . . . It's basically an assumed thing that the most wealthy class is responsible for a lot of the inequality because they have the resources to control various things."

Affluent students were put on the defensive in some courses by comments from other students. Two lower-income white females spoke of classes in which negativity or hostility were directed toward the wealthy. Amy reported on a class in which:

> If you say something about being rich, you get knocked down really quickly as feeling you're superior to others and stuff like that. Yeah, we had this one discussion about popped collars and their meaning,

and the girl sitting next to me with the popped collar kept her mouth shut the whole time as people were just bashing on what that meant. And I felt really bad for her.

The other lower-income white, Megan, reported negative connotations attached to being "the very, very, very highly affluent in society. When we were talking about the distribution of wealth in America, even though there were no personal attacks, it wasn't like, 'All rich people are cold hearted and evil,' but it was like, 'This is unfair.' I thought it was fairly presented, but there was still negative shading to it." David, an affluent white, felt that students in a classroom directed scorn at the "idea of the WASP, and sort of put a lot of negativity into it." Kevin, an affluent black, was also sensitive to negative feelings about the affluent. "I think that the people that are affluent are made out to be the villains. The rules are skewed for them."

Hannah, an affluent white, felt criticized by some of her professors because her family was affluent:

Some professors do make [comments], not about poor students, but about highly affluent students. They'll make a comment like, "You don't realize what you have," or "You guys are all rich anyway." I've heard implications of, "You guys don't know what it is like because some of you have grown up in this thing where you don't need to think about this."

Emily, a lower-income white student, had heard a similar comment from a professor in a different course. She found it offensive that the professor implied that all students in the classroom came from wealth, and felt unfairly put down. Andrew, an affluent white, said that he had "definitely heard professors joke about the popped collar issue," making fun of a style of dress adopted by affluent students. Jeremy, a lower-income white, said his professor had called "people 'WASPs' and stuff like that. I feel if I considered myself to be a WASP from that background, I could have been offended by things he said."

Some affluent white students felt that the negative stereotype of the rich had been misapplied to them and, like the lower-income students, believed that they had to prove the stereotype wrong:

I feel that some people, because I went to private school, make assumptions about [me]. I feel like they make assumptions about the way you act, the way your parents are, the way your family is. But at the same time, once you're friends with people, and you tell them something about your past, they're sort of surprised. (Hannah)

Some people have joked that [my wealthy suburb] is really preppy, which I think isn't true, and I'm pretty much the opposite of preppy. I actually hate dressing up. I would refuse to go to a prom just because they would make you wear a suit. I hate fancy restaurants. (Geoffrey)

Another affluent white, Matthew, said that the clothes he brought to campus, such as his khaki pants, were left over from prep school. He did not own any jeans and had not purchased any because he had no idea what students might be wearing on campus:

Just based on the way I dress, a lot of people perceived me at the beginning of the year to be sort of a jerk and stuck up and whatever. And then they said, "When we got to know you we learned that's completely the opposite." One kid said, excuse my language, but he said, "I thought you were an asshole at the beginning of the year," and he was like, "And I never even met you, just based on what I saw."

Classroom Diversity

Students have the opportunity to learn about social class through the curriculum, and while few courses have a primary focus on social class, many addressed class issues from a variety of disciplinary perspectives. Based on a review of students' transcripts and their reports of taking courses that addressed class issues, lower-income students were learning more about social class through the curriculum than affluent students were. Over two-thirds of lower-income students said that they took a course that addressed social class (usually as a subtopic rather than the primary topic), while less than a third of affluent students did so.[10]

Learning can also occur in the classroom through the presence of peers from diverse class backgrounds. Many students reported having benefited from hearing personal experiences of peers in the classroom. Two in five students reported personal sharing by students of different social classes that caused them to change the way they understood social class or their class position.[11] Such comments often stood out and had a strong impact. "It's more the different backgrounds that people have grown up in that is interesting," said Emily, a lower-income white, about classroom discussions. Others agreed. David, an affluent white reported, "I think the most interesting things were when people in those classes really painted this picture of their lives." He felt that "it's hard sometimes to contextualize people," and he felt that he gained a lot from the disclosure of personal information about students from different backgrounds in classroom discussions.

Hearing a student's comment in class helped Larry, a lower-income white, become aware that some students on campus came from very low-income backgrounds. Students had watched the film *Hoop Dreams*, a documentary about black males trying to find success in life through basketball. A black student in Larry's class spoke of being in a similar situation:

> He was recruited right out of middle school and was able to go to a really good high school because he was really good at football. And hearing that was a shocking reminder that there are people here on campus that do come from very low-income backgrounds, and I don't think I'm aware of that constantly. I don't know how much of that is me being callous to it or of people not wanting to expose that right away.

The situation faced by families without means, something many affluent students never thought about, was brought into focus for some students in the classroom: the fact that "certain people can't afford the drugs to keep the people in their family healthy" (Monica, affluent black), or have "struggles to pay for healthcare and stuff" (Benjamin, affluent white).

Hearing students' comments in class helped to break down some class-based stereotypes. Affluent students shared aspects of their experiences in classroom discussions that helped challenge stereotypes about the wealthy. Such comments helped Brianna, a lower-income black, dispel some of her stereotypes of the rich: when affluent students explained, " 'Our parents don't give us everything we want,' it changed my view about upper-class society." She reported that an affluent female in the course, whose father was a professional, had spoken about her parents' expectations:

> Though they were paying for her college, they expected her to do a lot of things on her own, whereas the popular television image of the upper-class girl is where Daddy does everything for you. That changed my view because then it made me think, "OK, while there are still differences, the Hollywood image isn't necessarily correct."

Cross-Class Conversations

One of the hoped-for outcomes of bringing a diverse group of students to campus is that the students will learn from their differences. This was happening in a variety of ways with regard to social class. Much of the learning derived from friendships and conversations with students from different class backgrounds, hearing their life experiences and their perspectives. Three-quarters of the students in the study reported that they formed a close relationship with a student from a very different class background than their own, and of that group, over three-quarters reported that they had increased their understanding of social class through their relationships.[12] Conversations with people from different class backgrounds exposed students to life experiences and perspectives different from their own, enriching their understanding of that difference. Overall, 70% of students reported having had meaningful, honest conversations with peers about issues of social class during the year.[13] For a quarter of the students, conversations about social class occurred at least once a week.[14] For most students, however, discussions about class were infrequent, with three in seven reporting that they had been in a discussion of social class at most a few times a semester.

Some conversations addressed class issues in the society at large. Kayla, a lower-income white, for example, exchanged opinions with friends on "working-class immigrants and whether they can move up to the middle class, and whether in society they will always be kept subjugated, and where we fit in with that." More conversations centered on class issues on the campus itself. Students exchanged differing opinions on how big a role class played, and whether you could hide your social class in your self-presentation and pass for another social class. Students from all four groups agreed that the *Business Week* article had stirred up "a big debate," and students brought their own class-based perspectives to that debate. Heather, a lower-income white, was aware that her support for the initiative to increase the number of lower-income students at the college was influenced by being lower middle class. She felt that "lower-class kids definitely have something to offer"; even if they did not go to the best public schools, "once you get here, it's all just how well you absorb the knowledge and how easy it is for you to get help, which, here, is definitely very easy. So, if you're motivated enough, nothing should be able to hold you back." From the opposite side of the class spectrum, Rachel, an affluent white, seemed less concerned about social justice. "It seemed a lot of my friends and I sort of felt that academics should be the criteria and socio-economic class shouldn't really be looked at."

At times, conversations about class issues on campus became heated and challenging. Christopher, an affluent black, spoke of being "confronted" in the dorm by a lower-income student who felt "at a handicap at Amherst" and believed that unfair advantages accrue to affluent students. Christopher argued that lower-income students were "at a handicap in the long run, but at Amherst not so much."

Some lower-income students, black and white, felt that they offered insights and new vantage points to their affluent friends: "the other side really, a different opinion, and just a different perspective on things" (Dana, lower-income black). "We've been able to teach each other things" (Nicole, lower-income white).[15] Brianna, a lower-income black, felt that she provided insight on stereotypes that are associated with lower class, that they don't speak properly. I'm like, "Yeah. I'm from lower class and I do." I enjoy it. I take a delight in it. I don't agree with a lot of stereotypes because there's no way that you can judge an entire group of people. Even if the vast majority that an individual has personally encountered acts a certain way, you can't judge the entire group.

Justin, a lower-income white, spoke of an "assumption of wealth" among students. In conversations he was able to say, "'Hey, it wasn't like that for me, and this is what my experience has been like.' I think that I surprise people . . . especially students who came from private schools and who were only around people who had similar amounts of money." Megan, a lower-income white, said that her family had been "the recipient of federal aid. We had food stamps for a little while. I have some friends whose parents were on welfare and so if an issue like federal aid to the poor comes up, and people are against it, that's something I do feel strongly about." Brandon, a lower-income black, spoke of sharing experiences that wealthier peers "wouldn't have gone through, like maybe paying bills late, paying tuition late." Emily, a lower-income white, talked with her roommate about how things were for her own family, about "how my family lives, and how different this is for me. I really need to watch what I spend. I don't think she's ever come in contact with anyone who isn't from suburbia." Brandi, a lower-income black, had gone through a "really bad education system" and grew up in a world where "I feel like I've gone through a lot more than other people have, and having to work that much harder to get what you want. It's not handed to you. A lot of things are stacked against you coming from where I come from. Just going to college is a big deal, so I feel I have a lot more to bring."

Many students valued hearing different perspectives from friends of another social class and learning about their backgrounds. In speaking of such a friendship, Kayla, a lower-income white, said, "We come with different outlooks and we come from different backgrounds. Even if we get to the same answer, we get there very differently. I think it's very interesting for us to talk about how we see things and how decisions are based, how we get our information." Heather, another lower-income white, found taking in different class perspectives "enlightening" and said, "It's important and I've enjoyed it so far. I may not have changed too much from it. But it's still just good to talk about things and get things out there." Meeting wealthy students, hearing about their backgrounds, and hearing what they had to say got Larry, a lower-income white, "excited. . . . They seem really cogent in what they talk about, their ideas."

In talking about the opportunity to get to know some extremely wealthy students, Julian, an affluent black, said that these relationships "can give you new light":

You may have hated rich people because you thought they were all stuck up, and then you got introduced to this person and you didn't know he's rich and you become great friends and then he tells you he's rich, and now you have a new perspective on rich people. It can be very rewarding.

Likewise Marc, a lower-income black, felt that rather than "sticking to what you know and having the same sort of people surround you," relationships across class give you

different opinions, different outlooks based on all sorts of different background factors. I can see where people who don't have as much exposure to different sorts of class backgrounds can be resentful towards higher classes and vice versa, and why [rich people might think], "Can't these poor people just get a job and make things better for themselves?"

Breaking Down Stereotypes

When asked whether their experience living and interacting with people from different class backgrounds at Amherst had changed the way they saw people of their own social class or other social classes, approximately two-thirds of the lower-income students, black and white, and of the affluent whites said yes, as opposed to only a third of affluent blacks.[16] It is not clear why fewer affluent blacks reported a change in their perceptions. Alicia, a lower-income black, reported that her views of all social classes had changed. "My stereotypes are starting to break down, which is nice. I just see that there are very different values within different classes, and comparing all of that, one's not necessarily better than the other." As Christopher, an affluent black, put it, "I've been able to put myself in different people's shoes, which has really stopped me from judging so much."

When members of two different groups interact together, they can come to see the variability among the members of each group.[17] In line with these research findings, many lower-income students, both white and black, came to realize that many affluent students on campus did not fit their stereotypes of the rich. Jeremy, a lower-income white, noted that a lot of students "don't want to show off their wealth. That was a stereotype I had before." Marie, a lower-income white, noted that her tendency to "overgeneralize" had led her to think that most wealthy people were "stuck up": "I think I've gotten over that. I've become a little bit more open-minded, to not generalize [about] people based on their class."

The stereotype of rich students as "snobby" broke down for Corey, a lower-income black, who got to know students whose families had "millions of dollars." He realized: "They're just normal people. . . . A lot of them are very similar to me, it's just they happen to have more money." Danny, a lower-income white, similarly came to see that, in many respects, wealthy kids were not that different from people of other social classes. He too had expected the students on campus to be "snobby and all that," but discovered "they're really not. . . . It really makes you see how everybody's really pretty much just the same no matter where they came from." Trina, a lower-income black, saw that affluent students "aren't snobby and snooty," that they were "nice people." Trina realized that some affluent students "don't define themselves by being rich, like, 'I'm a rich kid and that's who I am.' It's made me see people as individuals."

Other lower-income students agreed that the rich were more heterogeneous than they had imagined:

> I had opinions coming in about really rich, snobby, prep school kind of people. And some people I've met have reinforced that and some people I've met have made me realize that it's not where they're from or how much money they have, but who they are. I wouldn't categorize them all together, but then there are the few kids that give the whole group a bad name. (Robert, lower-income white)
>
> I've come to realize that people from a higher social class, . . . not all of them feel entitled. . . . Some of my [affluent] friends, they still had to work in high school and they were given things but they still weren't spoiled or expecting "I should have this," which, based on the little experience I had had, was definitely an assumption I had which I don't anymore. (Nicole, lower-income white)

Alicia, a lower-income black, reported:

> Stereotypes I've held are changing—that not all really wealthy people are bad people or selfish. . . . I'm starting to see that it's a much more complicated issue than "Why are you whining? You're wealthy. You don't have anything to whine about." That's not true. [I'm] starting to figure out everyone has problems. Problems aren't [to be] devalued based on your social class. . . . It's very nice to have that happen.

Marc, a lower-income black, began dating an affluent student: "You hear lots of stereotypes that the rich will stay rich and they don't necessarily want to see things equaled out, that they want their perks." But talks with his girlfriend made it obvious to him that she would rather have things be on "equal ground and [she] doesn't want to make a big deal of 'I'm rich, I need to marry some rich guy.' I think that people are more understanding than [they're] given credit for."

Students, both lower-income and affluent, were sometimes unaware of how rich a fellow student was. One lower-income white, Robert, was at first unaware that his friend was from a much higher class: "We dressed the same, we talked the same. I actually assumed he was from a blue-collar family." It was not until Robert visited the student's home for Christmas that he realized that his friend was "actually very well off. And it made me respect him a little bit more, that he could afford polo shirts and could drive a BMW and all this stuff, but he chooses not to. I actually felt that was pretty admirable of him—he doesn't really need to show off his money."

For two affluent students, visits to a very wealthy student's home likewise contributed to a positive change in their conceptions of the very wealthy and a realization that all wealthy people do not show off their wealth. Christopher, an affluent black, went home with a friend for spring break and only discovered at that point his friend's wealthy background. The experience helped him come to terms with not stereotyping people: "I started thinking how many more kids are there like this, where you don't really put [your social class] out there. I was really happy with him. He doesn't have to put it in my face." On a visit to a friend over spring break, Katelyn, an affluent white, discovered just how wealthy his family was: "But he doesn't really behave like he can just flaunt that wealth." Growing up, she had wished that she were wealthier and that her parents "chose to spend more of our money instead of save it." She came to feel that the very rich, whom she had envied, did not have it all. She discovered that her friend would "rather live in a small house and have his parents care about him instead of working all the time. . . . So that helps to get rid of any lingering envy."

Greater Awareness of Privilege

While many lower-income students spoke of stereotypes of the rich breaking down, few affluent students spoke specifically about a breakdown of stereotypes about the lower social classes. However, much learning took place for affluent students both about their own privileged position and the struggles of those from lower social classes.

In the process of getting to know students with high financial need, some affluent students came to realize that they had lived in an insulated world, had paid little attention to people less fortunate than themselves,[18] and had failed to consider that what they had in life was not shared by most others in society. This finding parallels research showing that dominant groups tend to have less motivation to attend to those with less power.[19]

Through close relationships with students from less privileged backgrounds, Sarah, an affluent white, recognized that her home community "is a real bubble, and it's really hard to see outside the bubble." Sarah had a boyfriend and two best friends with high financial need. These relationships allowed her to "look outside my own social class, realize my own social class. I get this very communist attitude and I just want to make everything all the same and better. . . . I've just been more aware of other people's social classes and how that's affected them." Andrew, an affluent white, spoke of attending a private school in New York where everyone was very well off. Among students at his school the prevailing feeling was that students could do whatever they wanted in life:

> There would be no financial constraints in doing those things. Economic concerns weren't going to form decisions about what you were going to do. My high school was just so insulated from everything. . . . [It] just sort of pisses me off actually sometimes that I never noticed that earlier. It makes me feel like an ignoramus. [Maybe that's] the wrong word, but I don't really know how to describe it. I guess "isolated." But it really has to do with my just having no idea.

Whitney, an affluent black, felt that her private school experience distanced her from people of lower social classes. Meeting lower-income students made her "realize again that people like this *do* exist, people who might be living from paycheck to paycheck."

At times lower-income students challenged affluent peers about their failure to be more aware of those who have less than they do, and helped expose affluent classmates to another class perspective. Brandi, a lower-income black, said:

> Every time my dorm gets fined for dorm damage, I'm like, "Listen, you guys. My family is not rich. You need to stop doing dumb stuff so the dorm gets trashed. I don't care if it's six dollars. I don't want to pay six dollars for something I didn't do. Six dollars adds up over time." So I'm very honest with it. . . . I let people know what I'm thinking.

For these lower-income students, all expenditures involved a choice. Money for dorm damage could mean working extra hours to pay the bill or not having money for something else.

Amy, a lower-income white, reported on a discussion she had with a student who said her mother made $90,000 as if "that's the way it is, like that's so normal. And both her parents work. I looked at her and I was like, 'You should understand that not everyone's parents make that much money.'" Amy

felt that her affluent friend came to see that "people are different and not everyone can afford everything, and that [class] does do something in your life,
that it does have meaningful consequences."

Benjamin, an affluent white, had a close friend with high financial need
who made him aware of things he had not thought about before. The friend
talked about how rich white kids self-segregate: "He was pretty bitter about
it. I can't say that I'd noticed that very explicitly." But his friend stimulated
him to think about it. Nathaniel, an affluent white, was spurred by his
lower-income roommate to recognize that his friends were mostly affluent.
The roommate pointed out Nathaniel's failure to recognize other students on
campus who had less, and the fact that lower-income students occasionally
have to "cut back" or "can't go out to dinner sometimes."

Numerous affluent students, both white and black, spoke of learning
about the experiences of lower-income peers. Matthew, an affluent white,
had a roommate who was "at the bottom of the wealth gap" at Amherst. "He's
told me about his struggles. A lot of this is something I've never had to think
about really. And it does open your eyes to what's out there and the kind of
kids that are also at this college." Hearing his roommate's life story confronted Matthew with a very different class experience. He was impressed by
his friend's ability to support himself without any help from family:

> He had to pay the bills, do everything in his junior year of high school.
> He worked two jobs. I couldn't even imagine doing that. That's amaz-
> ing to me. . . . When I want to go out or mutual friends are going out
> to eat, he might say, "I don't want to go, because I can't afford it." And
> so you think about it a lot.

For Andrea, an affluent black, a best friendship with a student with high
financial need awakened her to different ways of thinking and being in the
world. Andrea noted that her best friend "appreciates things more" and "rolls
with the punches better in terms of money." When she did not get the financial aid she had expected, her friend assumed that she would "find a way to
make up for it"; she was also trying to pay off her loans early:

> I realize that she's just more aware [of] future problems or issues than
> I am. I don't think about that right now, or I don't know if I ever will
> have to. She has shown me that coming from a different social class
> makes you think a different way about how to deal with things now
> and in the future.

Sarah, an affluent white, came to see that she did not take the same approach to college as her lower-income peers because of her privileged economic

situation. "A lot of their efforts are put toward getting wealthy, and they see college as a way to get there. I've never seen that."

Affluent students heard from lower-income students about struggles to pay for college expenses, about the need to work several jobs to pay for campus living expenses, about worries that they might not have enough money to last through the month, about the need to make money during the summer, and about not being able to go home during the semester or to travel. Affluent students gained a greater awareness of their own privilege and came to feel "very lucky that I come from kind of a more affluent family" and "very grateful that my parents are still supporting me." One student realized, "I've had a pretty fortunate childhood," and another came to "appreciate the things I *have* a little bit more." Some expressed guilt about their privilege.

The lower-income students came from a wide range of social class backgrounds. Some lower-income students formed friendships with students whose families had fewer financial resources than they had; they, too, gained a new awareness of their relative privilege. Heather, a lower-income white, had friends who were poor: "I've definitely realized how fortunate I am in comparison to some of the people whom I'm friends with and how remarkable it is that they were able to get in here without as much help as I had, even being like slightly higher up on the social ladder." Amy, another lower-income white, had a close friend on a full scholarship. While talking about summer plans, she suggested that she might be able to visit her friend. Her friend responded:

> "There's probably not a lot of room." And I was like, "I'll just sleep on the floor." And she's like, "No, it's a one-room apartment and there are six of us living there." And I just had to think about what I said in that moment, just my assumption that, of course, there's always room for one more person to hang out even if you don't have a guest bedroom.

A number of lower-income students agreed. They came to realize that they were more privileged than they had thought, and to recognize "how relatively better off I am." "I'm not as disadvantaged as I self-imagined," one said. Another observed, "There are students here that have it much worse than I do."

Knowledge about the Wealthy

Part of the education lower-income students received at Amherst involved learning about prep schools and boarding schools, about the lifestyles and attire associated with wealth. Justin, a lower-income white, saw exposure to wealthy students as a "cultural education" that "just blows my mind." A close friendship with a wealthy student allowed Alicia, a lower-income black, to experience something of the lifestyle of the affluent. "Her parents took me and her and another one of our friends to [a vacation spot] for spring break, an all-expenses-paid trip, which was quite lovely."

Many lower-income students were exposed to a way of life and mindset on campus unlike anything they had ever experienced. There was much less pressure on campus than in their home environments to be practical rather than intellectual. Nicole, a lower-income white, marveled that at college she was "free to have this intellectual exchange" without concerns about paying bills and other obligations. She now had the leisure to sort out what she wanted to do:

> You come to appreciate the education side of [college] more. I can go to my liberal arts college and I can major in something and people [at the college] say, "What are you going to do?" And you're like, "Oh, I don't really know." Whereas everyone else back home thinks that's absolutely absurd. I think that's definitely a sign of the institution and a sign of having the cushions to be able to play around and think about what you want to do.

The elitism of the wealthy became salient to Peter, a lower-income white. Peter recognized that affluent people "tend to see themselves as sort of separated from the masses, seeing themselves not as part of general American society, [but as] sort of a more educated, a more reasonable group of people." He felt that there was "a tendency to feel that being here, you're exceptional and sort of separated."

Some lower-income students came to see that a college education was simply an assumed part of life for wealthy students. For many students on financial aid, Amherst was a precious opportunity that would set them on a new trajectory. It appeared that some wealthy students felt free to study less and focus more on enjoying themselves because they had a greater sense that their futures were assured. Nicole, a lower-income white, felt that she worked harder than some of her affluent friends because it was "such a big deal" being at Amherst. "I feel like I definitely have something to prove while I'm here and that I need to make the most of this opportunity, whereas I think for a lot of people it's kind of standard. . . . I might put more into it than some."

Commonalities across Class

Social scientists have found that inter-group contact can lead to the discovery of similarities between the groups, and, indeed, these benefits were evidenced on campus.[20] Students came to see commonalities they had not previously recognized with peers from very different class backgrounds. Dana, a lower-income black, "learned to not let [social class] get in the way of approaching someone. Before I'd be like, 'Oh, what if we don't have too much in common?' Then I'd be more hesitant about approaching them." But she came to ask, "Are we really that different? I don't think we are." Nicole, a lower-income white, had an "upper"-class friend and came to recognize that despite wide differences in their possessions, they had much in common. "It just shows you that there's really not that big of a difference because of social class, because we get along great. We're very much the same people." She said she was "learning that there's really not that big of a difference between people in general."

Through cross-class friendships, some students learned that social class is not a good predictor of character or values. Heather, a lower-income white, came to recognize that "people aren't that different just based on social class. It doesn't have as much of an influence as sometimes you'd expect it to have." Alicia, a lower-income black, became close friends with a black student who was wealthy, only to discover, she said, "We have very similar personalities but very different backgrounds." A relationship with someone from a very different class background "reaffirmed that class is not that much a dictator of personality in terms of who I am involved with. I find that while all my friends are similar, it has nothing to do with class. They're all from different class backgrounds" (William, affluent black).

Over time some students found that class became less of a barrier. Emily, a lower-income white, reported: "I think I've just accepted the fact that people come from different social classes and that that is just not really a factor to me anymore. I'm more interested in the person." David, an affluent white, reported that his friends had reached

> the point where we can talk about social class and it's not even a huge deal. But it is something that we're all aware of, which is good. It's not [that] we're aware of a bad thing or an awkward thing, it's like we know each other that well, which is nice. So I would say it has surprisingly small effect. I know that that's not true for everybody here, but I think that's sort of cool for my experience so far.

Some affluent students, too, reported discovering commonalities across class lines. Rachel, an affluent white, reported, "I kind of assumed that if I had a friend that was very different socially than I was, then it would be weird or whatever, but it's really not at all. It just doesn't come up with us, really, ever." Benjamin, an affluent white, formed a close friendship with a girl on full financial aid who was from an extremely poor school district. They talked openly about social class, and he learned that class "doesn't matter in the sense that once we're aware of it . . . it doesn't change the way we interact."

Class Categorization

Some students began to reflect on the fact that assigning individuals to particular class categories can be quite complex. A student from a currently affluent family could have been raised in very different financial circumstances, and a student with high financial need might have grown up with affluence. How, then, is a person's social class to be understood? Brianna, a lower-income black, formed a friendship with a student whose family had come from abroad. Before moving to the United States, the student's family was upper middle class, and her father held a professional job, but once here, their class standing changed dramatically. While her father was getting further training, the family of six lived on an annual income of $20,000. Over time, the family attained affluence. Brianna felt that the relationship gave her "a more open mind" about someone's class background.

David, an affluent white, realized "how inconsistent class is." He went on to describe a friend:

Last year, both his parents were working, and this year they both lost their jobs. And it's a huge example of how class can change instantly. And next year they'll have jobs again, but not right now. So his class is not the same right now. People have this idea that class is something that's sort of assured and constant, and it really isn't.

In David's statement, social class is equated with income, an oversimplification of the class system and the multiple components that define a person's social class.

Some students were trying to puzzle out what distinguishes people from different social classes. Was social class a placement on a scale of social advantage,[21] or was social class something one "performed" by enacting particular attitudes or behaviors, or by dressing in a particular manner?[22] David, an affluent white, was perplexed by what it meant to be white and upper class: "If you're not a WASP, are you really upper class? Or do you have to act a certain way to be really upper class? Do you have to know everything about wine and take dance classes to be upper class? Or do you have to have certain manners or eat a certain way?" He was struck by the fact that working on campus did not seem to be a good indicator of social class. Some of his friends came from families with such great financial need that they qualified for full scholarships that did not require them to work on campus. Yet David had affluent friends who worked eight hours a week, and a friend who "doesn't have money in his bank account. And it's not that he comes from a lower class, it's that his parents aren't giving him money. They're like, 'No, you have to work, make some money.'" In fact, holding a job was not an accurate predictor of having high financial need for students in the study. In the spring semester a third of the students in the study reported holding jobs, 30% of affluent students and 38% of lower-income students.[23] Nor was the number of hours students worked a good predictor of social class. Some affluent students, as well as some lower-income students, worked 8–10 hours per week.

Some students recognized a subjective and relative component to social class. Lower-income white students from communities with little class heterogeneity did not feel disadvantaged before coming to college. They were more likely to feel disadvantaged after arriving at Amherst, where they were exposed to a much wider spectrum of wealth. Marie, a lower-income white, realized, "Somebody who lives in wealthy suburbs can feel poor with a lot more income than somebody who lives in a rural area." Angela, a lower-income black, hadn't had "much of a sense of how relative class is. Being around international students I think . . . maybe I'm poor at Amherst, but in terms of internationally, we're all really privileged." Greg, a lower-income black, noted: "Kids that would say they were from lower-class backgrounds, generally when we had an honest conversation, would admit that they weren't poor, but they weren't rich. So I guess the lines were blurred initially."

Class May Go Unseen

Class-based diversity on campus did not guarantee that learning would occur. Some affluent students directed relatively little attention to students from lower-income backgrounds. They formed uniformly affluent groups of friends and demonstrated little awareness that all students did not share their privilege.[24] Nathaniel, an affluent white, saw the college as "a pretty homogeneous place." He remarked that students' spending money came from "what they've earned over the summer, which is $10 an hour, or at least that's what I made, $12 an hour working at the yacht club or a country club caddying or doing whatever. And you can make enough money where it's going to get you through the whole year." Apparently unaware that many lower-income students used summer earnings to pay some part of their tuition or pay off loans, buy necessities like a computer, or help out their families, Nathaniel went on to say, "We all go out to dinner together, and there's no one that really is held back yet." He hadn't as yet "really been part of something where a kid can't afford to do something."

Affluent blacks were the group least likely to have learned from the class differences among students on campus. Some students in this group showed little awareness of the economic diversity there. "I don't think there are a lot of people from a lower social economic class," said Devon. "I think [Amherst] is diverse ethnically but not really socioeconomically" (Whitney). "It's hard to tell the social classes, which I think is kind of a good thing," reported

Monica. "It's not like one social class is separate from the other. But mostly I feel there are a lot of people here from the same social class. I don't feel like there's like a definite group of lower-social-class [students]." Kimberly felt that "the class differences aren't really that apparent, and maybe it's just the people that I hang out with, but I don't really see any major disparities. I don't really feel like [class differences] have any negative or positive effect on anything." Marissa, also an affluent black, seemed unaware that everyone did not possess the social capital that she had. She had benefited from using her parents' connections for jobs and said, "Everybody I know has stuff like that, regardless of your social class. It's just people know people and it can help you out a lot sometimes."

Discussion

Class inequalities and divisions are deeply ingrained in our society. As a consequence, many students came to campus lacking personal knowledge of and experience with people from a very different social class than themselves, making them more prone to stereotypic judgments. As was the case with racial stereotypes, though to a lesser degree, societal stereotypes of the poor and the rich made their way to campus inside and outside the classroom. On occasion people at the lower end of the class spectrum were referred to, by some students, as poorly educated, as liable to bring down the college's standards, "white trash," "dumb low lifes," "hicks," and "hillbillies," as people who don't "work hard" or try to "better themselves." Lower-income students were referred to at times as "they," as if they were not members of the college community. At the other end of the spectrum, the very wealthy were seen by some students as "arrogant," "snobby," "off-putting," "spoiled," "entitled" and "very into their own group."

The college's policy of bringing a larger number of lower-income students to campus is based on a commitment to promoting social mobility, social justice, and equity. The findings suggest that a clear educational argument can be made for the benefits of class-sensitive admissions policies as well.[25] For many students getting to know students from different class backgrounds, and getting to know their life stories and perspectives both inside and outside the classroom, led to the breakdown of class stereotypes, the reduction of class prejudice, greater empathy and understanding, and the discovery of cross-class commonalities. Cross-class relationships helped some students rethink their preconceived ideas about social class and develop a more complex understanding of it. It helped some affluent students recognize their own privilege as well as their lack of awareness of the less fortunate, and helped some lower-income students overcome negative stereotypes of the rich. Overall, three in five students believed that living and interacting with classmates from different class backgrounds had changed their views of social class; two in five felt that they had benefited from class-based diversity in the classroom.

By the end of one year at college, many students showed increased awareness and understanding of, and sensitivity to, class differences, a finding that is quite positive. But some of the potential of living in a diverse community has not been realized. Lower-income students were twice as likely as affluent students to take courses pertaining to social class issues. Such learning provided lower-income students with an analytical framework for understanding their lives and families, and society as a whole.

At year's end, some affluent students, both black and white, lacked awareness of the economic diversity on campus and had not learned from it. In part, such learning is difficult to accomplish with few very low-income students on campus, many of whom do not feel comfortable revealing their family situations. But further change may need to occur in the student culture on campus—a movement toward placing greater worth on learning from peers different from oneself as part of what can be most valuable in a college education. Without this shift in culture, some affluent students may not be motivated to reach beyond what is most comfortable for them and get to know people from very different class backgrounds. Greater learning may yet occur over the next three years if students extend themselves to form deeper relationships with students from backgrounds unlike their own, if they select academic courses that address class issues, or if more structured opportunities are created on campus for greater openness and sharing between students about class stereotypes and class differences.

glass is half full or half empty.

8

Negotiating Racial Issues

Black students had to navigate social relationships both with other blacks on campus and with whites, and each group posed different challenges. Blacks in this study did not all define and present themselves in the same way. Their identities differed because of such factors as social class, the degree of centrality of blackness to their identities, and skin tone, and these differences added complexity to blacks' relationships with one another. In developing connections with whites, blacks had to cope with their own distrust and with concerns about where they stood, how they would be received, and whether whites had their best interests at heart. Black students had to handle those occasions when whites inadvertently made ignorant, insensitive, or offensive racial comments. Their relationships with one another and with the black community are the subject of the first part of this chapter. The focus then shifts to the issues blacks faced in building and sustaining relationships with whites.

[margin annotation: heterogeneity within black community.]

Relationships between Blacks

In the 1970s and 1980s, when concern grew at elite colleges and universities about the need to increase black enrollments, black students were few in number on those campuses and often felt like outsiders.[1] Many blacks in those decades felt that they were not fully accepted by whites and looked to one another for support and friendship. They also joined together to demand changes on their campuses to better meet their needs and to make a place for themselves there: they fought for black studies courses, black cultural centers, additional black faculty members, and additional black students, and they protested racial discrimination and ignorance on campus. Differences existed between blacks within the black communities on campuses in those decades, but those differences were often overlooked as these common concerns drew blacks together.

Today a larger number of black students are present at some elite colleges like Amherst, where students who self-identify as black currently make up 9% of the student body. The college now has a Black Studies Department and a Black Student Union, and racial discrimination has been reduced. But black faculty members are still few in number, and racial stereotypes are still present on campus. Racism has become less overt, but its presence continues to be felt by blacks on campus. Factors that drew blacks together in previous decades in a common struggle to change the status quo are present to a lesser degree and are felt to be more pressing by some black students than others. As this chapter will show, some differences between blacks that were previously overlooked are now being more overtly negotiated. This makes for a more complicated but also for a distinctly vibrant black community in which black students can learn from their differences.

Social Support Networks

Many blacks continued throughout the year to reach out to one another on campus, and at year's end three-quarters of the black students in the study reported that their race had opened up social opportunities for them. Being white and in the majority had social advantages for whites, helping them form connections with other students, but few whites were cognizant of this privilege. Only 15% of white students considered their race to have any social advantages.[2] Marissa, an affluent black, described the support from other black students this way:

> There's a big network based on being a student of color that you have access to. . . . You're invited to things. You meet people through activities that tend to [attract blacks]. The older students reach out to you if you're a student of color, especially a black student.

Similarly, Jason, an affluent black, said, "The African American community at Amherst College is not that big, but it's very tight knit, so I've gotten to know a lot of people, a lot of upperclass[men]."

Some black students spoke of a "need to connect with other people of the same race," of "being in the minority and wanting to stick together," and of the feelings of comfort, understanding, support, and help they derived from interactions with other black students.[3] Whitney, an affluent black, sought out other blacks because "you have something in common. . . . Honestly I've had more time with black people, so you can sit down and talk to them about more." If she were in trouble and needed to talk with someone, Andrea, an affluent black, felt that "maybe people of the same race can relate more to the issue than people of a different race, or maybe people of another race won't be there for you." Particularly when advice on how to handle a racial issue was needed, blacks turned to one another. Julian, an affluent black, felt that it was easier to talk with other blacks because they understood what it was like being at Amherst. Talking with whites involved some strain: "Sometimes I get tired of interacting with white students all the time, to be honest, but on the whole I came here knowing that I'd have to do it. And I had to do it for 12 years before this, and I have no problem." Some black students from predominantly black or mixed-race communities were used to socializing with other black students and missed being in an environment with more minorities. They chose to hang out with other blacks because frequently they were "the only black person around." In contrast to high school, where blacks in predominantly white schools returned to black families at the end of the day and could unwind, relax, talk about any racist incidents freely, and seek comfort, they were now surrounded by whites 24 hours a day, 7 days a week.

Talia, an affluent black, joined the Hip-Hop dance group rather than the modern dance group because "it's just nice to have other black people around." Five black students in the study joined that group (Dancing and Stepping at Amherst College). Corey, a lower-income black, found common ground with other blacks because of things they shared, like watching Black Entertainment Television. "There aren't going to be many white students that watch BET. So we couldn't really connect on the same level."

Marissa, an affluent black from a predominantly white community who had attended a high school that was only 10% black, felt that it was important to form connections with other blacks to show support for the black community on campus:

> My parents even said it's important for you to get to know the black
> students because there are not very many of you, so you should all
> know each other at least. And I think that was sound advice because I
> think that, at least in my community back home, all the black families knew each other, and it was kind of a way of networking, and that
> was just how I was raised.

Like most college campuses, Amherst has a black student organization, the Black Student Union (BSU), whose stated purpose is to serve as "a resource mechanism to foster the social, political, cultural and intellectual development of Black students at Amherst College."[4] Most blacks in the study did not become members of the BSU (four lower-income blacks and two affluent blacks did so), but many blacks attended some BSU events. For those who joined, the BSU provided a "sense of community," connections to other black students, and involvement in activities. Further, it connected first-year students with upperclassmen who could offer support and advice, look out for them, and serve as mentors. The BSU organizes two major events, Harlem Renaissance (a 1930s-style jazz club complete with dinner, dancing, and performances that showcase black talent on campus) and Kwanzaa (a celebration of African American culture with speakers and performances, followed by a dinner). Many black students, whether or not they are BSU members, plan and participate in both events. Many blacks also attend the Bi-Semester Worship Series, which includes a church service followed by a Sunday brunch.

Black students received overtures not only from the BSU, but also from other campus groups popular among black students. Marc, a lower-income black, spoke of being "tagged" as an African American to join "diversity coalitions" and "race identification" groups. Students were also invited to lectures, dance parties, and informal social gatherings. These invitations were met with mixed reactions from some black students, who did not want to join these groups or activities but felt that other blacks *expected* them to do so and would be critical of them if they did not.

Issues Negotiated between Blacks

The larger number of blacks on campus created an environment in which some differences between blacks needed to be worked through. Blacks formed a heterogeneous group, and the differences that divided blacks students were likely greater than those that divided white students. Blacks differed in social class, in the centrality of race to identity, and in cultural heritage (i.e., some were Caribbean American, some African American, some African; some were biracial, others mixed-race). They varied greatly in skin tone, in use of "black" forms of speech, in preferences for "black" forms of dress and music. They came from the North and South, from the inner city and the suburbs, and differed in their experiences of racism in society. Helpful and supportive as it was for many blacks to connect to others of their race, 30% of blacks in the study, regardless of class background, reported not feeling comfortable with some of the black students on campus.[5] And as noted in Chapter 5, a quarter of the blacks in the study stated that none of their close friends were black.

Whites notice and often comment on blacks sitting together at tables in the dining hall, an arrangement that gives some the impression that all blacks are part of a tight-knit black community. The vast majority of tables filled by students who are all white are overlooked.[6] Blacks who ate at the "black" tables were simply friends who chose to eat together, just as other tables were filled with friends eating together. But not all black students were part of these friendship groups. A number of affluent blacks said they chose not to sit with blacks in the dining hall: "My parents are wealthy enough to not have to receive financial aid. I don't really fit into the, as [a former student] calls it, the 'black hole' in Valentine, which is all the kids that are pretty much on financial aid sitting together in this one part of the cafeteria. And I've just never been able to sit in that group" (Christopher, affluent black). Another affluent black, Andrea, felt that the blacks sitting together in the dining hall formed a tight group, and she was reluctant to join them "because they all have these inside stories, and they're all really best friends," and she would have felt "out of the social loop."

These comments leave the impression that the tables at which blacks ate together in the dining hall were composed entirely of black students (they are in fact noticeably but not exclusively black), and that black students on financial aid were most at ease there. However, blacks from a wide variety of socioeconomic backgrounds sat at these tables, and not all the lower-income black students were comfortable sitting there. Alisa, a lower-income black, reported, "A lot of black people are in the middle part of the cafeteria, and I feel not so comfortable completely around them. . . . Yeah, they're black, but I don't know them." Trina, another lower-income black, noted, "They all sit there in Val. And I think they look down on me because I don't sit with them. . . . I feel that their self-segregation only heightens the racial tension in Val or in class."

Social Class

Differences among blacks in their social class backgrounds had to be negotiated. Lawrence Otis Graham, a bestselling author and commentator on race, politics, and class in America, writes that blacks "divide first by class, and later by race." Graham writes that members of the black elite are raised to view poor blacks as an out-group: "They don't relate to us and we don't relate to them."[7] The social distance between blacks raised in the inner city with few financial resources and blacks with wealth and social standing must be crossed. For blacks from lower-income families, a lot of distance had to be crossed to connect to wealthy blacks who had not shared their struggle, and with whom it was difficult to identify. Angela, a lower-income student, was aware of "black students who don't talk to other black students because they're from a different class." William, an affluent black, expected that "as an African American I'd have a lot in common with African Americans in general." But he discovered at college "that class is important. . . . Making friends with certain lower-class African Americans is a little complicated because some of them will say, like, 'sellout.' . . . I'd be willing to be friends with a lot of people who are more accepting."

Centrality of Race to Identity

Black students, both lower-income and affluent, differed on how central race was to their identities[8] and how much significance they accorded to it.[9] Thirty-six percent of the affluent blacks and 57% of the lower-income blacks gave race a rating of 6 or 7 on a 7-point scale of importance, while most of the remaining blacks gave ratings of 3 or 4.[10] As Devon, an affluent black, put it, "I don't know if this is politically correct or whatever, but there are black people and then people that don't really identify themselves as black people." Brandi, a lower-income black, said, "I love being black. . . . It's something that I'm proud of being. But I don't let it overshadow who I am." For Megan, an affluent black who had attended a predominantly white elite private school, race had low salience in her life, and she felt "a little bit isolated from the black community" on campus. "I am conscious that that aspect of black culture is not necessarily imbedded in me. I can't dance; I'm bad at rhythm; all those stereotypes." Megan's identity was built strongly around her academic interests:

> It's not like I'm purposely shunning the black community. I'm not one of those politically active people who join the Amherst College Diversity Coalition and everything and are gung ho. And I probably should be, but I was taught to not prioritize my race. I don't really see it in color, which is both an advantage and disadvantage in terms of my life.

Alicia, a lower-income black, joined the BSU at the beginning of the year because students in the BSU were "all really welcoming and orientation was wonderful," but she dropped out later in the year:

> A lot of people in BSU definitely *do* identify themselves mainly by their race. I don't do that. I don't identify with a certain group of people just because they're a certain color. And I think that was really hard for me to go through and have to decide, well, do I really want to be with these people who are really nice and open and welcoming? But I really don't feel comfortable because that's not how I define myself.

Assumptions about Associating with Blacks

While overtures from black students were experienced in a positive way as an entrée into a social support network, some black students felt that implicit in these overtures was the assumption that they *should* coalesce with other blacks around being black. Half the black students reported having felt some pressure to be with other students of their race.[11] Regardless of social class background, black students spoke of the expectations they felt some black students held that they should "stick together" and form relationships with one another. Some black students feared that if they chose not to socialize primarily with black peers, to join black groups, or to exclusively date other blacks, they might be seen as opposing the black community, which was not their intention.

Some blacks did not hold to the premise that their social world on campus should be centered on race:

> I feel that a lot of people assume that black people are always going to hang out with black people, they date black people, they hang out with them, they party with them. And I don't cut myself off to any other people just because they're not black. (Andrea, affluent black)

Another affluent black, Marissa, observed:

> If I didn't associate with anyone who was black, I would be looked down upon because I've seen people be judged before. People here who don't really talk to other black people are kind of judged. People are like, "I wonder why she doesn't," or "[I] wonder what's her deal or his deal."

Angela, a lower-income black, noted: "There's a certain way that black students look at black students who don't talk to other black students. There's a term for it. 'Incog-negro' is not talking to someone just because they look like you."

Criticism of blacks who did not socialize with many other blacks came from whites as well. Kimberly, an affluent black who did not have many black friends, reported that her white friends joked about that fact: "I want to say it's funny, but there's not really anything funny about it." Christopher, an affluent black, said, "A lot of times the black kids that hang out with the white kids get called 'Oreo,' black on the outside, white on the inside. It's usually black kids that say it. I mean, white kids [do] too."

The choice to join or not to join the BSU reflected differences in the importance students placed on a black community and a black support network, and differences in how much they wanted to devote themselves to promoting black culture and working toward making the college a better place for blacks, rather than other interests. Some blacks were reluctant to join the BSU because in the year they entered college the BSU was in the process of rebuilding and was not highly organized. Members hoped other black students would join them and extended many invitations to incoming students at the beginning of the year. Brandi, a lower-income black from a high school that was 7% black, felt that she did not need the support system the BSU offered. The college was "not a culture shock" for her, since she was not "transitioning from being with predominantly black people to white people." Similarly, Kimberly, an affluent black, did not "see the need for a group of people to get together, [where] the only commonality they have is the same skin tone. I've never really been a part of stuff like that . . . and I don't really want it to start being a big factor in my life." From the perspective of BSU members, these students' understanding of the organization was somewhat narrow, since the BSU's mission includes the goals of helping the campus deal more effectively with racial discrimination and making it a better place for black students.

When they did not follow up on invitations to join black groups or socialize primarily with blacks, a number of black students reported discomfort and disapproval from some black peers. Andrea, an affluent black who did step dancing in high school but chose not to do it in college, felt "put down" by blacks for not wanting to do it. Black students said to her, " 'But you should do it because you're black, and you have had previous experience.' It's like, yes, but that really pissed me off actually." Trina, a lower-income black who did not sit with other blacks in the dining hall, felt criticized by those who did. "They're like, 'Oh, the black freshmen are so complacent. They don't go to the BSU meetings. They don't sit at the table with all the black people.' " Alisa, a lower-income black, would be asked by other blacks, " 'Why aren't you into this event? All the other black people are going.' It was like, 'I don't want to go.' It was like, 'Why didn't you apply to be a Diversity Intern?' I want to work in the Admission Office. I don't want to have to just work with the Diversity Interns." The word "should" came up over and over again. Greg, a lower-income black, felt that he "should" hang out more with blacks, "just so as not to seem like I'm abandoning my race. I'm not trying to avoid them." William, an affluent black, talked about invitations he had not responded to, and felt that he "should network or connect better with the African American community. I haven't really done much to become part of, like, any union or done much at BSU."

Not living up to such expectations was harder for some than for others. Not all students experienced overtures from other blacks as pressure. Brianna, a lower-income black who chose not to attend a BSU meeting, believed other students were "accepting of her decision," and Brandi, another lower-income black, also felt that students were not going to say, " 'Come out with us because you're black,' at all. It's not even like that." Corey, a lower-income student, felt that the expectation "was around" to be with other blacks, but "not for me particularly." Over time the personal invitations trickled off and turned into e-mail invitations, which were much easier to ignore and facilitated black students' ability simply to make their own choices about how to spend their time and who to spend it with.

Being "Black Enough"

Defining what it means to be black is complex in this society. Race has been understood by some as a biological construct designating people who share phenotypic characteristics like skin color and facial and bodily features. But sociologists Michael Omi and Howard Winant speak for many when they argue that

> selection of these particular human features for purposes of racial signification is always and necessarily a social and historical process. . . . There is no biological basis for distinguishing among human groups along the lines of race. Indeed, the categories employed to differentiate among human groups along racial lines reveal themselves, upon serious examination, to be at best imprecise, and at worst completely arbitrary.[12]

Many agree that race is not a biological construct, but rather a socially created phenomenon, that racial groups are "a matter of social, political, and historical contingency, rather than transhistorical biological necessity."[13]

Various criteria have been applied to answer the question of who is black. Our society has used the "one-drop rule," meaning that a person with any black ancestry at all is categorized as black. Statutory definitions have varied by state: some states required one-thirty-second "black blood" to be black, others one-eighth or one-fourth.[14] Race has also been described by sociologist Sarah Willie as "relational, situational, and interpersonally dynamic."[15] In her interview study of African American alumni of historically black and white universities, Willie found that "race did not just *happen to* the men and women with whom I spoke (even if they happened to be born into racial categories)";[16] rather, her participants talked about race in multiple ways:

> black alumni described the ways they consciously *acted white* in certain settings and *acted black* in others. Although they saw themselves as black, that did not mean they understood blackness as something simple or simplistic. *The people with whom I spoke treated race as sets of behaviors that they could choose to act out*, as expectations they had of themselves and others, as physical difference, and as ethnicity and subculture.[17]

Given the complexity of what it means to be black, it should not be surprising that some students in this study struggled with questions about their blackness. Students differed, as described above, on how central race was to their identities and on the extent to which they accorded significance to it. But blacks on campus, as in the larger society, also faced external judgments by both blacks and whites about how "black" they were. Self-definition and external judgments of "blackness" by others were not always consistent. External judgments about where students fell on an implicit scale of "blackness" might be determined by skin tone, tastes, interests, forms of speech, and whether they hung out with blacks.[18] The closer students came to stereotypical images of urban black youth, the blacker they were considered to be.[19] Over half the black students reported that their blackness had been questioned by other students on campus—50% of the lower-income blacks and 62% of the affluent blacks.[20]

Marissa, an affluent student, spoke of expectations to "fit a certain stereotype to seem more black." In a room full of blacks, Marissa often felt like "the least black person in the room." Students could be considered "more black because of what they wear" (Carl, lower-income). When socializing with other black students, Dana (lower-income) felt accused of not being "black enough." Another lower-income black, Trina, was frustrated that black students made judgments about the "blackness" of others. "You hear what they say about other people, 'Oh, she's not really black!' I'm like, 'What is she?' Being black is a color. You can't not be black if you're brown." Some students felt quite vulnerable to such questioning and found it "really tough" to be "constantly having to prove that you're black" (Alicia, lower-income), while others felt more secure in their blackness and felt less pressure to meet expectations. Some of the questioning came from white students, but the more painful questioning came from other black students.

Skin Tone

Historically, prestige and mobility for blacks in this country and acceptance into elite black organizations have been associated with passing the "brown paper bag and ruler test"—that is, having a complexion lighter than a brown paper bag and hair as straight as a ruler.[21] Dark-skinned blacks in America experience significantly more discrimination than their lighter-skinned counterparts, earn less money, and complete fewer years of education.[22] The Black is Beautiful movement of the 1960s and 1970s reversed racist norms of beauty based on white standards but did not lead to permanent change in American culture. Lighter skin, as sociologist Sarah Willie argues, "can operate as a privilege whether the person who is so marked is conscious of it, wants it, or fails to exploit it actively."[23] Devon, an affluent black, recounted an incident in the dorm when a lighter-skinned friend offended her and her friends. When they came to this girl's door, the lighter-skinned friend, "trying to be witty," said, "'You can't come in, it's only light-skinned people, and you guys are too brown,' or something. And she closed the door in my face."

The situation could be reversed, and blacks with lighter skin could be subject to discrimination by blacks with darker skin. Through interviews with African American college women, sociologist Margaret Hunter found that many wanted lighter skin and eyes, which they felt would increase their attractiveness to men. Jealousy or resentment led them to keep lighter-skinned women out of their inner circle of friends.[24] Likewise, Hunter found that lighter-skinned African Americans and mixed-race (black/white) women who identified as black were ostracized by their dark-skinned peers.

Consistent with Hunter's research, skin color was found at Amherst to play a role in relationships between black women. Differences in skin tone divided them because of the preference for lighter-skinned women they had heard some black men on campus express. Adding to the complexity, some lighter-skinned blacks were made to feel that they could not legitimately claim their blackness because their lighter skin meant that they had not shared the same experiences in society as their darker-skinned peers. Marissa, an affluent black, spoke of a black friend who made her feel that there was something "I couldn't possibly understand because my skin was lighter than hers, like I couldn't have the same experience or know any of the same things." Devon, also affluent, spoke of a conversation with black friends, one of whom was "very into her blackness. . . . And she was basically saying how she doesn't like my two [biracial] friends. My [biracial] friend was like, 'Yeah, she just doesn't like us because we're too light or something, and she likes you because you're brown.'"

Alicia, a lower-income black from a predominantly white community, had never confronted the issue of "being black or the tone of my skin color not being really dark" before coming to college. She was light-skinned and now found that she had to "deal with constant comments about skin color. . . . Sometimes I feel excluded from this group of my friends who are very dark-skinned. And sometimes I don't. It all depends on what we're doing and what's up that day."

"Acting White"

Social scientists studying high school students have found that blacks who speak standard English, use a large vocabulary, enjoy classical music, rock music, ballet, opera, dress in clothes from the Gap or Abercrombie and Fitch, hang out with whites, or are high academic achievers (i.e., get good grades, go to the library, study hard) may be accused by other blacks not only of not being "black enough," but also of "acting white."[25]

Blacks in this study, both affluent and lower-income, were all high achievers in high school, and many had developed patterns of speech, styles of dress, and tastes in music that ran counter to the urban black stereotype and, in some cases, to the culture of their families and some peers.[26] As a consequence, their "blackness" had been questioned by family and peers as they were growing up, and accusations of "acting white" were common. Marissa, an affluent black, said that her dad made fun of her taste in music and called her "white-black." Students spoke of being teased about "acting white" or "sounding white" or being "a little white boy" by siblings and relatives because of their speech. Students' blackness had been called into question by peers in high school. The difficult position of young affluent blacks is reflected in Andrea's account of being "ridiculed a lot of times for not speaking Ebonics, I guess you could call it, with the 'yo' and the 'whatsup' and stuff." Andrea had never been taught to speak that way, but "people would say I don't speak like a black person. I don't dress like a black person. I was called 'white' a lot. And it did bother me." As Alisa, a lower-income black, put it: "I seem black here, but if I were at my home high school, yeah, 'You're white.' It's just I didn't act like them."

While most blacks at Amherst had been accused of "acting white" in high school because of their high academic achievement, that was *not* the case on campus. Academic achievement was expected and highly valued for all students, regardless of race. However, the racial authenticity of blacks could be questioned because their tastes, interests, speech, clothes, and knowledge of black culture did not fit a particular black urban stereotype.[27] "Acting white" could result in social sanctions from black peers, ranging from comments about one's blackness to exclusion.[28]

Layers of meaning might be ascribed to the forms of dress black students wore on campus. As Christopher, an affluent black, reported, "Let's say I'm wearing this, and black people say, 'Oh, he's trying to act white.' Let's say I wear my hat backwards like this. White people will say, 'Oh, he's trying to act black.'" Greg, a lower-income black, felt that his blackness might be questioned "on a Saturday night when I leave my room wearing some 'white' clothing." Andrea, an affluent black, didn't own "the typical black clothing name brands," but had "no problem not owning it." When she mentioned where she shopped for clothes, she received comments from students like "'Oh, you shop there. That's a really white store.' And I'm like, 'What the hell does that mean?'"

Many black students, regardless of class background, had their blackness questioned by black and white friends because of their cultural preferences. Whites were surprised to encounter blacks who did not fit their preconceived notions of blackness, blacks who *did not* listen to rap music, or who *did* listen to rock music. An affluent black reported that students did a "double take" when hearing the music she listened to. Marc, a lower-income student, raised the eyebrows of some of his white friends because of the music he listened to:

> I don't necessarily listen to rap, which is supposedly stereotypical of black music or jazz or anything like that. I think my music tastes are

very eclectic and varied, and as a result, they'll go, 'Wow, you listen to that. You know about that band.' And it's like, 'Well, yeah, it's just music.' So there have definitely been some stereotypes about that.

Alicia, a lower-income black, felt that on campus "societal stereotypes really come into play. . . . I don't have the proper speech of a black person to talk about a certain issue. . . . If you don't use that slang, then you're not black. You don't fit the black mold. And I have never used slang like that in my entire life." Conversing with a student who had "very dark skin and she's very black power," Alicia used the word "fun" while her friend used the word "hot." "We actually got into a big argument about it because I was like, 'I can say "fun." Don't pick on me and rag on me because I say "fun" versus you saying "hot." It doesn't matter.' "

Students faced a choice: move closer to the cultural stereotype to prove their blackness, or be black in another way. Steven, an affluent black, expressed the difficulty of that choice:

Now that I hang out with black kids I feel kind of pressured to use slang and lingo and things. That makes me uncomfortable because it doesn't come that naturally to me. And also the way I dress. I don't dress like the rest of them normally. And that makes me kind of uncomfortable when I go into large social situations where there's lots of people that I don't know. Because then I stand out a lot.

In talking about a friendship, Marissa, an affluent student, recognized that there were many valid ways to be black:

I don't think that anybody should fit a certain stereotype just so that they can seem more black. In the past I probably would have tried to fit in and act differently so that [my friend] would like me or accept me more, but now coming here I realize my blackness is not worse or less valid than hers just because I don't like the same things.

Finding a black student on campus who provided a different model of being black and who did not adopt the urban version of blackness was helpful to Christopher, an affluent black, in resisting perceived expectations. Worried about what he was wearing to a party, whether his "white" clothes were "OK to wear," Christopher was excited to see another black student "wearing a polo shirt, and wearing his hat properly! I was like, 'Wow, this is where I should be!' " Some blacks would take issue with his use of the word "proper" because of its implicit devaluation of the urban version of blackness.

Empowerment

One of the benefits of being in a community with students of different races was that it enabled some black students to experience a genuine sense of empowerment around their own blackness, primarily through their relationships with whites but also with other blacks. Corey, a lower-income black, noted: "A lot of my white friends, they just assume that I'm an example of someone who's black. They're not around black people all the time. They don't know. So to them, it's just, 'I am a black person.'" Marissa, an affluent black, reported: "My quintessential struggle with the race growing up was, I wasn't white enough and I wasn't black enough and I was somewhere in the middle, and I had to negotiate or reconcile." To most people "it's just 'What do *you* know?'" But at Amherst Marissa came to see herself in a new light through a relationship with a white friend because she got to illuminate and explain for her friend things about "being black or about black culture." She found that for her white friend, "I'm black enough." The experience was "validating" of her blackness, and being black enough in her white friend's eyes led to feeling "accepted in the same way by other black students here."

Negotiating Inter-Group Relationships

In our society interracial interactions can be strained or fraught with anxiety. Members of minority groups are often anxious about facing prejudice or rejection.[29] Whites tend to fear embarrassment about saying the wrong thing. Indeed, occasions arose when white students said things blacks took to be ignorant or racially offensive. A quarter of the black students reported hearing whites make what they felt were insensitive or ignorant comments about race, which contributed to inter-group tension.[30] Most blacks on campus said that they rarely, if ever, encountered overtly racist comments. For some blacks, it was only by narrowing their focus to classes and activities that they avoided noticing racial slights, which they otherwise noticed frequently. They coped with everyday racism by directing their attention elsewhere.

On occasion some overtly racist comments appeared under the cloak of anonymity on the *Daily Jolt* website. "People will say things like 'Minority students don't contribute anything to campus life. Why is [race] a factor in admissions?'" (Angela, lower-income black). Such racially insensitive comments, when they appeared, were experienced as alienating by black students. Dana, a lower-income black, felt that racist comments were often made in ignorance, without intent to offend: "One of my white friends used the word 'nigger,' but I don't think she realized what she was saying." Many blacks would have taken offense. Megan, an affluent black, spoke of a white friend who made racial jokes: he "doesn't realize that he's being offensive to us because we're good friends with him." Megan went on to say:

> I always had this thought in my head that if somebody was racist they would be really malicious about it and just be like, 'Ha ha, I'm racist and evil.' But [my white friend] probably is the most racist person I have ever been close to ever. He just doesn't realize that he's being offensive because that's the way he grew up.

Classroom Issues

Blacks who took courses where racial issues were under discussion were more likely to hear racist or ignorant comments by whites, as whites' beliefs and biases about race were more likely to be exposed in this context. For example, Jason, an affluent black, reported a white student in his class saying, "If I went to some uncivilized country in Africa full of savages, I could take it over and build myself an ideal society." Devon, an affluent black, reported hearing a white student argue against affirmative action because "black people have the same opportunities as white people." When comments reflecting racial bias and lack of knowledge went unchallenged by other white students in the class, this fostered black students' perceptions that other whites shared the same ideas and perspectives. Amber, a lower-income white, expressed concern about what she considered to be "dumb" and "really insensitive and ignorant remarks" made by a white male in one of her classes. She and her classmates "worried that the nonwhite people were going to judge us based on [his comments]."

Christopher, an affluent black, spoke about a classroom discussion about racial profiling in which he found whites' attitudes to be offensive. "I couldn't believe I was at Amherst. I felt like I was in the South." The professor posed the following situation: a police chief in New Jersey has information that a very small group of individuals are engaged in drug trafficking, but 85% of that group are minorities, "young black males, basically." The professor called on a student and said:

> "OK, you're the chief of police. Would you issue the mandate so that your police force [is] allowed to pull over based on race?" And this kid was like, "Yeah, it's a statistic. You're not being racist, but you have a statistic." And then [the professor] was going around the room, four or five kids saying, "Yeah, it's OK, I guess."

Even the absence of racially offensive comments was not fully reassuring to some black students. Trina, a lower-income black, believed that the absence of ignorant or racist classroom comments by whites might simply be an attempt to mask their real feelings because a black person was present. Being black, she believed,

> adds a different dynamic to the class. People are more conscious of their words. I don't think it stops people from thinking racist thoughts, but it stops them from expressing them. I don't know if that's a good thing or a bad thing. I'd rather people be truthful about what they're thinking and allow me to say, "No, that's not correct," rather than [their] saying, "Oh, that black girl's going to get upset so I'm not going to say what I want to say, but I'm going to think it."

It was not uncommon for a black student to report being the only black student in a classroom or one of a few, a situation that could pose difficulties when racial issues were under discussion.[31] Joe Feagin and his colleagues, in a study of blacks at a predominantly white university, found that black students often became the "objects of attention when racial issues arise in class," which put them in an awkward position.[32] Christopher, an affluent student, spoke of feeling "uncomfortable" in a large lecture course; it was "awkward to be one of 6 black kids out of 150 students, to be sitting there like everyone's looking at you." One student recalled the time the professor "looked right at me because I was the only black person in the class, and he was talking about black people, and he kept looking at me" (Devon, affluent). When students were reading slave narratives aloud and they came to "the N-word": "You can see the eyes looking around the classroom and thinking, 'Oh boy, is he going to be offended?'" (Marc, lower-income). Brandon, also lower-income, found it awkward when "some teachers or students look to you to give your perspective."[33] Dana, another lower-income student, spoke of a class in which students read a book about a young black woman at a predominantly white school: "A lot of the white kids were like, 'Oh, was this really what it's like to come from a black background?' And then they'd look at me, and I was just, 'I can't answer it for my race.' It was just a little uncomfortable when everyone just looks at you and expects you to answer." Another lower-income student, Trina, found being looked to for the black perspective difficult:

> People just assume that I'm African American. . . . They just see all black people as being the same culturally. I'm actually a first-generation immigrant. I know little about black cultures, so when I'm in black studies class, don't expect me to be informed on everything black because I'm learning about it just as much as you. I'm not in black studies to be a second teacher to you, but to learn as well. And I felt that

not just in black studies classes, but in my First Year Seminar. I think a lot of people turned and asked me a question about "How does the black community feel?" I'm a first-generation immigrant. I have no idea. And I don't think there's one person on campus that walks around with the encyclopedia of everything black.

Black students can be put in an untenable position, singled out to speak for their race as if a single racial perspective existed. They are expected to take on the role of educating white peers. As Feagin and his colleagues put it, black students feel "the burden placed on them by whites to act as defenders and explainers of their group."[34]

Racial Joking

As blacks and whites on campus tried to cope with the multiple occasions when racial misunderstandings, disagreements, or social missteps might occur, they drew at times on humor to deal with racial stereotypes or challenges to racial authenticity. Martin, a lower-income black, said blacks and whites "joke about race all the time on our floor. We give each other a hard time all the time." Over half of the blacks in the study said they had heard racial comments framed as jokes, while just under 20% of whites reported hearing such jokes.[35] Blacks, too, joked with each other about racial stereotypes, in part to make painful realities about race more manageable. Alicia, a lower-income black, said, "Everyone makes jokes about race, just like racial slurs said in a joking manner or just joking. I think that's very present on campus."

Some of the challenges to students' blackness discussed above were framed in a joking manner by whites. Julian, an affluent black, reported that when he put on a country song, whites would say, " 'Oh man, you're not black anymore, we're losing you. You're playing country and you actually know the words to it.' " Black students reported comments framed as jokes about their departure from racial stereotypes: for example, listening to less rap music than a white friend did, not sounding "black," not liking fried chicken, attending private school.

Joking occurred about blacks being indistinguishable from one another. Martin, a lower-income black, said that another black student hung out on his floor a lot, and occasionally whites would intentionally call them by each other's names, making fun of the notion that one black person was interchangeable with another. Racial terms were applied in a joking manner. Danny, a lower-income white, spoke of teasing that went on between his black and white friends. One black friend was referred to by the name of a black TV figure. "He knows we're kidding, and most people know we're kidding, so we're very insensitive if somebody didn't know us, but we're just very good friends and we know each other's kidding and nobody takes offense to it." The black male, in turn, "calls us all his honky friends."[36]

Groups must negotiate which forms of joking are appropriate within the moral boundaries of the group.[37] What is a joke to one member of the interaction may be offensive to another, and although a joke may have been meant well, it may be taken as an affront. Students had to discover the limits to what they could say. Whites had to figure out in the context of friendships with blacks whether they were good enough friends that they could joke about racial issues, or whether such jokes would be experienced as insulting.

In the experience of some white students, racial stereotypes framed as jokes were simply humorous: "It's acceptable because we know they're joking and it's funny because we know each other so well" (Jeremy, lower-income white). In many instances blacks talked about the racial teasing as "just a joke," as just "completely joking around"; they felt that "it's not ever intended to offend." But the joking at times cut more deeply—for example, when it involved accusations of getting into college because of race.[38] Julian, an affluent black, said that one of his close friends "joking around" would say: " 'You only got in here because you're black.' I know he's joking around. And I'll be like, 'Whatever. There's no quota here or anything like that.' And he'll be like, 'Whatever, they still want black kids.' And I'm like, 'Whatever, that might be true, but that's not why I got in.' " Christopher, an affluent black, said he and a white friend "always make fun of each other. . . . Obviously neither of us are really serious, but we're just teasing each other." Christopher would tease his friend about getting admitted because he was "a dumb football player," and his white friend would say, "Oh, you just got in here because you're black." Christopher went on to say that racism was never "blatant," that students "joke around about things. But at the same time it has a little truth to it. . . . I've heard a lot of 'getting in here because you're black.' That's a big thing."

Racial joking at times was seen by blacks as racist and the use of humor by whites as a thin disguise for racist feelings. The problem, as Whitney, an affluent black, put it, was that a lot of people joke about race, but "you never know if it's a joke or not." She went on to say that in a situation where whites were joking with blacks and using racial stereotypes, "When is it enough? When do you laugh and when is it serious? But also, not that I believe this, but a lot of people think all white people are racist and that when they're behind closed doors, they just say whatever they want to say about other races."

Responding to Racial Offenses

When whites unwittingly went too far and said something that was racially offensive and upsetting to blacks, blacks spoke of seeing several ways to respond, none of which they found to be adequate. The first option involved confrontation—expressing the anger they felt and informing the white student that they experienced the comments as racist and hurtful. Trina, a lower-income black, described a white friend in her dorm whose racial joking had gone too far. A bunch of students on the floor confronted him, and when he claimed he was "just joking," they were insistent: "No, you have to stop"; his behavior was hurtful to his black friends. Angela, a lower-income black, experienced a white friend's comment on slavery as ignorant and upsetting, and it provoked her to anger. Her friend, who had been reading the slave narrative by Harriet Jacobs, said that "slavery in the South wasn't that bad" and that whites and their black slaves were "like families and some of the [sexual] relationships were consensual. And I just got really angry with her. We fought over that."

Direct confrontations and expressions of anger often did not lead to a good outcome, and black students struggled with whether to express angry feelings. They were concerned that through their expressions of anger, they would fulfill whites' stereotypes of the militant, angry black person, the Malcolm X or militant Black Panther, the person who accuses whites of explicit or implicit racism and of being bad people. After such a confrontation, the relationship with the white student would become fraught with anxiety and might lead the black and the white student involved to avoid one another. It was clear that blacks and whites had not yet found a way to get beyond expressions of anger by blacks in response to provocation by whites. Blacks were also concerned that their expressions of anger violated the expectations of the academy that people must not be emotional, but should talk about things in a more intellectual manner.

A second option blacks saw for responding to offensive comments or other instances of perceived racism was to mask their feelings in order to keep the interaction on a positive footing. This tended to be a prevalent choice. In such cases blacks might afterward go back to black friends, discuss the encounter, and vent their frustration. This choice, however, also incurred serious costs. Feagin and his colleagues describe this response as a "black survival technique" but note, "The psychological pain of not being able to respond more actively is clear."[39] An additional price is paid as well. The relationship might continue, but unbeknownst to that white student, trust has broken down. Black students spoke of being likely to write off such a relationship as one that could go no deeper. While blacks might continue to hang out with the white student involved, they would, to protect themselves and gain greater personal control, probably keep the relationship at the level of acquaintanceship.

The third choice blacks described, which required considerable maturity on their part, was to step back from an interaction and try to educate white students about their comments. Rather than seeing whites as racist, blacks

framed the situation differently and attributed whites' comments to ignorance. Impressively, in many situations black students in this study took this
approach. Brandi, a lower-income black, described it this way:

> Sometimes [whites] just don't know, and you can't fault them for not
> knowing. I just see this as a chance for them to meet people and to
> learn new things. If you take everything personally that everyone
> says, you will get offended a lot because sometimes people say things
> without even meaning to say it, or it comes out the wrong way. Of
> course, yeah, there are definitely times where I have to sit there and
> just cover my mouth or turn my face. . . . A lot of the times I just keep
> my cool because shouting at someone is not going to help them at all.
> You have to explain things to them.

Blacks felt pressure to "be the bigger person," to step back from their anger and model themselves after figures like Martin Luther King. This option,
too, had its drawbacks. It could be burdensome always to have to be the edu-
cator and "the bigger person." From their perspective, blacks were called
upon to learn about whites, but they felt that whites must also be held ac-
countable for their lack of knowledge about blacks.

Racial Terms

Students had to negotiate what language was appropriate in referring to
blacks: which terms were acceptable and which might offend. Some students
came from communities in the United States where use of the word "nigger"
was commonplace. Emily, a lower-income white, felt that the people of her
almost entirely white home community "don't mean it in a bad way"; they
used the term "in ignorance, not necessarily in a racist way." William, an affluent black, had heard white students use the word, "not in a negative way,
but they use it anyway. . . . I guess they didn't realize I was around. One of
them apologized to me once."

The word "nigger" holds multiple meanings depending on who uses it
and in what context. Today, the word is considered by many to be so noxious,
derogatory, and offensive that it has been replaced by the euphemism "the
N-word." [40] Its use by whites is considered to be racist, yet black comedians
and rap artists have appropriated it for different purposes. Some blacks use it
as an affectionate salutation and to signal solidarity with other blacks, while
others find it so disparaging that they would like to see it eradicated.

Alicia, a lower-income black, took offense at blacks *and* whites who used
the "N-word" in a joking manner. She had "a very big issue" with the word:

The N-word has traditionally been used as a horribly derogatory term, and I don't care if [blacks] want to own the word, I still think it's a derogatory term. And why would you want to own something that's been putting you down for many years and used so negatively? Why would you want to even own that word? So I just have issues with that word in general. But it's used a lot. And usually I'm like, "Hey, can you please not say that word around me. I really don't like it. It really bothers me." And they're like, "Ha, ha, ha." [They] pick on me about not wanting to [hear it], but it's just, "You know, that's how I feel. I really don't like that word, so please don't use it."

Because the word has been appropriated by rap artists, white students have unintentionally offended some black students by listening to these songs and singing them. William, an affluent black, spoke about a rap using the N-word that he heard played on the computer of a white classmate: "I don't like that [word]. I guess everything else in rap is funny and they all enjoy it, but I just don't like it at all. I in fact leave the room and get upset about it, while they enjoy it."

Some whites, too, felt uncomfortable when a black friend used the word. Kayla, a lower-income white, realized that blacks' use of the term took the "negative connotation" and "power" out of it, that they used in "in jest, in friendship," but it evoked "uncomfortable feelings" for her because it had been "engraved" in her head that the word was "not an OK thing to say."

Through lack of knowledge, whites used other terms that some blacks found offensive. A white student was unaware that since the civil rights movement of the 1960s, the term "Negro" had taken on pejorative connotations and that blacks now referred to themselves as "African American," "Black," or Black American."[41] When a white student said to Julian, an affluent black, "I didn't know you guys didn't like to be called Negroes," Julian instructed him, "Yeah, I wouldn't do that any time soon."

Discussion

The black community on campus offered many blacks comfort, understanding, and support. But the black students on campus were a very diverse group and did not define their racial identities in the same way. Not all blacks chose to center their social lives on the black community or to define their identities primarily around their race. Thus, being part of a diverse black community on campus today meant that blacks must actively negotiate the differences between them, as well as negotiate relationships with whites and wrestle with any racial misunderstanding or ignorance that arises.

The model of racial identity by educational theorists Bailey Jackson and Rita Hardiman (discussed in Chapter 6) provides one perspective on issues going on among and between black students.[42] While Hardiman and Jackson talk of "stages" of racial identity development, they acknowledge that a person may not actually move neatly from one stage to another: "In reality most people experience several stages simultaneously, holding complex perspectives on a range of issues and living a mixture of social identities."[43] Thus it may be most useful to think about some students as showing attitudes reflective of different stages in different situational contexts, or at different points in time.

Hardiman and Jackson describe a stage of resistance, which is marked by increasing awareness of racial oppression. At this stage blacks move toward acquiring a deeper understanding of how racial oppression works and begin to value all that is black. This understanding can be accompanied by anti-white sentiments and hostility to fellow blacks who, in their view, collude with whites in their own victimization. Attitudes and emotions reflective of resistance were expressed by a number of blacks on campus. These students may be at the stage of resistance, but as Hartiman and Jackson suggest, such attitudes may be evoked by particular contexts and may reflect only one aspect of a student's perspective. A racist incident, for example, may induce resistance attitudes in a person who might otherwise not exhibit them. From the standpoint of a student in this stage, blacks who take racial jokes in good humor could be viewed as colluding in their own racial oppression, and blacks on campus who did not join the black community, who were not focused on fighting racial injustice, who did not listen to rap or jazz, could be seen as "not black enough" or "acting white."

Other black students on campus presented a different image of what it means to be black. Their identities were defined around nonracial interests or issues, and they gave lower salience to blackness and black culture in their self-definitions.[44] These students chose not to join black groups or activities, not to hang out primarily with blacks, or not to reject things deemed "white." Some students did this while remaining secure in their blackness; they were self-confident about their priorities in regard to race. Others did this with some feelings of guilt or insecurity.

Black students on campus were experiencing and responding to the very same divisions that exist among blacks in America today over what it means to be a black person. While all students defined themselves as black, they had to deal with the way that others perceived their blackness and whether they were seen as black enough. Blacks were negotiating complicated differences in racial identity without support and guidance from those with more experience. Provided with a way to understand their differences, to understand the feelings those differences evoke, and to bridge those differences when they arise, the potential is there to turn their differences into greater learning opportunities.

Likewise, in forming a healthy community of blacks and whites, interracial interactions need to be more openly discussed and worked through. Racial joking and racist comments inside and outside the classroom must be acknowledged and addressed. The joking may often be a sign that strong bonds of affection between blacks and whites allow them to joke about potentially offensive matters; conversely, it may at times reflect racist attitudes or racial anxieties that often go unaddressed. Instances occurred when whites wittingly or unwittingly offended blacks with insensitive or racist comments, or used derogatory racial terms. If racist remarks go unchallenged, they foster a climate of distrust among black students, and a belief that these remarks represent deeper racist attitudes harbored by whites.

Such racially offensive comments by whites, while disquieting, present an important opportunity for learning. But how is that learning to take place? The burden is too often put on black students to educate white classmates inside and outside the classroom. They are treated not as individuals but as representatives of their race, called upon to speak for their race as a whole. Blacks found it problematic to confront white students about racist comments, but likewise found it problematic to ignore such comments, or take on the role of educators.

Research by psychologist Linda Tropp has shown that a history of experiencing prejudice against one's group can lead a member of a minority group to lower his or her expectations of getting along with, trusting, or feeling comfortable with members of the majority group.[45] Thus racist expressions must be addressed if meaningful relationships between blacks and whites are to develop. If blacks choose not to address racist comments that offend them, whites will continue to offend blacks without knowing it, and relationships between blacks and whites will become blocked and remain superficial. Students could benefit from structured conversations inside and outside the classroom to help them understand the attitudes behind these comments and their consequences for black students and for black-white relationships on campus.

That said, the incidents black students described in this chapter were a part, but not the prevailing part, of their experiences on campus. Many black students saw these experiences as something they unfortunately had to learn how to cope with in daily life as a black person in our society. As psychologists William Cross and his colleagues have found, many blacks on campus were able to "filter out racist information, and to let non-racist experiences, relationships, transactions, and opportunities flow through."[46] The racial incidents or hassles did not keep most blacks from feeling positively about their overall experience on campus, as will be discussed in the following chapter.

9

As the Year Ended

As the academic year drew to a close, students in the study were asked to reflect on how the year had gone for them academically and socially. How had they fared academically, and did they think race and class had an influence on their academic experience? Had they found a place for themselves on campus, gotten involved in activities, and made a satisfying social adjustment? In what ways had race and class played a role in students' relationships with families during the year? Did race and class make a difference to maintaining ties with family, friends, and communities left behind? The answers to these questions are the focus of this chapter.

Academics

Just over three-quarters of the students felt that race had *not* made a difference academically.[1] Those blacks who felt that it had spoke of its effect on classroom dynamics or their decision to select courses in black studies, as discussed in earlier chapters. They did not believe that race had had an impact on their academic achievement. As for social class, in reflecting back on the year, a third of lower-income whites felt that their social class position had made them less well-prepared for the academic demands at Amherst than their peers, four times the percentage of students in any of the other three groups.[2]

At the end of the year, when some of the lower-income whites and one lower-income black as well reflected back on their first interviews, they realized that at that point they had not yet become aware of the deficiencies in their academic preparation. The lower-income whites in this study came primarily from public schools that were lower in quality than either the private schools attended by many of their classmates or the public schools attended by classmates from affluent communities. Many lacked a real understanding of the sort of academic work other entering students had done in high school. Some lower-income students had never written a research or analytical paper or taken a foreign language or an Advanced Placement course because these opportunities simply were not available in their high schools. Some had gotten little feedback to help them improve their writing. High school courses and assignments were described by many lower-income students as neither "rigorous" nor requiring them "to think." Some lower-income students faced extremely different academic expectations and demands at Amherst, and soon discovered that they had serious catching up to do.

What is most striking is that despite the academic underpreparation experienced by some lower-income whites, social class was not a good predictor of final grades for white students. At the end of the year the grade point average (GPA) of lower-income whites in the study was 3.50 on a 4.0 scale; for affluent whites it was 3.66.[3] Many lower-income white students spoke of working very hard, and while the academic confidence of some may have dropped after the early weeks, by the end of the year most had regained a belief in their academic abilities. Students began *and* ended the year showing little difference from one group to another in their levels of academic confidence.[4]

Blacks ended the year, on average, with a B average (the GPA for blacks was 3.17), which was much lower than the B+/A- average attained by whites, whose average GPA was 3.58.[5] The racial difference may be due, in part, to blacks having entered the college with lower SAT scores than whites, though the explanation for the racial differences are many and go beyond the scope of this research.[6] William Bowen and Derek Bok similarly found in their large-scale study of 28 elite colleges and universities that blacks' GPAs were lower than whites'.[7] Social class background, however, was not predictive of the academic performance of black students in the study: the average GPA for lower-income blacks was 3.19, and for affluent blacks it was 3.14.[8] This may be due to the fact that the majority of the lower-income blacks at the college had attended private high schools and had excellent educational opportunities during those years.

In a study of blacks who attended a predominantly white university, Joe Feagin and his colleagues found that half the black students reported being mistreated by white professors and had difficulties with such things as differential grading.[9] Blacks at Amherst perceived that their race made academic integration (i.e., being taken seriously by professors, forming relationships with professors, and earning good grades in coursework) slightly more difficult, while whites felt that their race made academic integration slightly easier.[10] Class was not perceived to have an impact on academic integration.[11]

Race and class did have one additional effect on students' academic experience. Some lower-income students, black and white, as well as some affluent black students, felt that they carried the burden of seeing their grades as a reflection on the academic capabilities of members of their race or social class. Affluent whites, by contrast, thought about their own academic performance in more individualistic terms.[12] Brianna, a lower-income black, felt that she was representing her whole race. She believed that if African Americans who are famous "do something good, it's like, 'Black people did something good.' They do something bad, it's like, 'Yeah, all black people are like that.'" If she did not do well academically, blacks would be seen as less capable academically, fulfilling negative stereotypes. Some lower-income whites, too, feared that if they did not do well academically, lower-income students in the future would not be afforded the same opportunity to come to the college.

Growth, Well-being, and Adjustment

Looking at several measures of self-reported growth, well-being, and adjustment at the end of year, students in all four groups were strikingly similar in their favorable assessments of their experience. *Regardless of race and class background*, students gave comparable positive self-reports in five areas of psychological and social well-being: their psychological health, their social lives, their feelings of comfort and inclusion in relation to their peers, and the extent to which they had grown as a person and had found a place at the college.[13] Only a few students (from 2% to 16%) gave low ratings on any of these five measures.[14]

The four groups gave similar assessments of whether either their race or their class affected the ease or difficulty of getting invited to social events.[15] Race and class were not experienced as obstacles to social invitations. Nor did the four groups differ in their assessments of whether social class made their social integration and comfort either easier or more difficult: that is, feeling comfortable on campus, being included in informal activities with classmates, finding like-minded friends, and/or finding refuge on campus when things were going badly.[16] Blacks, however, did feel that their race made social integration and comfort a little more difficult for them, while whites felt that their race made social integration easier.[17] Blacks' ratings fell only slightly above the point that indicated "neither easier nor more difficult," so the findings should not be interpreted to mean that blacks saw race as contributing a major obstacle to social integration and support. However, blacks faced more complexities socially, as discussed in earlier chapters: they had to cope with being part of a small minority on campus; they were wary about the reception they would receive from whites and had to cope with fears of potential discrimination; they had to deal with whites' racial stereotypes about blacks; and they also had to manage concerns about negotiating relationships with other blacks.

Looking at three additional measures of students' social experiences, race and class were again found to make little difference. Students in all four groups had gotten involved in a similar number of extracurricular activities: on average, they joined two extracurricular activities.[18] Students in the four groups did not differ in self-reports on the extent to which they had gotten to know people of different races well, nor did they differ in self-reports of whether they had gotten to know people of different class backgrounds well.[19]

What the study found, then, were primarily individual differences among students within each of the four groups on growth and adjustment to college. Race and class were not determinants of students' overall self-assessments of their growth, well-being, involvement, and adjustment.

Families and Home Communities

While social class was not a major determinant of overall well-being and adjustment on campus, it did have an influence on several issues pertaining to students' families and home communities that have not been discussed to this point. First, lower-income students faced more difficulties than affluent classmates *seeing* family members during the year. They were less able to go home for family visits, and family members were less able to visit them on campus because of the expenses entailed. Second, because the parents of lower-income students had more limited education than the parents of the affluent students, they were more likely to be living vicariously through their children's experiences on campus, and at times living out parents' dreams and expectations could feel burdensome. And, finally, the growth and development that occurred over the course of the first year of college brought changes for lower-income students that made it harder for them to maintain their connections to family, as well as to friends and communities left behind. The growth of affluent students did not involve dislocation from family and people in home communities. These three issues are discussed below.

Visits

Lower-income students felt that their social class position made it more difficult to go home for family visits or occasions, and to have parents or family members visit campus, while affluent students felt that their class position made these types of family visits easier.[20] Students, however, did not feel that their race posed obstacles to visits home or family visits to campus.[21] Most families of lower-income students who lived at a distance from the campus could not afford to visit it for family weekend or for performances or athletic competitions. The costs of transportation, meals, and housing were prohibitive. In addition, the college campus was an environment unfamiliar to the parents of many of the lower-income students, and one in which they might well feel some discomfort. Without campus visits, the new lives, friends, and activities of lower-income students remained unseen by parents, creating distances to be bridged. Lower-income students were likewise more prone than their affluent peers to miss out on important family events because they could not afford to travel home.

Although students with high financial need experienced more difficulty *seeing* their families during the semester, they remained in contact with them by phone. Over 80% of the students in the study talked on the phone with their families at least once a week, though the length or content of these conversations is unknown.[22] Approximately 60% of lower-income students, black and white, talked to parents at least two or three times a week.[23] Many students in all the groups were also in contact with family members by e-mail.[24]

Hopes and Expectations

Depending on their race and class backgrounds, students carried different types of family expectations and dreams. The families of many lower-income students, black and white, were eager for their children to enter occupations that would bring the type of financial resources they had been unable to attain; they did not fully understand the value of a liberal arts education that provided no "practical skills." As a first-generation college student, Angela, a lower-income black, was expected by her family "to get a degree that will lead to me making a lot of money, instead of writing poems." Marc, also a lower-income black, spoke of being "the first-generation college student in my family," which expected him "to finish and go on to have a great job." Only one affluent white student, versus a third of students in the other three groups, spoke of parental expectations to choose courses and majors that would lead to a well-paid job upon graduation.[25]

Some parents and family members who had not had the opportunity to attend college at all, or who had not attended a college like Amherst, were vicariously living through their children's experiences. Most parents of the affluent white students had completed a bachelor's degree at a prestigious college or university, and while they were highly interested and invested in their children's college experiences, their children were not living out dreams that they had not had the opportunity to experience. Only 2 of 10 affluent whites felt that family members were vicariously living through them; by contrast, 7 of 10 lower-income white students felt this. The two groups of black students fell in between.[26] For many students in the lower-income white group and in the two black groups, one or both parents did not have a BA; those parents who had spent some time in college or had received a BA had not attended elite institutions; and often they had gone back to college later in life. Those parents were reported to be highly invested in their children's opportunity to live out experiences that they had missed.

Lower-income whites spoke of a parent who "missed out on living on campus and being a college student" (Marie, lower-income white), family members "excited to see me have this opportunity because it's something they would have loved and [had] not been able to do" (Nicole, lower-income white); a "really, really smart" sibling who "only had the opportunity to attend a small state school" (Larry, lower-income white); a parent who would "love to be in this kind of atmosphere" and to be "doing the same kind of things if she could" (Robert, lower-income white). Whitney, an affluent black whose mother had not attended college, said that her mother was "always telling me to take advantage of things." Among affluent blacks whose parents had a BA, not all parents had a liberal arts education. Kimberly, an affluent black, described her mother, who had attended an undergraduate professional program as an older student: she was always "curious about what classes I'm taking and sort of wishes she had gotten the chance to do the liberal arts thing, because she's interested in a lot of stuff. But she didn't really have the opportunity to go to college." Kimberly's dad had not attended a liberal arts college, "so they're both very, very curious and very actively interested in what I'm doing here. . . . I feel like my mom more so than my dad might be living vicariously through me."

Many lower-income black students spoke not only of immediate family members, but in many cases of extended family, friends, and communities vicariously living through them. A number of students with limited family education spoke of "everybody, my whole family" (Trina, lower-income black); or of "everyone—family, friends, friends of family, [people] just closely related to me" (Brandon, lower-income black) living through their experiences, and of being reminded by family members how "lucky" they were.

Having opportunities that their parents and family members did not, however, could also be a burden. Megan, an affluent black, had a father who had grown up in poverty, had overcome great obstacles, and "worked really hard so I don't have to deal with anything like [he did]. But as a result, I sometimes feel like I have to do things the way he wants me to. . . . There's a lot of me juggling doing what I actually want to and doing what I feel my dad wants me to do." Marc, a lower-income black, said, "My mom will go on the [college] website and be like, 'Why aren't you doing this? Why aren't you doing this? I see these groups doing that.' And I'm like, 'I can only do so many things, Mom, and I have my own interests and stuff.'" Marc took her advice "every now and then" and would explore a suggested option. Brianna, a lower-income black, said her family expected her to become "this really, really successful doctor" and to "make a lot of money." She was trying to hold on to "the type of life that I want" and resist the pressure to have "the life that they want for me." Another lower-income black, Dana, said her mother was "intent on my becoming a doctor" and would ask, 'Why don't you take all these science courses and become a doctor or nurse?' And I'm like, 'I'm not really interested in that at all.'" Being a doctor had been her mother's unattained dream. Danny, a lower-income white, spoke of his mother "just always pushing me. . . . She really wants me to get my degree because neither of my parents did." Rebecca, a lower-income white, said that her immigrant parents "just sacrificed so much to come to this country and for me to go to Amherst College. . . . They just want to see that I take advantage of the fact that they sacrificed so that I can establish myself." These pushes toward specific choices or career paths were not often reported by affluent white students.

For both lower-income students and black students, success in college would be living proof that it was possible to make it to another level in society, but this expectation left little room for failure. Brianna, a lower-income black, felt pressure to go further than others in her family had, a pressure that seemed to be experienced more heavily by the black students in the study. At the beginning of the year, she sensed these family expectations "weighing me down." Trina, another lower-income black, felt that high family expectations could be a positive force because "when people expect a lot from you that means that they think you're capable of it." But she went on to describe "a constant fear of letting them down." A third lower-income black, Dana, called the family expectations "a bit large, and grander than I would have thought, and I don't think I can fill those expectations." These pressures extended to affluent blacks as well—Marissa described the pressures she lived with:

> It's hard because I want to do well for myself, but sometimes I can give myself a day off or I can say, 'I'm going to put this off.' But then I can't do it 'cause I know that I have to do better. And I know that I can't do that 'cause so many people are counting on me, so many people are going to know my grades like this summer. In my family, grades are not a personal thing.

Alisa, a lower-income black, also said that her grades were public, shared not only with family members, but with people all over town, putting additional pressure on her to excel.

Cultural and Social Capital

Gradual growth and change occurred over the course of the year as students encountered new people and experiences. The self-presentation of some students shifted to bring them closer to whatever they perceived to be the norm on campus; for example, they bought or wore different clothes, or tried to downplay regional accents or forms of speech. But in both the on-line surveys and face-to-face interviews, students in *all four groups* reported that they had not changed a lot to try to fit in at Amherst.[27]

Changes were occurring, however, that went beyond speech or dress—changes that took place gradually and often less intentionally. In contrast to their affluent classmates, lower-income students were changing in ways that would distance them from their families, friends, and the communities left behind.

Research by sociologists and psychologists suggests that the college experience leads to the acquisition of new forms of cultural capital.[28] Many lower-income students began to adopt "a more intellectual stance," new tastes, interests, preferences, styles, and ambitions that would make them unlike their family members. Angela, a lower-income black, was aware that after a year of college, "the whole way you think is different." Some lower-income students spoke of having gained skills and self-assurance in interacting with people of higher social classes, skills most affluent peers already possessed. Trina, a lower-income black, felt that the college made students more "comfortable" and "self-confident speaking to people of a [higher] social class," and more "socially capable in those situations." Corey, a lower-income black, said that on campus, "you're talking to people of a [higher] social class all day and you're with them all the time in the dorm. So I guess it just prepares you to be with them for the rest of your life." Lower-income students learned how to socialize and make "small talk," and the proper etiquette for a sit-down dinner.[29] Rebecca, a lower-income white, said she would now present herself differently in an interview. "It's little things . . . like making eye contact and trying to address everyone present and remembering names and things like that."

The cultural capital of the affluent students also included knowledge of how to get access to scarce rewards: for example, how to talk to teachers and administrators to make situations work to meet their needs. These were skills that many affluent students had seen modeled by their parents and had internalized growing up.[30] Jeremy, a lower-income white, spoke of learning from the behavior of his more affluent peers:

> I don't really go to office hours and talk to teachers a lot. But I feel people who *do* are more likely to be more successful in their classes,

just having the connection to the teachers. I figure even after they graduate, staying close to teachers, beyond having a good friend and being someone you are close to, will also help you out in terms of getting more connections and having more opportunity.

At the beginning of the year, Alisa, a lower-income black, had been unaware that it was acceptable for her to ask a professor a question during a science exam, or to ask if she might rewrite a paper she had not done well on. She was just learning that these were requests many affluent students felt entitled to make, and made regularly, to their advantage.

Lower-income students were being educated about the importance of social capital, and some were already building upon the connections the college afforded them. Justin, a lower-income white, said, "I've spoken to a lot of alums, tried to have relationships with them. . . . You need to have a network, and coming in with none, I need to be ambitious and be very assertive and try to set one up for myself." But many lower-income students still lacked the boldness, the confidence, and the sense of entitlement to connect to successful alums.

Maintaining Ties

The acquisition of cultural capital would contribute to lower-income students' material success down the road, but it would also make them different from and distance them from family and friends at home. Lower-income students were on a path of upward social mobility and would ultimately, in all likelihood, surpass their parents in education and occupational attainment.[31] By the end of the first year of college, some had already exceeded their parents' educational attainment. Some lower-income students were eager to come to Amherst precisely because it would give them entrée into a wealthier world. The college was known to provide "plenty of connections," and to enable students to "go on and make lots of money" (Danny, lower-income white). Brandon, a lower-income black, thought students were attracted to the college because "it has that reputation of getting [you] into the socially elite class and the socially elite workforce." Marc, a lower-income black, agreed that students come to the college because it provides "the potential to move up into a higher class," gives students an advantage in the job market over someone from a state school, and facilitates becoming "a lawyer or doctor or things like that, professions that will enable you to become high class and elite."

But already lower-income students were paying a price for their entrée into a higher social class. Some now found themselves with one foot in the affluent world of Amherst and another in their home communities.[32] A third of the lower-income students felt that they were juggling two worlds, while only a single affluent student had this feeling.[33] Some lower-income students were beginning to wonder whether they would be able to go back to home communities and fit in as they once did, given the ways they were changing. And they wondered whether they would ever truly feel at home in the new world they were entering.

Parents

The transition to college, a major adjustment in any parent-child relationship, was especially disruptive for students from lower-income families. Larry, a lower-income white, spoke of a growing separation from his father, who had not gone to college, because Larry was gaining knowledge and experiences his father did not have, and was becoming more liberal than his father politically. The father was "very afraid that he's going to lose touch with me completely." Amy, a lower-income white, said, "I think it's just that I have had a different experience. And as much as I want to talk to my family about what I'm doing, they haven't experienced it with me, and they don't know everything that's happened." Family (and friends) tended to ask few questions about their experiences on campus, being unfamiliar with their lives and not knowing where to begin, and a large part of their current experiences and development simply remained unknown to family members.

Other lower-income students began to see their parents through a new lens. Comparing them with the parents of their friends on campus, they struggled not to feel judgmental. After spending time with the wealthy and high-powered family of an Amherst friend, Justin, a lower-income white, reflected, "My parents gave me so much with the means that were available and the experiences they had, but there is definitely a lot more out there." Alisa, a lower-income black, now looked at her parents' lives as a cautionary tale: "I want a job where I'm not expendable, because they both lost their jobs and now, well, my dad found a job that he really wants and my mom's looking, but she's lowering her standards. So I just want to be in a spot where I'm not expendable. So I do look at them differently."

Friends

Some lower-income students also encountered difficulties in maintaining relationships with friends who had stayed back home, had not gone to college, or had gone on to community colleges, state colleges, and large state universities where their college experience was different intellectually and socially. By contrast, many of the close high school friends of the affluent students had left home for colleges and universities, and many were having similar college experiences.

Some lower-income students came to Amherst because they grew up feeling different from many around them because of their intellectual focus and ambitions, and were seeking an environment in which new aspects of themselves could develop. For these students, Amherst provided the first environment in which it was acceptable to use "big" words and engage in conversations about books and ideas with friends. They felt that a part of themselves was beginning to blossom in college, but it was difficult to share new intellectual interests with old friends who were not academically focused. Nicole, a lower-income white, spoke of downplaying intellectual interests at home: "Many times it does feel I have 'Amherst' and I have 'home' and they don't totally fit together." Amy, a lower-income white, talked about steering away from talking about her academic interests "just because I don't want [my friends] to think that I'm snobby for going to a school out of state."

The problem of maintaining ties to old friends was most prevalent for lower-income white students. Almost half the lower-income whites talked about difficulties maintaining connections with friends they had left behind, six times the percentage of any of the other three groups.[34] Robert, a lower-income white, reflected on where his life was headed, and worried that after college, if he went on to graduate school and to "some business job in New York," it would be difficult "going back and having beers with a bunch of guys who work at the mill. I think our lives are definitely going in different directions." Emily, a lower-income white, felt that for her friends at home it was like "they're still in high school," because they were going to a college close to home with the same people. "I feel like they haven't had any new experience, whereas I definitely have had a completely new experience that has made me change." Danny, a lower-income white, found that his experience at Amherst was "completely alien" to his friends back home, who talked of "rarely going to class" and partying "all the time," yet were "still getting good grades." Friends at home commented on how different the lower-income students had become, seeing them already as outsiders. Because it was hard to find parallels with friends' experiences, some students found that reminiscing about the past was the way to reconnect: "We always end up talking about stuff that's happened to us in the past" (Amy, lower-income white). By contrast, many of the new friendships at college were experienced as much richer and deeper.

Some lower-income students said that friends from home experienced their decision to leave home communities as an implicit negative judgment of them. Further, old friends felt that lower-income students were making an implicit negative judgment of them if they talked about exciting experiences or opportunities they had at college or fascinating people they had met. Some lower-income students struggled, too, to avoid being judgmental. Rebecca, a lower-income white, said she wasn't "better" than her friends at home, but felt that she had "moved on ahead a little bit," while many of her friends' lives "haven't changed that much."

Home Communities

Some lower-income students found themselves becoming more critical of their home communities. Larry, a white student, said, "I remember going back home for Christmas break and spring break and being, 'Wow. It's a lot more homogeneous here than I remembered.' . . . And it was definitely a feeling of, I'm definitely not on the same wavelength anymore." Emily, from a rural white community in a conservative state, said:

> When I first got here I was more proud of the people at home, just the way that they got by and could make things work, and didn't have a lot of outside help. As I've gone through the year, I've turned to seeing people at home as being more closed-minded, and more judgmental of people. . . . I definitely feel there are two worlds. When I go home, it definitely is a different world, it's completely different. It's like going back in time. It really is. It's completely white. It's completely isolated. It's completely ignorant of the outside world. . . . I definitely feel like I'm more defensive of here when I'm at home, and more defensive of home when I'm here.

While she still felt pride in people from home, regardless of those feelings, she was now viewed as an outsider because she had changed.

Jeremy, a lower-income white from a rural state, went home over January interterm and saw people through a new lens. He worried about how he was changing and who he was becoming:

> I noticed the country bumpkin people, and I went to go get a haircut at this place, and the people there were really the stereotype, not country, but ignorant in their opinions. They're not knowledgeable. That wasn't something I noticed before. I knew I was from a place like that, but I hadn't felt it so strongly. It didn't make me feel good, how much I noticed the difference. I wasn't sure if it had to do with being here, and I didn't really like the way it made me feel. The first week I was home I was really uncomfortable being in that community. I was worried that this place was changing me too much. I've lived in [my home state] for the last 10 years now, but I don't feel that attached to it and I don't plan on staying there. But the fact that I was so uncomfortable in that situation with those people made me worried that I was somehow becoming someone who couldn't handle

people who weren't at the same intelligence level as people here or something like that.

A serious challenge for lower-income students was to find ways to maintain the connections with family, friends, and home communities while continuing to grow and change at college.

Another set of potential issues confronted some lower-income blacks. They were caught not only between two different worlds based on social class, but also between two cultures based on race.[35] Many affluent blacks faced this issue as well. Marissa, an affluent black, described interacting with blacks and whites as "moving between two different worlds" in which she experienced herself as "two different people." Particularly for black students coming from predominantly black communities, the style of speech, dress, and interaction in home neighborhoods was quite different from that on campus. Just as some lower-income whites worried about where they were now headed and how they would fit back into home communities, Angela, a lower-income black, raised a concern that, if not already on the minds of many black students in this study, could well be in the future. She had some fears about the direction in which her education was leading her. Would it remove her from the black community, and what might her place be in the white community?[36]

> You have choices to make. For me it's being someone who's going to have this education, and who could probably segue into the middle class, upper middle class. Am I just going to be a token? You know what I mean? I don't want to be the *one* black friend basically. I had a professor talking about a [black] friend who's upper middle class and very educated, has a PhD in something. And she has all these white friends and goes horseback riding and fox hunting and all this other crap. But one, she hasn't had a date in five years, and [two], she's not going to get married. None of those people will marry her.

A concern for blacks was whether they would find romantic partners, whom they would find, and where they would find them. If their partners were white, would their choices alienate them from the black community? Would they still fail to be accepted by the white community?

Discussion

Given the challenges lower-income and black students faced on campus, their reports on how the year had gone for them are especially encouraging. In general, as students, black and white, lower-income and affluent, approached the end of their first year, they gave similarly positive reports on their overall well-being, their growth, their social lives, and their adjustment to college. Over the course of the year, the majority of students in all four groups felt comfortable and confident in their relationships with peers, had established a positive social life, and had found a place for themselves on campus.

Academically, the finding that blacks' GPAs were lower than whites' is consistent with data from larger-scale studies of blacks at elite colleges and universities.[37] The extent to which this gap is due to precollege influences (e.g., academic preparation) or factors in the college environment (e.g., vulnerability to negative racial stereotypes about their abilities)[38] cannot be determined by the data collected, and the question goes beyond the present study. The unanticipated result, however, was that despite the fact that some lower-income students entered the college academically underprepared in comparison with many of their classmates, their GPAs did not differ statistically from those of affluent students at the end of the year. A variety of factors contributed to their academic success. First, both institutional selectivity (i.e., the extent to which an institution sets high standards for the selection of incoming students) and financial support by an institution have been found to be predictive of GPA.[39] Amherst is highly selective, is able to pick students with great academic potential, and meets the financial need of all the students it accepts. The college thus provides lower-income students greater chances of success than students at institutions that do not have these characteristics. Another predictor of college grades is high school grades,[40] and outstanding academic performance in high school is necessary for admission to Amherst. Further, lower-income students, as discussed in earlier chapters, were in general deeply appreciative of the investment the college was making in them, and highly invested in succeeding at Amherst so that they might attain greater material success. Thus they were highly motivated, experiencing college as a precious opportunity that could not be squandered.

The education Amherst provides, however, is a double-edged sword. Success at Amherst is beneficial for future success, but it comes with some costs. Lower-income students were changing in ways that most had never anticipated, and a gulf was beginning to grow between them and family, friends, and home community. Finding common ground with family and friends left behind, whom they now viewed through a new lens, posed challenges. Some were already beginning to feel like outsiders in their home communities, and some were coming to be seen as outsiders as well. When lower-income students tried to share their excitement about new interests, or about meeting interesting new people, they could be seen as arrogant, elitist, and condescending. As they deepen their knowledge of, ease with, and comfort in the world of the affluent, and the opportunities it offers them, the dislocation from families and home communities may increase as well. Blacks, both lower-income and affluent, experienced an additional form of dislocation and concern about where their education was leading them. As they became acculturated to the affluent white world, they were uncertain what their relationship would be to the black community.

Students with a foot in two different worlds, however, *were* finding ways to manage. By changing the way they expressed themselves to match the people they were speaking with, students made interactions more comfortable, and made themselves easier to understand and relate to. Some lower-income students, black and white, spoke of "code-switching," [41] changing their speech depending on whom they were with. They used more colloquial speech, smaller vocabularies, and more slang with people at home than at college, and avoided more intellectual topics of conversation with family and friends at home as well. A few lower-income black students spoke of putting on "a little of a ghetto accent," to match the speech of family and friends at home. Some blacks noted that different aspects of themselves became prominent when interacting with blacks at home and with whites at college, just as different aspects of themselves became prominent when interacting with groups of black friends and groups of white friends on campus. Steven, an affluent black, described the switch in his self-presentation:

> If I'm with a bunch of black guys, I act more "black." . . . And then when I'm with white people I act more "white." . . . I seem to find that I can definitely identify with each race better if I acclimate to their kinds of speech and their music and different trends. . . . I'm kind of like a chameleon.

Some students bridged divides of race and class with less difficulty than others, and these were skills that will likely develop further as divides deepen. Lower-income and black students' ability to move between affluent and lower-income, between black and white, despite the difficulties, will enable them to have a broad range of experiences on campus and in society.

10

Meeting the Challenges
of Diversity

Like many elite colleges and universities, Amherst is going to great lengths and expense to identify and attract to campus talented students who are not affluent and white. Its efforts are directed at offering opportunities for social and economic mobility to these students, at providing some measure of social equity. Bringing a diverse group of students to campus also creates opportunities for all students to have their previous notions of race and class challenged, and their understandings deepened, through interactions with one another. Opportunities abound. What actually happens? In following 58 students, black and white, affluent and lower-income, through their first year at Amherst, I was able to get and, hopefully, give a sense of what they experienced, with a focus on these two questions: what were the specific challenges that arose for these students of different races and classes in being part of a diverse community, and what did students actually learn from the diversity around them?

Several major conclusions can be drawn from this study. Lower-income and/or black students faced many more challenges than affluent whites in becoming part of a predominantly affluent white academic community, but their reports on how the year had gone indicated that most had quite positive feelings about their experience on campus and had been able to deal effectively with the difficulties that confronted them. If we look at students' self-reports at the end of their first year in regard to their academic, social, and psychological well-being and adjustment, students from all four groups were remarkably similar in their favorable descriptions of their experience.

As for the learning that occurred from diversity, the outcomes were variable. On the whole, important learning did take place, but some students gained much more from living in a diverse community than others. Some students got to know students of different races and classes well; others did not. In earlier chapters, findings were presented *separately* for the learning that occurred about race and class. When those figures are combined, 30% of students reported changes in the way they saw people of *both* different races *and* classes as a result of living in a diverse community, and an additional 32% reported having learned something about people of *either* other races *or* other classes from this experience.[1] Of the remaining 38% of the students, just over half felt that they had gained something from the classroom comments of peers who differed from them in race and class. These findings are positive. That said, given the potential that existed for learning from one another, it seems fair to add that much potential went unrealized.[2] Let us turn now to summarizing in more detail both the challenges students faced and the learning that took place.

Challenges for Blacks

Black students faced a variety of challenges that are likely faced by black students at other predominantly white campuses.[3] Many of these issues were not pervasive but presented themselves on occasion: racial stereotyping, comments perceived to be racially offensive or "ignorant," being made the targets of racial jokes (e.g., about affirmative action) that went too far and became insulting. The presence of such attitudes and behavior, however infrequent, produced a degree of distrust and wariness for many black students about the kinds of antiblack sentiments whites might harbor.

As a minority, blacks were constantly in the position of having to break into groups of whites. This was something some black students were completely comfortable doing, but others had anxieties about whether they would face prejudice or rejection, and had to overcome stereotypes of whites as racist, rich, and unconcerned about blacks. When racial issues were under discussion in the classroom, eyes often turned toward blacks to provide "the black" perspective, as if a single black perspective existed. Black students were expected to educate whites. When some blacks formed close friendships with other blacks and ate together in the dining hall, whites took notice, and some were critical of blacks for self-segregating, while groups of whites socializing or eating together went unremarked upon.

Many blacks felt that they carried the burden of being representatives of their race. Affirmative action has been questioned from many quarters on the grounds of merit and fairness, and whether diversity goals have given students with weaker academic records the places that would have been given to students with stronger ones.[4] In response, a number of black students felt pressure to do well academically to prove that blacks deserved the opportunity to attend Amherst.

Blacks made up a very heterogeneous group, one in which not all members felt comfortable with one another. Issues experienced by blacks in society at large were present on campus. Differences existed between blacks in social class, skin tone, the importance of race to identity, and attitudes about interracial dating, and these differences had to be negotiated. Some black students spoke of pressures to be with other students of their race, as well as questions about their not being "black enough." Blacks faced the challenge of bridging two different worlds, one black, one white, as they moved between groups of blacks and groups of whites on campus, and between blacks at home and whites at college. And they faced uncertainty about where their education was leading them.

Despite these challenges, the majority of black students in the study felt positively about the year. When asked in their interviews at the end of the year what the college could do to make it a better place for them, many black students spontaneously spoke of the college being "a great place" or "the best choice for me"; they praised the college for "making students comfortable" and for making it easy to relate to students from different social classes. A few offered suggestions related to racial issues that could have made the experience better for them, most of which will be considered below.[5]

Certain social advantages came with being black. A subgroup of black upperclassmen was welcoming and supportive to incoming black students, facilitating their transition to college. Blacks had the opportunity to join extracurricular groups that addressed blacks' interests and concerns: the Black Student Union, Dancing and Stepping at Amherst College, the Gospel Choir. While many blacks did form friendships with other black classmates, and derived feelings of comfort, understanding, support, and help from these relationships,[6] blacks could *not* be viewed as self-segregating: 96% of the blacks reported getting to know two or more whites well, and only two blacks in the study reported having only black friends. In fact, the findings in this study support and extend previous research that shows students of color as less likely to be self-segregating on campus than white students.[7]

Evidence was lacking that the environment was an unhealthy one that made it difficult for blacks to survive socially. As a group, they did not show signs of isolation and alienation on campus.[8] The self-reports on which this study is based indicated that blacks had made good adjustments to the college and felt positively about their social lives. Those black students who were highly aware of and sensitive to racist slights and offenses had developed ways to buffer themselves against everyday encounters with racism and to benefit from nonracist experiences and opportunities. While some blacks spoke of the problems that came from having a foot in different worlds, one black, one white, many had learned ways to successfully move back and forth between those worlds.

Challenges for Lower-Income Students

Lower-income students, black and white, faced a number of challenges as well. In many cases they lacked the economic, cultural, and social capital of their affluent classmates, which at times led some to experience themselves as existing outside a culture shared by wealthy peers. Class differences were felt strongly when students arrived on campus and moved their possessions into dorm rooms and conversations turned to travels abroad, to the private schools they had attended, to operas and Broadway plays. Class differences became prominent at other moments during the year as well (e.g., during January intersession and spring break, lower-income students could not afford the trips taken by wealthy classmates). Throughout the year lower-income students, with limited discretionary income, had to make choices when it came to eating out and ordering food in, or buying tickets to off-campus concerts and plays; to spend money on one thing meant giving up another or working extra hours. On occasion lower-income students encountered references to themselves as "they," as outsiders, as well as negative stereotypic assumptions about people without means.

On the whole, the lower-income whites had less prior exposure to wealthy people, more limited family education, and greater financial need compared with the lower-income blacks in this study, the majority of whom had attended private schools with wealthy white classmates. Lower-income whites thus experienced more anxiety about forming connections to affluent classmates and about being excluded or judged in a negative way because of what they did not have.

Lower-income students, black and white, carried a number of burdens that their affluent peers did not. They felt academic pressure to prove wrong those who felt they were bringing down the college's standards and to demonstrate that they deserved a place at Amherst. Some had to work harder academically than their affluent peers to make up for the academic underpreparation that came from attending poorer-quality high schools. Those with a parent or parents who had not graduated from college often carried pressures from home to attain things family members had not been able to achieve in their own lives, to live out dreams parents had not been able to realize.

Many of the lower-income students experienced greater physical and psychological disconnection from families than affluent students. Family members were less able to visit them during the year, and they were able to make fewer visits home. Once home, they faced difficulties sharing their experiences with family, friends and community. For many, the opportunity to attend an elite college had costs they had not expected: a divide between home and school. The lower-income students were becoming upwardly mobile and were being perceived by some people at home as possibly arrogant or condescending, or as outsiders. They themselves saw parents, friends, and communities at home through a new lens and struggled not to be judgmental. Some worried about where their journey was leading them and where they would ultimately find their places in society.

Very much as black students had when asked about racial issues, the majority of lower-income students, black and white, when asked at the end of the year what the college could do to make it a better place for them, responded with positive feelings about the year.[9] Some students expressed love for and enjoyment of the school, reported that the college had been a good place for them, and had words of praise for the opportunities and resources they had been offered and the good job the college had done in helping them along the way. Only four lower-income students had suggestions to offer about how the college might have improved their experience based on their social class; two of those students suggested that it bring in more students from lower-income backgrounds.[10]

Despite being surrounded by more affluent students, lower-income students generally voiced positive feelings about who they were and what they had. Many of them valued character traits they felt they derived from the economic constraints they had grown up with, traits they perceived to be lacking in numbers of their more affluent peers. Some spoke critically of wealthy peers who were not appreciative of or did not have to work hard for what they had, or who they felt lacked self-reliance and independence. As a rule, lower-income students did not believe that the affluent students had it all; they saw drawbacks that came with being wealthy. The lower-income students had many reasons to feel satisfied with the way their lives were turning out: they were on a trajectory of upward social mobility, the embodiments of the dream that if you work hard you can rise in society.

At year's end, lower-income students, black and white, did not differ from the affluent students in self-reports of their psychological well-being, of their social lives, and their feelings of comfort and inclusion around peers. Most did *not* feel marginalized by very wealthy peers; they had chosen alternative friendship groups in which they felt valued, respected, and included.[11] Lower-income students certainly lacked the kinds of connections wealthier students had to summer jobs and internships, but they were learning that in addition to their own hard work and determination, they could draw upon the connections that being at the college provided, connections made through other students' families, through professors, and through alumni.

At the end of the year, the majority of lower-income students reported that class was not highly salient to them on a day-to-day basis. Activities on campus were free. Meals were paid for. In fact, many students, affluent and lower-income, found class to be difficult to discern in daily campus life, since most students dressed casually and markers of class like students' homes and cars remained unseen (first-year students are not allowed to bring cars to campus). Many students agreed that class could be disguised or downplayed on campus. Both lower-income and affluent students were motivated by a desire to find common ground, which meant at times that both tried to play down class differences.

Learning from Diversity

As discussed in Chapter 1, social science research has identified a variety of optimal conditions for reducing prejudice and facilitating learning. A residential college such as Amherst meets those conditions. It provides strong institutional support for diversity;[12] equal-status contact takes place between students from different groups in pursuit of common goals (e.g., athletic teams); the number of black and lower-income students on campus makes cross-race and cross-class interaction likely; contact is personalized, and sufficient time is present for cross-group friendships to develop. Belonging to this diverse academic community, however, had much more influence on some students' attitudes, beliefs, and behaviors than on others'.

Race

Overall, just over a third of students reported that living and interacting with classmates of different races had changed their views of people of different races or their own race, while an additional 21% talked of personal sharing in the classroom by students of another race that had changed the way they understood race or racial issues. But the group differences were striking. Affluent and lower-income whites had an equal opportunity to learn about race from black peers or through the curriculum, but almost twice as many lower-income whites as affluent whites reported getting to know two or more blacks well (93% versus 54%); more than twice as many took a course in the Black Studies Department or with "Black" or "Africa" in the title (20% versus 8%); more than twice as many reported that their experience living and interacting with students of different races at the college had changed their views of race (47% versus 21%). Affluent whites, on the whole, made less use of the opportunity to learn from diversity and showed the greatest propensity to self-segregate by race. Many lower-income whites, students who had little prior exposure to blacks beyond the media, took advantage of these opportunities to get to know blacks and establish friendships. And many were able to form such relationships and to learn from them. As for blacks, almost all of them got to know some whites well, but only a third felt that they had gained new insights about members of other races from the diversity on campus, most likely because of considerable prior contacts with whites.

While the variability was great, it is clear that a good deal of learning about race did take place. Some students discovered commonalities across race lines that had previously gone unrecognized. Some white students reported encountering blacks who defied and helped break down their personal stereotypes. For example, they met wealthy blacks and blacks who did not fit their images of "hip-hop black culture" and "popular culture." Many white students who formed cross-race friendships benefited from hearing black students' experiences with and perspectives on issues such as racial profiling and affirmative action. This sharing deepened their understanding of many blacks' position in society and of their own white privilege. Some whites came to realize that racism persists and became more sensitive to issues of racial prejudice and discrimination. Some black students came to see that not all whites were rich, or preppy, or snobby, or racist, that some whites were genuinely knowledgeable about black culture and interested in getting to know blacks, and that whites could become their close friends. Many blacks learned about race through the curriculum as well, acquiring a critical lens or analytical framework from which to view race.

Class

Turning to social class, the data suggest that an *educational* argument can be made for the benefits of class-sensitive admissions policies,[13] and that bringing lower-income students to campus has benefits beyond promoting social mobility, social justice, and equity. The majority of both affluent and lower-income students reported becoming well acquainted with students from a very different class background than their own, and many found more commonality across class lines than they had imagined possible. Through personal cross-class relationships and through diversity in the classroom, students heard the life stories and perspectives of classmates whose class backgrounds were different from their own, which led, in some cases, to the reduction of class prejudice and greater empathy and understanding. Some affluent students heard the experiences of students whose families had been on federal assistance, had struggled to pay bills, and had had to be much more self-reliant than they had, and these affluent students came to recognize for the first time or in a new way their own privilege, as well as the lack of thought they had previously given to others less fortunate than themselves. Many lower-income students had their negative stereotypes of the rich challenged and their prejudice reduced as they got to know affluent students who were not spoiled, entitled, and arrogant. They got their first exposure, too, to the world of those who were wealthy.

As with race, group differences emerged in the extent to which students were learning about social class from living in a diverse community or through the curriculum. More lower-income students, both black and white, reported learning about class through living and interacting with diverse peers than did affluent students (69% versus 48%), and more reported taking courses that addressed social class issues as a subtopic or major focus (69% versus 25%).

Fostering Further Learning

This study looked only at the first year of college. It may well be that students will have more cross-race and cross-class experiences in the next three years, experiences that will lead to changes, or further changes, in their attitudes. Over the course of the year, as relationships deepened and students established themselves to one another as individuals, they spoke of moving toward greater openness and comfort in revealing information about their social class backgrounds. If this unfolding continues, further learning may occur. Social science research suggests that inter-group contact can produce more favorable attitudes not only about out-group members who are in the immediate situation, but about the entire out-group.[14] Only time will tell whether the changes in attitudes that occurred over the first year of college will generalize to other out-group members.

Clearly more potential exists on campus for learning through diversity than is being realized. How can we inspire students of different races to recognize the benefits of being inclusive and to take the difficult first steps to reach out to classmates dissimilar from themselves? How can we enable students to negotiate differences in order to create more meaningful black-white, black-black, and cross-class relationships? What can we do to help students examine internalized racism and be more attuned to the existence of racism on campus? How can more affluent students, black and white, be helped to gain a greater awareness of and sensitivity to the experiences on campus of those who do not share their privilege? These are some of the challenges that face us, and the first year of college is a critical year. If this type of learning is an institutional priority, it appears that more active steps need to be taken to ensure that learning will take place.

Institutional Change

Blacks and lower-income white students were being asked to adjust to the culture of a wealthy elite college, but institutions, too, need to consider ways in which they may need to adjust in order to facilitate the incorporation of a more diverse student body and to benefit from the mix of students on campus. Amherst, like many other colleges and universities, has taken steps to do so, and continues to make changes. What other steps might a college like Amherst take if it wants to provide additional support to the students it now accepts to enable them to thrive, and if it wants to promote greater learning from diversity? Given the emphasis of this study on the personal and interpersonal realms, the results do not go as far as one might hope in providing answers to these questions. In the following section I draw on what can be gleaned from the present study, along with the work of other researchers who have written cogently about how best to transform educational institutions to meet the challenges of diversity.[15]

As on every college campus, some degree of racism exists toward blacks, but because it is often subtle, whites, both students and faculty, tend not to fully recognize its manifestations and significance for black students. In my more than 30 years at Amherst, the faculty as a body has not addressed the issue of everyday racism on campus. This may be because the faculty sees this as an issue of student life that falls outside its purview, or perhaps the faculty assumes that the "liberal education" being offered at the college adequately addresses the issue. The importance given to educating students about the realities of racism is a matter of institutional values and goals that needs to be discussed by everyone on campus. Feagin and his colleagues have argued that "by not educating white students to the reality of everyday racism, the predominantly white faculties at most universities participate as accessories in its maintenance and perpetuation."[16]

Structured Dialogue

The college has invested much in diversity but may need to invest further in programming to enrich learning from the greater mix of students, if it takes that to be an important goal. Some students come to campus lacking experience with cross-race and cross-class interactions, and with no knowledge about or experience with working through difficulties that might arise in such relationships. How do we better enable students to bridge their differences? Race and class issues were very much on students' minds, yet few safe avenues existed for discussion of these matters over the course of the year. Without such help, it can be easier for students to back away from complex cross-race and cross-class interactions, to gravitate toward others like themselves rather than engage with those who are different.

When asked what the college could do to make it a better place for them, a few black students and one white student spoke of the need to do more to bridge the gap between blacks and whites and of the need for more dialogue about racial issues. Dialogues about racial issues have taken place, as when the college community mobilized to respond to a racist incident, or when black students demanded to be heard around a specific issue. But these conversations are not part of the ongoing fabric of life on campus. They do not address day-to-day racial tensions. Many more structured dialogues about race *and* class issues might well be useful so that students can reflect on and learn more from the experiences they are having. Dialogues such as these have been found to be highly successful in helping students engage effectively across racial differences.[17] Such conversations require trained facilitators who know how to create an environment in which students feel safe in both expressing what they honestly believe and having those beliefs examined, and who know how to help students manage the strong emotions and differences of opinion that are likely to arise as beliefs are expressed and examined.

The study points to many topics deserving of dialogue between blacks and whites, and among black students. Blacks and whites could benefit from talking together about their perceptions and assumptions about each other, about the difficulties that arise in black-white relationships and how to get past them, about racial joking, the functions it serves and its impact on black students, and about the benefits and disadvantages of trying to remain "color blind." It would be helpful for black students to talk together about their differing perceptions and expectations about what it means to be black or "black enough," about expectations to socialize with blacks and be a part of the black community, about interracial dating, and about how to bridge differences in social class or skin tone.

Class issues call for discussion as well. Cross-class conversations are needed about students' class-based perceptions of one another, about the negative stereotypes that abounded about the very wealthy and the poor. Dialogue could help students sort out feelings about their differences in economic, cultural, and social capital; lower-income students' sense of exclusion—from trips, eating out, buying tickets for off-campus activities; affluent students' feelings about having so much more than some classmates. Lower-income students could benefit from conversations among themselves about the challenges they face, such as growing apart from family and friends at home, and the guilt they may feel about their new status and privileges relative to those they have left behind.

Leadership

How can a college create an environment that fosters such structured dialogue between students and one in which students and faculty can safely explore diversity issues together? As many have argued for decades, a strong message needs to come from those who lead a college about the importance of addressing race and class issues on campus. Leadership is needed to rein-force the commitment to diversity goals, the commitment to being an insti-tution that welcomes difference and that is willing to take needed action to meet the challenges that come with that diversity.[18]

Diversifying the Faculty and Administration

Amherst, like many of its peer institutions, has made great strides in diversi-fying the racial and socioeconomic profile of the student body. But more is required to become a diverse "community" and to promote learning from diversity. Colleges have long understood the need to bring greater diversity to their faculties and administration to create such a community. This has been difficult to accomplish, but the changes in the student body make such diver-sification even more imperative.

Many arguments have been put forth for the benefits of a diverse faculty. To help counter negative race- and class-based stereotypes, it is important for every student to see outstanding teachers, scholars, and administrators who come from all races and classes. Lower-income and minority students can profit greatly from finding role models from their own race and class on the faculty and in the administration, and these individuals can bring an addi-tional dimension to mentoring because they may recognize aspects of their own experiences in these students. Further, when faculty and administrators come to campus with a broad range of backgrounds and life experiences, important alternative points of view and solutions can be brought to decision making at every level.

Finally, it is important that faculty and administrators who are members of minority groups and from lower-income backgrounds be present on cam-pus in sufficient numbers in order to be regarded as individuals and avoid their being viewed and treated as "tokens," as spokespersons of their respec-tive groups. If few in number, these individuals can be overwhelmed by mentoring students similar to themselves and by being placed on numerous committees to represent their race or class. Minority faculty will themselves need mentors to help them handle this minefield of student and administra-tive demands without compromising their teaching and research.

Academic Issues

A variety of academic issues must be considered to better address the needs of a diverse student body and to help students benefit from the diversity on campus. Are race and class adequately addressed in the curriculum and are students selecting courses that address these issues? Are members of the fac-ulty adept at handling potentially charged discussions of race and class? Are

students with weaker preparation able to attain academic success in the rigorous curriculum?

Bringing a more diverse group of students to campus has highlighted the
need for the faculty to reexamine and broaden the curriculum. As blacks,
Latinos, Asian-Americans, and lower-income students have been admitted
in greater numbers to colleges like Amherst, students in these groups have
pressed for the development of courses and majors that cover historical, economic, social and cultural dimensions of race and class, that provide theoretical and analytical frameworks to better grasp the systems that have produced
race and class inequalities. Such material, often absent or on the margins,
needs to have a more central place in the curriculum.

Courses that address race and class are of great interest to many blacks
and lower-income students because they often help them to understand their
personal experiences and those of other members of their race and/or class.
Not surprisingly, more blacks than whites in this study took courses pertaining to blacks and racial issues, and more lower-income students than affluent
ones enrolled in courses that addressed class issues. But many whites, as well
as blacks, lack an analytic framework for understanding race, just as many affluent students lack such a framework on social class. Diversity-education
scholar Joyce King has argued that whites from "economically privileged, culturally homogeneous backgrounds are generally unaware of their intellectual
biases and monocultural encapsulation."[19] Their knowledge and understanding of social inequalities is limited. Lacking a critical perspective on the social
order, they tacitly accept dominant norms and privileges. Most affluent whites
at Amherst have not made the courses on race and class a priority and may
well graduate without that "critical perspective on the social order."

At present, it is not part of the stated mission of the college that students
examine their intellectual biases with regard to race or class and/or the racial
and class inequalities that surround them. It is, however, the goal of a liberal
education to enable students to question assumptions, to become more critical of their own and others' presuppositions, and to think analytically. Given
the history of race in this country and the presence of racism today, and
given the growing inequalities in wealth, *should* students be encouraged to
direct some of their attention to questioning these matters? This is a question
of values—whether this subject matter should be privileged over others—and
is a question that needs discussion.

Another set of concerns relates to whether faculty members are comfortable and skilled at addressing issues of race and class in classroom discussions. Many students reported learning from diverse peers in the classroom,
but talking about racial and class issues in a classroom with students from
diverse backgrounds can be a complicated matter. Discussions can become
heated. Insensitive, racist, or classist comments may come up; terms may be

used or assumptions and perspectives put forth that are offensive to some students. Such remarks, if unaddressed, can create a classroom climate that is detrimental to black and/or lower-income students. Professors have an important role to play in these situations, creating an atmosphere in which students feel safe to state their opinions *as well as* to have those opinions examined. Faculty members are trained to teach a particular subject matter, but most are not trained to handle these types of discussions. The institution must consider what it currently offers in terms of faculty development and what types of programs it might undertake to better enable faculty to manage discussions of course material that deal with matters of race and class, discussions that may be difficult to handle.

Students across the four groups in this study entered the college with academic confidence. As the year got underway, however, some lower-income students discovered that they were academically underprepared for the rigors of the curriculum. Relying on the style that had helped them succeed in the past, many of these students worked even harder, drew on their independence and self-reliance, and didn't reach out for help. It can be difficult to disclose weakness. Many lower-income students lacked the sense of entitlement possessed by more privileged peers who turned to faculty, deans, and other campus resources more readily to help them succeed. How, then, can all students be helped to attain academic success?

A major challenge that colleges face will be to develop ways to identify students' academic needs early on and successfully address those needs. This will likely require the introduction of new courses, changes in pedagogy in existing courses, or other creative initiatives to put students on an equal footing. A further complexity emerges, as students who could most benefit from help do not always access available resources. Professors hold office hours, but not all students feel comfortable approaching their professors outside of class, or revealing their weaknesses to them. Colleges have developed resources like writing centers or help sessions to make it possible for all students to succeed, but these resources can only work for students who feel comfortable asking for and entitled to such help. Mechanisms must be developed to enable students to take advantage of resources without singling out those in need and making them feel further like outsiders. Should all students be required to use specific resources, be they office hours, problem-solving sessions in science courses, a writing center, thus giving the message that these resources are designed to benefit every student?

Student Affairs

In order to create a more welcoming and inclusive environment for a diverse student body, an institution needs to examine some traditions and practices that may have been in place for generations of students—for example, orientation or holiday breaks. What messages do students infer from these practices? Are they messages of inclusion, or must some of these traditions and practices be rethought to meet the needs of a more diverse student body?

Orientation

As part of the preparation for the year ahead, there is great value, starting in their first days on campus, to sensitizing students to their diversity and the value the college places on diversity. This is an excellent opportunity to identify and discuss the different issues that students from different classes and races may well be dealing with.[20] Orientation is an important time to set the tone that students should take advantage of the chance to learn from their differences—to see these differences, as Amherst president Anthony Marx put it, as their "best gifts to each other."[21]

Colleges differ in their orientation programming for incoming students. At Amherst, for many years, gender and sexuality were major issues addressed in the orientation program. Although some time was devoted to issues of race, class issues received little attention in the orientation for the students in this study.[22] Orientation programming addressing race and class issues would be extremely important for incoming students. Many students in the study came from environments where people were primarily of their own race and social class. Even those students who had experience interacting in diverse communities may have lacked experience in how to discuss race and class issues, discussions that can easily evoke strong emotions and create misunderstandings. Orientation is a time to begin giving students the motivation and skills to engage with and learn from students who differ from themselves.[23]

Lower-income and black students gave examples of information that would have been useful to them but had not occurred to orientation planners. The information ranged from when financial aid checks would be arriving to where black women could get their hair done (a concern raised by a number of black women in the study). I note these as examples of obstacles that some incoming students faced alone, but that could be addressed if systems were in place to solicit and act on concerns, large and small, faced by lower-income and black students.[24]

Thanksgiving, Winter Break, and Spring Vacation

Assumptions have been made by the college and practices have been put into place that made sense historically, based on a different student body, but now need updating. For example, the institution can no longer assume that all students will leave campus for college breaks. Some lower-income students cannot afford a ticket home for the Thanksgiving vacation and end up remaining on campus for the 10-day holiday period. College breaks can be very lonely times on campus, especially when a student is away from family on Thanksgiving Day or left behind over spring vacation while most classmates leave, with some off on exciting travels. The dining hall stops serving meals, and lower-income students are not only left on their own but have to bear the costs of eating out.[25] Through consultation with students who cannot afford to leave campus for these college breaks, plans could be made for how best to provide for them.[26]

Directions for the Future

The study answers some questions but raises many others. I attended closely to gender in analyzing the data, but given the small sample size, few sex-specific patterns were apparent and thus the study cannot shed light on the way in which gender interacts with race and class in the issues discussed. Likewise, the sample was too small to differentiate between the experiences of black students who were biracial, African American, or Caribbean American, between the experiences of blacks who attended public high schools or private schools, between lower-income students who were poor and those who were middle class, or between lower-income students with college-educated parents and those who were the first generation to go to college. These questions are there for future research. The study focused solely on students who were black and white; it remains to be determined whether issues faced by black students are unique to that group or extend to Latinos and Asians.

The study has followed students through the first year of college. Growth and change are likely to occur over the next three years. In order to determine how much students ultimately learn from diversity over the course of their education, I plan to assess these students again at the end of their four years in college to explore what challenges they confronted, new, old, or both, and what obstacles they have faced along the way.[27]

I have looked at group differences, but an important finding of this study is the considerable variability within each group when it came to the nature of their experiences on campus. For example, some black students were highly sensitive to racism on campus and perceived numerous incidences of it; other black students perceived much less.[28] Some lower-income students noticed class markers (e.g., designer labels on students' clothes and accessories) and perceived many affluent students to be flaunting their wealth, while other lower-income students were less highly attuned to these class signals or were not put off by them. Some students who were poor were able to form connections to those who were rich; others found the differences too great to bridge. In thinking about what students' needs are and how to meet those needs, the variability in student experience must be kept in mind.

As an elite, highly selective, well-endowed residential college, Amherst is not typical of most institutions of higher education. Nor are its students typical of most college students. But in many ways the matters of race and class that students were dealing with on campus are not unique to this institution. They are issues being dealt with or avoided throughout the larger society. What can be learned at Amherst has important implications beyond its campus.

Appendix A
On-Line Survey Measures

DEMOGRAPHICS AND BACKGROUND INFORMATION

In the fall semester students were asked to report their sex, age, race, race of parents, type of high school they attended (public, private, religious), whether they were receiving financial aid, their self-perceived social class, the highest level of education attained by parents, the college attended if the parent had obtained a BA/BS, and parent's primary occupation during his/her working years. In the spring students were asked the percentage of students at their high school who were members of their social class and members of their race, and the percentage of people in their home neighborhoods who were white or black.

ACADEMIC CONFIDENCE

In both fall and spring semesters students were asked to indicate on a 7-point scale (1 = not at all confident, 7 = very confident) "how confident you feel about each of the following": your academic preparation, your writing skills, your general academic knowledge, your intelligence, your ability to express your ideas, and that you merit being at Amherst College. Scores on these six items were averaged to form a measure of Academic Confidence (Chronbach's alphas in the fall and spring were .89 and .86 respectively).

FEELINGS OF COMFORT AND INCLUSION IN RELATION TO PEERS

In both semesters students were given a list of 13 bipolar adjectives and asked to indicate the point on the 7-point continuum between the two poles that "best described your feeling in the past week." The list of adjectives included comfortable/uncomfortable, included/excluded, insider/outsider, adequate/inadequate, optimistic/pessimistic, not intimidated/intimidated, capable/not capable, distant/close, valued/not valued, knowledgeable/ignorant, listened to/unheard, superior/inferior, and appreciated/unappreciated. Scores on these 13 items were averaged to form a measure of Feelings in Relation to Peers (Chronbach's alphas in the fall and spring were .89 and .86 respectively).

OVERALL WELL-BEING, GROWTH, AND ADJUSTMENT

In both semesters students were asked to rate their psychological health and social life on a 7-point scale (1=poor, 4=good, 7=excellent). Spring semester students were asked to indicate on a 7-point scale (1=not at all, 4=somewhat, 7=a lot), "up to this point in your college career, how much you feel you have": grown as a person, gotten to know people well from different class backgrounds, gotten to know people well from different races, changed in order to fit in at Amherst College, found a place at the college. The items were derived from those developed by Cantor and Prentice (1996).

GRADES AND SCHOLASTIC APTITUDE TEST SCORES (SAT)

In both semesters students were asked whether they were willing to release their grades and SAT scores on file at the college.

ITEMS STUDENTS BROUGHT TO CAMPUS

In the fall semester students were asked whether they brought any of the following items to campus: a laptop computer, a desktop computer, an iPod, a television, a DVD player or VCR, a stereo system, a microwave or kitchen appliance, a rug, a couch, other furniture.

IMPORTANCE OF RACE AND SOCIAL CLASS TO IDENTITY

In the fall semester students were asked to rate the importance to them of "my race/ethnicity" and "my social class" on a 7-point scale (1=not at all important, 7=extremely important). In the spring they were asked to use the same scale to rate how important they felt each of those characteristics had been in shaping their experience at Amherst College.

DIFFICULTIES POSED BY SOCIAL CLASS AND RACE

In the spring semester students were asked to rate 12 items on a 7-point scale (1=much easier, 4=neither easier nor more difficult, 7=much more difficult) indicating whether being a member of their social class made each item easier or more difficult. They were then asked to rate the 12 items again indicating whether being a member of their race made each one easier or more difficult. The items were based on those developed by Cantor and Prentice (1996). Three items were highly inter-correlated: be taken seriously by professors, form relationships with professors, and earn good grades in coursework. They were averaged to form a measure of Academic Integration (Chronbach's alphas in regard to social class and race were .80 and .69 respectively). Four items were highly inter-correlated: feel comfortable on campus, find like-minded friends, find refuge on campus when things are going badly, and be included in informal activities with classmates. Scores on these 4 items were averaged to form a measure of Social Integration and Comfort (Chronbach's alphas in regard to social class and race were .80 and .66 respectively). The remaining 5 items did not highly inter-correlate and were retained as single items: make friends of different races/social classes, make contacts for the future, get invited to social events, go home for family visits/occasions, and have parents or family members visit you here at Amherst.

FRIENDSHIPS ACROSS RACE AND CLASS

In the spring students were asked: Have you gotten to **know well 2 or more** students who are white? Have you gotten to **know well 2 or more** students who are black? Have you gotten to **know well 2 or more** students who are from much wealthier families than your own? Have you gotten to **know well 2 or more** students who are from much poorer families than your own? How many close friends do you have at Amherst College? How many of those close friends are members of your social class? How many of those close friends are members of your race?

SALIENCE OF RACE AND CLASS

In the spring students were asked: "Over the past month, how much thought have you given to your social class? Over the past month, how much thought have you given to your race? Approximately how often do you: Discuss racial issues with other students? Discuss issues of social class with other students?" Response categories included: daily, 2 or 3 times per week, once a week, a few times a month, a few times per semester, never.

CONTACT WITH FAMILIES

In the spring students were asked: "During the academic year, how many times have your parents or family members come to campus to visit you? Approximately how often do you: Talk by phone with family members? E-mail family members?" Response categories included: daily, 2 or 3 times per week, once a week, a few times a month, a few times per semester, never.

PARTICIPATION IN EXTRACURRICULAR ACTIVITIES AND WORK

In the spring students were asked to list the extracurricular groups that they belonged to (e.g., athletic teams, religious groups, performance groups, community outreach, ethnic/cultural groups). They were also asked if they had a job on or off campus, and how many hours they worked.

Appendix B
Interview Questions

I would like to begin the interview by asking you some questions about social class.

Social Class

- What social class do you identify with?
- Is your social class an aspect of yourself you have thought about before coming to Amherst College? What kinds of thoughts have you had?
- What difference do you think social class has made in your life? In the things you have done? Can you cite some examples?
- Were there any things that were made easier in your life because of your social class? Were there any things that were made harder?
- Suppose that it were possible for you and all of your family to be born all over again. Would you want to be born into the same social class, or a different social class? Why?
- What differences do you think your social class background will have on your experience here at Amherst College, if any, academically? What about socially?
- Since you arrived at Amherst College, how much thought have you given to your social class? Is this a change since before coming to Amherst?
- Since you arrived, has class ever been a factor in your interactions with your classmates on campus?
- Has there ever been an incident here on campus where you felt your class position caused you to be left out, put down, dismissed, or discriminated against?

- Are there times when you have felt being a member of your social class opened up social opportunities for you, or allowed you to be included?
- Would you say your social class is expressed in the way you present yourself physically, in your clothing, jewelry or hairstyle? Would you say your social class is expressed in your speech? In the way you interact with others? How so?
- In choosing your friends and/or romantic partners here at college, do you think that social class will make a difference? Please explain.
- Do you feel you have something special to contribute here at Amherst because of your class background? How has that manifested itself? Are there values you bring because of your social class?

Race
I would like to turn now to some questions about race. [The questions above were asked again, substituting "race" for "social class."]

General
- Were there things you purchased to come to Amherst, e.g., a computer, printer, bedding, clothing? What kinds of things did you buy?
- What could Amherst College have done so far to make this a better place for you?

SPRING INTERVIEW
I want to begin generally by finding out how things have gone for you this year academically and socially. How does that compare to what you expected? What has been most surprising?

Social Class
- What differences, if any, do you think your social class background has had on your experience here at Amherst academically and socially? Can you give me some examples?
- How often do you think about the differences in wealth between students on campus? What kinds of thoughts have you had?
- Have you had meaningful, honest conversations with students about issues of social class? [If yes:] Could you tell me about any of those conversations and whether they caused you to see something differently?
- Has there ever been an incident here on campus where you felt your class position caused you to be left out, put down, or dismissed?
- Are there times when you have felt being a member of your social class opened up opportunities for you, or allowed you to be included?
- Do you feel there are cliques of students based on social class from which you feel excluded? [If yes:] Could you describe them? Are there cliques of students you have avoided because you wouldn't be comfortable with them? [If yes:] Could you describe them?
- Have people ever made assumptions about you because of your class background that you feel are incorrect? [If yes:] Please describe the assumptions. How com-

fortable do you feel interacting with people from a very different class background than your own? Is this a change from how you felt when you first arrived?

- Have you ever felt uncomfortable around peers about your family's resources, what you or your family has or doesn't have, or ever felt the desire to hide your class origins? [If yes:] Could you tell me about a situation when this has come up and what feelings were evoked?
- Do you feel your class background has given you values or qualities that make you different from students on campus who have much more or much less wealth than your family does? [If yes:] What are they?
- Has personal sharing occurred by students of different social classes in any of the courses you took this year that caused you to change the way you understand social class or your class position? [If yes:] What was said and how did it influence your beliefs or assumptions?
- Have you ever felt that negative stereotypes were presented in the classroom about people who are either poor or who are highly affluent? [If yes:] Please describe. How did this affect you?
- Have you developed a close relationship with a student who comes from a very different class background than you do? [If yes:] Could you tell me about that person? Are there things you have learned about yourself or about social class through this relationship?
- How important is forming a close relationship with someone from a very different class background to you personally?
- Do you feel your experience at Amherst living and interacting with people from different class backgrounds has changed the way you see people of your own social class? [If yes:] How so? Of other social classes? [If yes:] How so?
- Do you feel you have contributed something special because of your class background? [If yes:] What do you think you contributed? Can you give me a specific example to illustrate this?

Race

The questions above were asked again, substituting "race" for "social class." In addition, black students were asked:

- Have you felt any pressures to be with students of your race?
- Has your "blackness" ever been questioned, or have you been accused of "acting white"?
- How comfortable do you feel interacting with students who are white? Is this a change from how you felt when you first arrived? [If yes:] To what do you ascribe the change?
- Have you developed a close relationship here with someone white? [If yes:] Could you tell me about that person? Are there things that you have learned about yourself or about your race through this relationship? Has it influenced your thoughts about whites?
- How important is forming a close relationship with someone who is white to you personally?

White students were asked:

- How comfortable do you feel interacting with students who are black? Is this a change from how you felt when you first arrived? [If yes:] To what do you ascribe the change?
- Have you developed a close relationship here with someone black? [If yes:] Could you tell me about that person? Are there things that you have learned about yourself or about your race through this relationship? Has it influenced your thoughts about blacks?
- How important is forming a close relationship with someone who is black to you personally?

General

- How important is having connections to becoming a success, that is, connections through one's family, students at Amherst and their families, Amherst faculty and alumni?
- Are you aware of having changed in any ways to "fit in" at Amherst, for example, bought different clothes, adopted different ways of speaking or interacting? [If yes:] Please describe.
- Have you ever felt you were juggling two worlds or cultures, one at Amherst and one at home, where you must change how you speak or dress or act as you move up and back between them? Could you give me some examples?
- Are there people at home, i.e., family or friends who are vicariously living through you, who want you to live out things they didn't? [If yes:] What do they expect from you? What are your feelings about these expectations?
- In what ways, if any, do you view your parents differently now that you've been at Amherst? Do you think they view you differently? How so?
- Have the changes you've made brought you closer, or made you more distant from family? [If more distant]: Do you feel you have developed ways to help bridge differences?
- In what ways, if any, do you view your friends at home differently now that you've been at Amherst? Do they view you differently? How so?
- Have the changes you've made brought you closer, or made you more distant from friends at home? [If more distant:] Do you feel you have developed ways to help bridge discontinuities?
- What could Amherst College do, if anything, to make this a better place for you?

Notes

CHAPTER 1: BECOMING A MORE DIVERSE COLLEGE

1. The percentage of students from private schools ranged from 30% to 44% for classes entering Amherst between 1967 and 1987. For classes entering since 1987, the percentage of students from private schools has ranged from 32% to 42%.

2. See Karabel (2005) for a discussion of changes in admissions practices at Harvard, Yale, and Princeton over the past century. Parallel changes occurred at other elite colleges.

3. Karabel (2005), p. 382.

4. Rudenstine (2001), p. 45.

5. Bowen & Bok (1998); Karabel (2005).

6. The pattern of change at Amherst mirrors that described by Karabel (2005).

7. Leonhardt (2004).

8. Bowen, Kurzweil, & Tobin (2005), p. 162.

9. Summers (2004).

10. Hanson (1994).

11. Marx (2004).

12. Marx (2006).

13. See http://www.prepforprep.org/prepforprep/, retrieved August 19, 2007.

14. See http://www.abetterchance.org/, retrieved August 19, 2007.

15. See http://www.questbridge.org/students/index.html, retrieved August 19, 2007.

16. See Bowen & Bok (1998); Cantor (2004); Chang (2001); Duncan, Boisjoly, Levy, Kremer, & Eccles (2003); Gurin (2004); Gurin, Dey, Hurtado, & Gurin (2002); Gurin with Dey, Gurin, & Hurtado (2004); Gurin, Nagda, & Lopez (2004); Orfield & Whitla

(2001). Much of this research was used to argue for race-conscious admission in the Supreme Court case *Grutter v. Bollinger et al.*

17. Allport (1954), p. 267.

18. See Dixon, Durrheim, & Tredoux (2005); Pettigrew & Tropp (2006). In a meta-analysis involving over a quarter of a million participants and looking at the relationship between inter-group contact and prejudice, Pettigrew & Tropp (2006) found that greater inter-group contact is associated with lower inter-group prejudice, but the relationship was stronger for majority- than minority-group members. Pettigrew & Tropp found Allport's conditions to be facilitating rather than essential to achieve positive outcomes. Moreover, they found that the benefits of inter-group contact extend beyond the contact situation—through inter-group contact, attitudes not only become more favorable toward out-group members in the immediate contact situation, but extend to the entire out-group.

19. Gurin, Dey, Hurtado, & Gurin (2002).

20. While most white students come to college without considerable exposure to minorities, most minority students have had considerable experience with whites (Pettigrew, 1998a).

21. See Brewer & Brown (1998); Fiske (1998).

22. See Pettigrew (1998b); Stephan & Finlay (1999). In addition to the potential to reduce prejudice, living in a diverse community provides new challenges that foster cognitive growth. According Gurin, Nagda, & Lopez (2004, p. 20): "Cognitive growth is fostered when individuals encounter experiences and demands that they cannot completely understand or meet, and thus must work to comprehend and master the new (or at least not completely familiar) and discontinuous demands." This argument reflects what Piaget (1975) referred to as disequilibrium—i.e., a discontinuity and discrepancy between one's current cognitive structures and incoming information that spurs cognitive growth in order to make sense of new situations and information. Cantor (2004, p. 9) argues that "disequilibrium matters. It encourages us to pay attention, to see ourselves and the world in a slightly new light. To achieve this social disequilibrium, in which peers shed that new light, it helps to have diversity, in which the person in the next seat may well ask a question from a different perspective."

23. Cantor (2004), p. 12.

24. Devine & Vasquez (1998), p. 237.

25. Devine & Vasquez (1998), p. 261.

26. Devine & Vasquez (1998), p. 262.

27. Douthat (2005), p. 24.

28. The term "cultural capital" comes from the work of Pierre Bourdieu (e.g., 1977; 1984). Through family socialization people of different social classes acquire different forms of cultural capital, which includes not only "knowledge of or competence with 'highbrow' aesthetic culture" (Lareau & Weininger, 2003, p. 568), but also the abilities that "provide access to scarce rewards" (p. 587).

29. Personal accounts by poor and working-class individuals who attended college and smaller-scale empirical studies show that upward mobility may be accompanied by feelings of alienation, discomfort, pain, ambivalence, and displacement (Adair & Dahlberg, 2003; Dews & Law, 1995; Granfield, 1991; Hoyt, 1999; Lawler, 1999; Lubrano, 2004; Megivern, 2003; Ostrove, 2003; Ryan & Sackrey, 1984; Skeggs, 1997; Stewart & Ostrove, 1993; Tokarczyk & Fay, 1993).

30. Aries & Seider (2005).

31. D'Souza (1991); Margolis & Romero (1998); Rodriguez (1982); Steele (1990).

32. D'Souza (1991), p. 422.

33. Feagin, Vera, & Imani (1996), p. 159.

34. See Bowen & Bok (1998); Crosby (2004). Summarizing social science research on affirmative action, Crosby (2004, p. 168) found that while self-doubts may exist among affirmative action recipients, there is "scant evidence for the deleterious effects of affirmative action."

35. Bowen & Bok (1998).

36. Studies at elite preparatory schools document the challenges faced by lower-income and minority students. At an elite boy's prep school, boys from blue-collar families and African American boys found themselves socially on the margins and felt that the wealthy students "excluded poorer students, acted insensitively towards them, or simply failed to see them" (Kuriloff & Reichert, 2003, p. 761). African American girls from middle-class families in a predominantly white, elite, all-girls preparatory school also described themselves as outsiders, as not fitting in and belonging or being recognized as full members of the school community (Horvat & Antonio, 1999). These girls felt that "they could never achieve the unquestioned comfort and sense of belonging that came so easily and innately to many of the white and privileged girls" (p. 335). In a follow-up interview study of former participants in A Better Chance (ABC), a program that enables inner-city minority students from impoverished backgrounds to attend elite, predominantly white independent high schools, ABC graduates reported being intimidated by the possessions of other students and excluded from peers' conversations about their travels (Zweigenhaft & Domhoff, 1991).

37. Pope, Miklitsch, & Weigand (2005).

38. Astin (1993), p. 398.

39. These chapters focus on what social scientists have called informal interactional diversity, by which they mean the frequency and quality of interaction among diverse groups on campus, mostly outside the classroom (Gurin, Dey, Hurtado, & Gurin, 2002).

40. Van Dick, Wagner, Pettigrew, Christ, Wolf, Petzel, Castro, & Jackson (2004, p. 220) have found that "the simple fact that an individual has friends from other groups is not the key to reducing intergroup prejudice in itself. Rather, what is critical is the subjective appraisal of a valuable interpersonal relationship that is functional for the individual's goals."

41. Pettigrew (1998a), p. 70.

42. Gurin with Dey, Gurin, & Hurtado (2004). Through classroom diversity students will hear points of view that may increase their awareness of complexities and challenge their assumptions (Gurin with Dey, Gurin, & Hurtado, 2004). Gurin et al. (2004, p. 145) argue: "A growing body of research confirms that sharing, reflection, and dialoguing (especially when it is integrated with content through lectures, readings, and didactic learning), can be a powerful educational tool." Hurtado (2001, p. 198) has found that having "studied with someone from a different racial/ethnic background appears to have more pronounced effects than curricular diversity on self-reported growth in critical thinking and problem solving skills."

43. See Feagin, Vera, & Imani (1996).

44. Not only do race and class shape students' school experience; school experience, in turn, leads to the acquisition of new forms of cultural capital, and involves

changes in judgment, taste, preferences, and practices (Stewart & Ostrove, 1993). Over time lower-income or minority students who enter elite colleges acquire middle-class ways and adopt a different way of speaking and dressing (Almanza, 2003; Aries & Seider, 2005; Dahlberg, 2003; Kuriloff & Reichert, 2003; Lubrano, 2004; Megivern, 2003; Sullivan, 2003; Zweigenhaft & Domhoff, 1991). They struggle to maintain connections with family and friends at home without becoming judgmental (Aries & Seider, 2005; Lubrano, 2004). One student who grew up in poverty felt caught "in the margins between upper-class academe and my poor and working-class roots" (Megivern, 2003, p. 128); others are described as "unable to 'go home,' and with no community to which she can truly belong" (Dahlberg, 2003, p. 75).

CHAPTER 2: INVESTIGATING RACE AND CLASS MATTERS ON CAMPUS

1. Fifty-one percent of these students had attended public schools.

2. Statistics about the class of 2009 were derived from the Fifty-Ninth Annual Report to Secondary Schools, Amherst College.

3. Rubin & Rubin (1995), p. 4.

4. The approach was based on grounded theory, which begins with a close analysis of the data itself and allows important and relevant ideas to emerge (Glaser & Strauss, 1967; Strauss & Corbin, 1990).

5. Inter-rater reliability on these counts was 95% in the fall and 92% in the spring.

6. For some thematic categories data are missing because an interviewer skipped a question, or a student's response was equivocal or could not be reliably determined. Thus the sample sizes for the groups vary slightly from one analysis to another. The sample sizes for each group on which percentages are based are presented in the endnotes.

7. The majority of blacks in the study did not have typically African American names, and thus they were assigned names commonly used by both blacks and whites.

8. I have included inferential statistics in the endnotes. Inferential statistics assume that random samples have been obtained from a population (in this case, Amherst College students) in order to draw conclusions about that population. I began with a cluster sample, taking only students in the class of 2009 as a cluster out of all Amherst College admits. Within that cluster I further stratified by race and class. Within these strata the black groups were invited in their entirety and were not randomly sampled, and a few additions were made to those groups. Disagreement exists about whether inferential statistics should be calculated, given the nature of the sample. Because the students I have selected in each group have a high probability of being representative of the larger groups from which they were chosen, inferential statistics were calculated despite the concern about nonrandom selection. With regard to the frequency data, because of the small sample size, many of the expected values were less than five. Chi-square tests are inappropriate in these cases and were not calculated. For readers interested in doing follow-up tests where χ^2 tests are significant, or for readers interested in looking at confidence intervals for the percentages in each group for each variable, and determining whether each confidence interval overlaps the other three confidence intervals, the data necessary for such calculations are included in the endnotes.

9. Kerbo (1996, p. 12), for example, defines social class as "a grouping of individuals with similar positions and similar political and economic interests within the social stratification system."

10. Eighty-six percent of affluent whites and 93% of affluent blacks had at least one parent with a graduate or professional degree.

11. See http://www.usnews.com/usnews/edu/college/rankings/brief/t1natudoc_brief.php, retrieved September 8, 2006.

12. The characterization of parental occupations is modeled on occupational characteristics described by Lareau (2003, see app. C, p. 279). Lareau, however, fails to distinguish middle class from upper middle class, a distinction pertinent to parents in this study.

13. See Gurin, Dey, Hurtado, & Gurin (2002).

14. In the class of 2009, 57% of the students had attended public school.

15. Only one white student, a lower-income white, had attended parochial school.

16. One lower-income black and two affluent blacks had attended parochial schools.

17. Pettigrew (1998b), p. 275.

18. One lower-income white, one affluent white, and three affluent black students were not willing to release grades and SAT scores.

19. $N = 26$, $SD = 76.72$.

20. $N = 25$, $SD = 81.45$.

21. The SAT scores of blacks were significantly lower than those of whites, $F(1, 47) = 81.65$, $p < .001$, $\eta^2 = .64$.

22. Percentiles were acquired from the College Board.

23. Using self-reported racial identity, the average combined SAT for whites was 1469 and for blacks was 1272.

24. See Bowen & Bok (1998); Vars & Bowen (1998).

25. White students have been found to score higher than African American students on tests of vocabulary, reading, and mathematics as well (Jencks & Phillips, 1998). While the gap in test scores has narrowed since the 1970s, it has persisted and has been attributed to such overriding factors as "the culture of poverty, the scarcity of two-parent black families, and genes" (Jencks & Phillips, 1998, p. 10).

26. See Bowen, Kurzweil, & Tobin (2005).

27. For affluent students $N = 24$, $SD = 121.68$; for lower-income students $N = 27$, $SD = 135.67$. For lower-income whites $N = 13$, $M = 1480.77$, $SD = 81.70$; for lower-income blacks $N = 14$, $M = 1268.57$, $SD = 85.47$; for affluent whites $N = 13$, $M = 1496.15$, $SD = 73.88$; and for affluent blacks $N = 11$, $M = 1304.55$, $SD = 75.02$. The test for significance of the effect of race is reported in note 21 above. The effect of class was not significant, $F(1, 47) = 1.32$, $p > .05$, $\eta^2 = 03$. The race by class interaction was not significant, $F(1, 47) = 0.21$, $p > .05$, $\eta^2 = .004$.

28. For academic confidence: lower-income whites $N = 16$, $M = 5.08$, $SD = .61$; lower-income blacks $N = 14$, $M = 4.81$, $SD = 1.27$; affluent whites $N = 14$, $M = 5.12$, $SD = .97$; and affluent blacks $N = 14$, $M = 5.35$, $SD = .77$. The effect of race was not significant, $F(1, 54) = 0.01$, $p > .05$, $\eta^2 = .00$. The effect of class was not significant, $F(1, 54) = 1.41$, $p > .05$, $\eta^2 = .03$. The race by class interaction was not significant, $F(1, 54) = 1.08$, $p > .05$, $\eta^2 = .02$.

29. See Bowen, Kurtzweil, & Tobin (2005).

30. Bowen, Kurzweil, & Tobin (2005).

31. More aggressive outreach and recruitment has brought lower-income and black students into the applicant pool and into the college. The Office of Admission does direct mailing to high-scoring students of color identified by the Educational Testing Service. It has a travel budget to enable lower-income and black students who show interest in the college to visit the campus. It hires students of color to serve as interns in the office and do outreach to prospective students. College representatives visit high-quality, high-diversity high schools in the United States.

CHAPTER 3: FIRST ENCOUNTERS WITH RACE AND CLASS

1. These students had a parental contribution of $3,800 or less (personal communication from Dean Case, director of financial aid).

2. Sixty percent of lower-income white students ($N = 16$), 71% of lower-income blacks ($N = 14$), 77% of affluent whites ($N = 13$), and 79% of affluent blacks ($N = 14$) purchased computers. A χ^2 test was not calculated because four cells have expected values less than five.

3. Eighty percent of lower-income whites ($N = 16$), 79% of lower-income blacks ($N = 14$), 92% of affluent whites ($N = 13$), and 79% of affluent blacks ($N = 14$) purchased bedding. A χ^2 test was not calculated because four cells have expected values less than five.

4. Eighty-six percent of students in both of the affluent groups ($N = 14$ in each group) brought iPods to campus in contrast to 44% of lower-income whites ($N = 16$) and 57% of lower-income blacks ($N = 14$). A χ^2 test was not calculated because three cells have expected values less than five.

5. Bourdieu and Passeron (1979).

6. Lamont and Lareau (1988, p. 156) define cultural capital as "*institutionalized, i.e., widely shared, high status cultural signals (attitudes, preferences, formal knowledge, behaviors, goods and credentials) used for social and cultural exclusion*" (emphasis in original).

7. There was a significant relationship between group membership and students' perceptions that class would make a difference, χ^2 (3, $N = 55$) = 8.15, $p = .006$, Cramér's $V = .39$. For lower-income whites $N = 15$; for lower-income blacks $N = 12$; for the other groups $N = 14$.

8. The coding categories for having thought about social class were: "very little to not at all," "some," and "a lot." Based on the interview data, 29% of lower-income whites ($N = 14$), 15% of affluent whites ($N = 13$), and 0.0% of blacks ($N = 14$ for affluent blacks, $N = 12$ for lower-income blacks) reported having thought about social class "a lot." Blacks were most likely to have thought about social class "very little to not at all": 67% of lower-income blacks and 64% of affluent blacks versus 36% of lower-income and 23% of affluent whites. A χ^2 test was not calculated because five cells had expected values less than five.

9. See Stuber (2008).

10. Ninety-five percent of the students reported that their social class position had never caused them to feel left out, put down, dismissed, or discriminated against; 90% reported that they had never been judged by class stereotypes; and 75% reported that social class had never been a factor in their interactions on campus.

11. Forty-seven percent of lower-income whites ($N = 15$), 62% of lower-income blacks ($N = 13$), 71% of affluent whites ($N = 14$), and 57% of affluent blacks ($N = 14$) felt that clothes and appearance did not necessarily reveal class position. The relationship between group membership and reports on whether clothes and appearance revealed class position was not significant, χ^2 (3, $N = 56$) = 1.89, $p > .05$, Cramér's $V = .39$.

12. Other studies found that characteristics that distinguish one individual from others such as ethnicity (McGuire, McGuire, Child, & Fujioka, 1978) or gender (McGuire, McGuire, & Winton, 1979) become more salient.

13. Carter (1997).

14. Fifty-seven percent of lower-income whites ($N = 14$) and 43% of affluent whites ($N = 14$) reported that they had given little or no thought to their racial identity, compared with 0.0% of lower-income blacks ($N = 14$) and 8% of affluent blacks ($N = 13$). A χ^2 test was not calculated because four cells had expected values less than five.

15. See Helms (1990).

16. Thirty-six percent of lower-income whites ($N = 14$) and 50% of affluent whites ($N = 12$) thought race had had an impact on their lives, versus 93% of lower-income blacks ($N = 14$) and 85% of affluent blacks ($N = 13$). A χ^2 test was not calculated because four cells had expected values less than five.

17. Over 65% of African Americans have experienced racial discrimination (Sellers, Morgan, & Brown, 2001). Sue, Capodilupo, Torino, Bucceri, Holder, Nadal, and Esquilin (2007, p. 273) argue that racism today primarily takes the form of racial microaggressions, which they define as "brief and commonplace daily verbal, behavioral, and environmental indignities, whether intentional or unintentional, that communicate hostile, derogatory, or negative racial slights and insults to the target person or group." They review research showing that the cumulative effects of microaggressions can be devastating for persons of color.

18. Eighty-five percent of lower-income blacks ($N = 13$) and 77% of affluent blacks ($N = 13$) said that their race had opened up social opportunities for them, versus 8% of lower-income whites ($N = 13$) and 0% of affluent whites ($N = 12$). Group membership was significantly related to students' perceptions of whether race opened up social opportunities, χ^2 (3, $N = 51$) = 30.93, $p < .001$, Cramér's $V = .78$.

19. See Cross, Strauss, & Fhagen-Smith (1999) for a discussion of blacks' search for meaning and support through affiliations and attachments to other blacks.

20. Seventy-seven percent of lower-income blacks ($N = 13$) and 69% of affluent blacks ($N = 13$) thought that race would make a difference for them socially, versus 43% of lower-income whites ($N = 14$) and 31% of affluent whites ($N = 13$). The relationship between group membership and perceptions of whether race would make a difference socially approached significance, χ^2 (3, $N = 53$) = 7.50, $p = .058$, Cramér's $V = .38$.

21. Stephan & Stephan (1985).

22. Stephan & Stephan (1985), p. 162.

23. Forty-seven percent of lower-income whites ($N = 15$), 31% of affluent whites ($N = 13$), 21% of lower-income blacks ($N = 14$), and 14% of affluent blacks ($N = 14$) worried that blacks would self-segregate. A χ^2 test was not calculated because four cells had expected values less than five.

24. See Tatum (1997).

25. Major & Eccleston (2005).

26. Fifteen percent of lower-income whites ($N=13$), 15% of lower-income blacks ($N=13$), 8% of affluent whites ($N=12$), and 14% of affluent blacks ($N=13$) felt that race would affect friendships. A χ^2 test was not calculated because four cells had expected values less than five.

27. For social confidence in relation to peers: lower-income whites $N=16$, $M=4.50$, $SD=.84$, lower-income blacks $N=14$, $M=4.73$, $SD=.79$, affluent whites $N=14$, $M=4.82$, $SD=1.00$, and affluent blacks $N=14$, $M=4.87$, $SD=.77$. The effect of race was not significant, $F(1, 54)=0.40$, $p>.05$, $\eta^2=.01$. The effect of class was not significant, $F(1, 54)=1.04$, $p>.05$, $\eta^2=.02$. The race by class interaction was not significant, $F(1, 54)=0.17$, $p>.05$, $\eta^2=.003$.

28. For social life: lower-income whites $N=16$, $M=4.81$, $SD=1.17$, lower-income blacks $N=14$, $M=5.57$, $SD=.94$, affluent whites $N=14$, $M=5.14$, $SD=1.17$, and affluent blacks $N=14$, $M=5.14$, $SD=1.23$. The effect of race was not significant, $F(1, 54)=1.62$, $p>.05$, $\eta^2=.01$. The effect of class was not significant, $F(1, 54)=0.03$, $p>.05$, $\eta^2=.001$. The race by class interaction was not significant, $F(1, 54)=1.62$, $p>.05$, $\eta^2=.03$. For psychological health: lower-income whites $N=16$, $M=4.94$, $SD=1.84$, lower-income blacks $N=14$, $M=5.93$, $SD=.73$, affluent whites $N=14$, $M=5.43$, $SD=1.28$, and affluent blacks $N=14$, $M=5.64$, $SD=1.39$. The effect of race was not significant, $F(1, 54)=2.71$, $p>.05$, $\eta^2=.05$. The effect of class was not significant, $F(1, 54)=0.08$, $p>.05$, $\eta^2=.001$. The race by class interaction was not significant, $F(1, 54)=1.13$, $p>.05$, $\eta^2=.02$.

29. Dovidio, Gaertner, Hodson, Houlette, & Johnson (2005). For more information on the Common Ingroup Identity model, see also Gaertner, Dovidio, Nier, Ward, & Banker (1999); Dovidio & Gaertner (1998).

CHAPTER 4: NEGOTIATING CLASS DIFFERENCES

1. These responses derive from the fall interviews in which students were asked to talk about the role that social class had played in their lives, whether their class position had made things easier or more difficult, and whether, if it were possible for them and their family to be born over again, they would want to be born into the same social class or a different one.

2. Seventy-nine percent of affluent whites ($N=14$) and 79% of affluent blacks ($N=14$) described themselves as fortunate versus 7% of lower-income whites ($N=15$) and 39% of lower-income blacks ($N=13$). Group membership was significantly related to perceptions of oneself as fortunate, $\chi^2 (3, N=56)=21.10$, $p<.001$, Cramér's $V=.62$.

3. Eighty-six percent of whites ($N=14$) and 87% of blacks ($N=14$) mentioned that their class position had given them access to a superior education.

4. See Lareau (2003) for a discussion of this form of socialization, which she refers to as the "concerted cultivation of children."

5. Ninety-three percent of affluent whites ($N=14$) and 93% of affluent blacks ($N=14$) spoke of their class privilege in relation to those who had less.

6. Thirty-six percent of affluent whites ($N=14$) and 43% of affluent blacks ($N=14$) described themselves in relation to the wealthiest and most advantaged. Veblen (1899) argued that individuals have a tendency to classify themselves in comparison with their neighbors; he described their struggle for competitive standing, their desire to "rank high in comparison with the rest of the community in point of pecuniary strength"

(p. 31), and to "excel everyone else in the accumulation of goods" (p. 32) in order to gain self-esteem.

7. Sixty-seven percent of lower-income whites ($N = 15$) and 85% of lower-income blacks ($N = 14$) described themselves in relation to the wealthiest and most advantaged. Group membership was significantly related to describing oneself in relation to the most advantaged, χ^2 (3, $N = 57$) = 9.04, $p = .029$, Cramér's $V = .40$. Fifty-three percent of lower-income whites ($N = 15$) and 43% of lower-income blacks ($N = 14$) spoke of their class position in relation to those who had less. A χ^2 test looking at the relationship between group membership and describing oneself in relation to those who had less was not calculated because four cells have expected values less than five.

8. For lower-income whites $N = 15$, and for lower-income black groups $N = 14$. For lower-income students being black or white was not significantly related to wanting to be born into "a higher social class" versus wanting to be born again into "the same or a lower social class," χ^2 (1, $N = 29$) = 1.66 with Yates' correction for continuity, $p > .05$, Cramér's $V = .31$.

9. Researchers have found that social class becomes salient in college when individuals encounter people from very different class backgrounds (Aries & Seider, 2005; 2007).

10. See Crocker & Quinn (1998); Twenge & Campbell (2002). System justification theory has shown that people are motivated "to hold favorable attitudes toward the existing social system and the status quo" (Jost, Banaji, & Nosek, 2004, p. 912).

11. Similar findings have been reported by Aries & Seider (2005; 2007); Ostrove & Long (2001); and Stuber (2008).

12. Kay & Jost (2003), p. 823. As a self-protective strategy "people are driven by ethnocentric motives to build ingroup solidarity and to defend and justify the interests and identities of fellow ingroup members against those of outgroup members" (Jost, Banaji, & Nosek, 2004, p. 882).

13. The amount that parents were expected to contribute toward a student's tuition and fees was based on data submitted by parents regarding family income, expenses, assets, debt, the number of persons in the family household, and the number of children in the household who are enrolled full-time in college (Financial Aid Packaging Overview—2007–2008, Office of Financial Aid, Amherst College).

14. Lareau (2003). Extended family members' lives were interwoven; they were in frequent contact and pooled resources and energies.

15. The percentages by group for having desired at times to hide class origins were as follows: 43% of lower-income whites ($N = 14$), 43% of lower-income blacks ($N = 14$), 36% of affluent whites ($N = 14$), and 54% of affluent blacks ($N = 13$). Group membership was not significantly related to wanting to hide class origins, χ^2 (3, $N = 55$) = 0.92, $p > .05$, Cramér's $V = .13$.

16. Fourteen percent of affluent whites ($N = 14$) and 23% of affluent blacks ($N = 14$) had been teased about family wealth. No lower-income whites ($N = 15$) and 7% of lower-income blacks ($N = 14$) had been teased about family wealth. A χ^2 test was not calculated because four cells have expected values less than five.

17. Negative societal stereotypes have been found to exist about members of lower social classes (e.g., Cozzarelli, Wilkinson, & Tagler, 2001; Hoyt, 1999; Landrine, 1999).

18. Sixty percent of lower-income whites ($N = 15$), 57% of lower-income blacks ($N = 14$), 64% of affluent whites ($N = 14$), and 92% of affluent blacks ($N = 13$) rarely thought about differences in wealth when asked at the end of the year. A χ^2 test was not calculated because four cells have expected values less than five.

19. Lower-income whites ($N = 14$) reported that 44% of their close friends were the same social class as themselves, and lower-income blacks ($N = 14$) reported that 55% of their close friends were the same social class as themselves.

20. Being a member of a low-status group does not necessarily result in low self-esteem (Crocker & Lawrence, 1999; Crocker & Quinn, 1998; Twenge & Campbell, 2002). See also Crocker & Major (1989); Snow & Anderson (1987); and Turner, with Hogg, Oakes, Reicher, & Wetherell (1987).

21. See Sennett & Cobb (1972).

22. Hartup (1993).

23. See Kuriloff & Reichert (2003); Stuber (2006).

24. E.g., Bourdieu, (1977); Lareau (2003); MacLeod (1995).

CHAPTER 5. RELATIONSHIPS ACROSS RACE AND CLASS

1. See Devine & Vasquez (1998); Stephan & Stephan (1985).

2. Bowen & Bok (1998).

3. For whites being affluent or lower-income was significantly related to getting to know two or more blacks well, Fisher's Exact test, $p = .029$. (A χ^2 test was not calculated because two cells have expected values less than five.) For affluent whites $N = 13$; for lower-income whites $N = 15$.

4. Hartup (1993) reports that adolescents choose friends who are similar in age and sex.

5. Nathan (2005).

6. For whites $N = 29$, $M = .65$, $SD = .25$; for blacks $N = 26$, $M = .34$, $SD = .33$.

7. For the percentage of close friends of the same race: lower-income whites $N = 15$, $M = .52$, $SD = .24$; for lower-income blacks $N = 14$, $M = .43$, $SD = .35$; for affluent whites $N = 14$, $M = .80$, $SD = .18$; and for affluent blacks $N = 13$, $M = .25$, $SD = .29$. There was a significant effect of race, $F(1, 52) = 19.07$, $p < .001$, $\eta^2 = .27$ qualified by a significant race by class interaction, $F(1, 52) = 10.36$, $p = .002$, $\eta^2 = .17$. The effect of class was not significant, $F(1, 52) = 0.46$, $p > .05$, $\eta^2 = .01$.

8. $N = 14$ for lower-income blacks.

9. Twenty-nine percent of affluent whites ($N = 14$) had exclusively white friends.

10. Thirty-eight percent of affluent blacks ($N = 13$) reported that none of their close friends were black.

11. Appel, Cartwright, Smith, & Wolf (1996). See also Feagin, Vera, & Imani (1996), p. 72; Nathan (2005).

12. Tropp & Bianchi (2006).

13. Sixty-four percent of lower-income whites ($N = 14$) and 69% of affluent whites ($N = 13$) felt that it was important to make a close friend who was black. For whites being affluent or lower-income was not significantly related to perceptions of the importance of making a close friend who was black, Fisher's Exact test, $p = 1.00$. A χ^2 test was not calculated because two cells have expected values less than five.

14. Van Dick, Wagner, Pettigrew, Christ, Wolf, Petzel, Castro, & Jackson (2004).

15. Forty-six percent of lower-income blacks ($N=13$) and 42% of affluent blacks ($N=12$) felt that it was important to form relationships with whites. For blacks being affluent or lower-income was not significantly related to perceptions of the importance of forming relationships with whites, χ^2 (1, $N=25$) $=0.00$ with Yates' correction for continuity, $p > .05$, Cramér's $V=.045$. Datnow & Cooper (1996) found that African Americans at elite independent schools, while valuing their relationships with other African Americans, recognized the importance of forming friendships with whites.

16. Thirty-three percent of lower-income white students ($N=15$) and 21% of affluent white students ($N=14$) reported becoming more comfortable interacting with blacks over the course of the year. For whites being affluent or lower-income was not significantly related to this development, Fisher's Exact test, $p=.68$. A χ^2 test was not calculated because two cells have expected values less than five.

17. Fifty-seven percent of students in each of the white groups ($N=14$ for each white group), 36% of lower-income blacks ($N=14$), and 39% of affluent blacks ($N=13$) felt that it was important to make a close friend from a different class background. Group membership was not significantly related to students' perceptions of the importance of making a close friend from a different class background, χ^2 (3, $N=55$) $=2.25$, $p > .05$, Cramér's $V=.20$.

18. Bowen & Bok (1998).

19. Sample sizes for reports of having gotten to know students from a much wealthier family than their own were as follows: for lower-income white students $N=15$; for lower-income black students $N=14$; for affluent whites $N=14$; for affluent blacks $N=13$. A χ^2 test was not calculated because four cells have expected values less than five.

20. Thirty-three percent of lower-income whites ($N=15$), 57% of lower-income blacks ($N=14$), 100% of affluent whites ($N=14$), and 92% of affluent blacks ($N=13$) reported having gotten to know well two or more students from a much poorer family. A χ^2 test was not calculated because four cells have expected values less than five.

21. Eighty-seven percent of lower-income whites ($N=15$), 71% of lower-income blacks ($N=14$), 71% of affluent whites ($N=14$), and 73% of affluent blacks ($N=11$) reported having made a close friend from a very different class background than their own. A χ^2 test was not calculated because four cells have expected values less than five.

22. For percentage of friends of the same social class: lower-income whites $N=14$, $M=.44$, $SD=.22$; for lower-income blacks $N=14$, $M=.55$, $SD=.25$; affluent whites $N=14$, $M=.54$, $SD=.31$; and affluent blacks $N=13$, $M=.64$, $SD=.24$. The effect of race was not significant, $F(1, 51)=2.40$, $p>.05$, $\eta^2=.05$. The effect of class was not significant, $F(1, 51)=1.86$, $p>.05$, $\eta^2=.04$. The race by class interaction was not significant, $F(1,51)=0.00$, $p>.05$, $\eta^2=.00$.

23. Sixty-nine percent of affluent blacks ($N=13$) versus 43% of students in the other three groups reported that over half their friends were of the same social class. For lower-income whites $N=15$; for both affluent whites and lower-income blacks $N=14$.

24. For lower-income whites $N=15$. One affluent white ($N=10$), one lower-income black ($N=12$), and 33% of affluent blacks ($N=12$) reported growing more comfortable

with students of a different social class than their own. A χ^2 test was not calculated because four cells have expected values less than five.

25. See Aries & Seider (2005).

26. Along with the pre-existing connections to classmates came connections to those students' parents, who could provide help when affluent students were searching for summer jobs and internships.

27. For lower-income whites $N=15$, $M=4.67$, $SD=1.54$; for lower-income blacks $N=14$, $M=4.43$, $SD=1.22$; for affluent whites $N=14$, $M=2.93$, $SD=1.27$; for affluent blacks $N=13$, $M=3.00$, $SD=.71$. The difference between lower-income students and affluent students on ratings of whether social class made it easier or more difficult to make contacts for the future was statistically significant, $F(1, 52)=22.84$, $p<.001$, $\eta^2=.31$. The effect of race was not significant, $F(1, 52)=0.06$, $p>.05$, $\eta^2=.001$. The race by class interaction was not significant, $F(1, 52)=0.22$, $p>.05$, $\eta^2=.004$. For whether race made it easier or more difficult to make contacts for the future, overall $N=56$, $M=3.75$, $SD=.88$. The effect of race was not significant, $F(1, 52)=2.04$, $p>.05$, $\eta^2=.04$. The effect of class was not significant, $F(1, 52)=1.48$, $p>.05$, $\eta^2=.03$. The race by class interaction was not significant, $F(1, 52)=0.43$, $p>.05$, $\eta^2=.01$.

28. See Aries & Seider (2005).

29. For lower-income whites $N=15$, and for lower-income blacks $N=13$. Fourteen percent of affluent whites ($N=14$) and 15% of affluent blacks ($N=13$) said that there were cliques from which they felt excluded. A χ^2 test was not calculated because four cells have expected values less than five.

30. Stephan, Boniecki, Ybarra, Bettencourt, Ervin, Jackson, McNatt, & Renfro (2002).

31. More negative contact between black and white students is associated with more inter-group anxiety. As inter-group anxiety is reduced, more favorable feelings are generated (Stephan, Boniecki, Ybarra, Bettencourt, Ervin, Jackson, McNatt, & Renfro, 2002).

32. Tropp & Pettigrew (2005a).

33. See Tatum (1997).

34. Individuals may withdraw from situations in which they anticipate being excluded, and rather than basing their self-esteem on the evaluations of individuals who might exclude them, they seek alternative bases for inclusion in order to feel valued (Major & Eccleston, 2005).

CHAPTER 6: LEARNING FROM RACIAL DIVERSITY

1. See Allport (1954); Fiske (1998).

2. Fiske (1998). Racial stereotypes tend to be overgeneralizations, exaggerations, or inaccurate depictions of group members.

3. Beyond stereotyping, racial categorization has profound consequences from employment to housing and the allocation of resources (Omi & Winant, 1994).

4. Fiske (1998), p. 379. See Fiske (1998) for a review of the research on stereotyping and social prejudice.

5. Wittenbrink, Judd, & Park (1997).

6. Gaertner & McLaughlin (1983).

7. Gaertner & Dovidio (1986), p. 62.

8. For example, see Banaji & Greenwald (1995); Gaertner & McLaughlin (1983); Wittenbrink, Judd, & Park (1997).

9. See Bell (1997); Cross (1991); Hardiman (2001); Hardiman & Jackson (1992; 1997); Helms (1984); Jackson (2001).

10. See Banks (1970); Johnson, Lecci, & Swim (2006).

11. Fifty percent of lower-income blacks ($N = 14$), 54% of affluent blacks ($N = 13$), and 47% of lower-income whites ($N = 15$) reported hearing incorrect assumptions made about them because of their race. For affluent whites $N = 14$. Group membership was significantly related to hearing incorrect assumptions based on race, χ^2 ($3, N = 56$) = 8.24, $p = .041$, Cramér's $V = .38$. Watson, Terrell, Wright, Bonner, Cuyjet, Gold, Rudy, & Person (2002, p. 69) similarly found that minority students believed "assumptions were often made about them based on their minority group membership."

12. See Feagin, Vera, & Imani (1996) for a discussion of blacks' perceptions of differential treatment by white professors.

13. Moynihan (1965).

14. See Cross (1991); Hardiman & Jackson (1992).

15. Fiske (1998); Waters (1999).

16. Many minorities are poor because they live in a racist society where they do not have access to excellent schooling or better job opportunities.

17. In their fall interviews, 79% of lower-income blacks ($N = 14$) and 69% of affluent blacks ($N = 13$) felt that they had something to contribute based on race. For blacks being affluent or lower-income was not significantly related to perceptions of having something to contribute based on race, Fisher's Exact Test $p = .68$. A χ^2 test was not calculated because two cells have expected values less than five.

18. Gurin, Dey, Hurtado, & Gurin (2002).

19. Gurin, with Dey, Gurin, & Hurtado (2004). Students report greater growth in critical thinking and problem-solving skills from having studied with someone from a different racial/ethnic background than from curricular diversity (Hurtado, 2001).

20. Fifty-seven percent of lower-income blacks ($N = 14$), 46% of affluent blacks ($N = 11$), 20% of lower-income whites ($N = 15$), and 8% of affluent whites ($N = 13$) took a black studies course or a course with "Black" or "Africa" in the title. A χ^2 test was not calculated because four cells have expected values less than five.

21. Ninety-three percent of lower-income blacks ($N = 14$), 82% of affluent blacks ($N = 11$), 53% of lower-income whites ($N = 15$), and 39% of affluent whites ($N = 13$) took a course in which race was a primary topic or subtopic. A χ^2 test was not calculated because three cells have expected values less than five.

22. Sixty-seven percent of the lower-income whites ($N = 15$), 43% of lower-income blacks ($N = 14$), 36% of affluent whites ($N = 14$), and 31% of affluent blacks ($N = 13$) talked about personal sharing by students in the classroom that caused them to change the way they understand race or racial issues. Group membership was not significantly related to whether students reported personal sharing in the classroom that changed their understanding of race, χ^2 ($3, N = 56$) = 4.43, $p > .05$, Cramér's $V = .28$. The lower percentage for affluent whites may be due to the fact that students in this group took fewer courses in which racial issued were addressed.

23. Pettigrew (1997).

24. Feagin, Vera, & Imani (1996).

25. Forty-seven percent of lower-income whites ($N=15$), 39% of lower-income blacks ($N=13$), 21% of affluent whites ($N=14$), and 31% of affluent blacks ($N=13$) saw their experience on campus as having changed their views of race. A χ^2 test was not calculated because three cells have expected values less than five.

26. When group salience (in this case the salience of race) is low, it is easier for people to perceive similarities (Pettigrew, 1997).

27. Pettigrew (1997).

28. Forty-three percent of lower-income whites ($N=14$) and 57% of affluent whites ($N=14$) had thought about racial identity, versus 100% of lower-income blacks ($N=14$) and 92% of affluent blacks ($N=13$). A χ^2 test was not calculated because four cells have expected values less than five.

29. DuBois (1993), p. 9.

30. Past research has shown that inter-group contact is less likely to lead to the reduction of prejudice for members of minority groups than for members of the majority (Tropp & Pettigrew, 2005b).

31. See Brewer & Brown (1998) and Fiske (1998). People who believe members of an out-group are similar to one another more confidently make stereotypic judgments about them than do those who believe that there is variability between members of an out-group (see Fiske, 1998).

32. Brewer & Brown (1998); Brewer & Miller (1984).

33. Learning about the out-group can contribute to improved attitudes toward that group (Pettigrew, 1998a).

34. Eighty-seven percent of lower-income whites ($N=15$), 64% of lower-income blacks ($N=14$), 43% of affluent whites ($N=14$), and 85% of affluent blacks ($N=13$) reported having had meaningful conversations about racial issues. A χ^2 test was not calculated because four cells have expected values less than five.

35. Forty percent of lower-income whites ($N=15$), 43% of lower-income blacks ($N=14$), 21% of affluent whites ($N=14$), and 39% of affluent blacks ($N=13$) reported having had meaningful, honest conversations about racial issues at least once a week. A χ^2 test comparing the four groups on frequency of meaningful conversations about race "at least once a week"/"a few times a month"/"a few times a semester or less" was not calculated because eight cells have expected values less than five.

36. Thirty-three percent of lower-income whites, 21% of lower-income blacks, 57% of affluent whites, and 23% of affluent blacks said they had meaningful, honest conversations about racial issues a few times a semester or less.

37. Childs (2005); Collins (2005).

38. See U.S. Bureau of the Census data at http://www.census.gov/population/socdemo/race/interractabl.txt, retrieved August 19, 2007. See also Childs (2005); Collins (2005).

39. See Childs (2005); Collins (2005); Davis & Smith (1991).

40. Childs (2005); Collins (2005).

41. Childs (2005).

42. See review by Pettigrew (1998a).

43. See Rockquemore & Brunsma (2002), p. 52.

44. See Daniel (1996).

45. For example, see Gibbs (1987); Sommers (1964).

46. Two studies using a smaller public-use subsample from a nationally representative data set reported negative outcomes for multiracial adolescents (Cooney & Radina, 2000; Milan & Keiley, 2000). However, based on the larger nationally representative data set, Campbell & Eggerling-Boeck (2006, p. 168) found that multiracial adolescents showed "no pervasive disadvantage associated with a multiracial heritage." Although biracial individuals experience ambiguities and strains, many blended individuals have been found to be comfortable moving between and among multiple ethnic groups in different contexts (Daniel, 1996). Their self-concepts have been found to be just as positive as those of monoracial peers (Field, 1996), and no clear relationship exists between biracial identity and self-esteem (see Bracey, Bámaca, & Umaña-Taylor, 2004; Campbell & Eggerling-Boeck, 2006; Field, 1996; Phinney & Alipuria, 1996; Pinderhughes, 1995).

47. This learning may make blacks less prone to blame themselves for shortcomings (Kuriloff & Reichert, 2003).

48. Hardiman (2001); Hardiman & Jackson (1992; 1997).

49. The model includes two final stages, *redefinition* and *internalization*, that are less often found in students of traditional college age and were not evidenced in the interviews.

CHAPTER 7: LEARNING FROM CLASS-BASED DIVERSITY

1. Thirteen percent of lower-income whites ($N=15$), 17% of lower-income blacks ($N=12$), 21% of affluent whites ($N=14$), and 23% of affluent blacks ($N=13$) felt that people had made incorrect assumptions about them or about members of their social class. A χ^2 test was not calculated because four cells have expected values less than five.

2. Lott & Bullock (2001).

3. Argyle (1994); Christopher & Schlenker (2000); Cozzarelli, Wilkinson, & Tagler (2001); Hoyt (1999); Johannesen-Schmidt & Eagly (2002); Landrine (1999).

4. Lawler (1999).

5. Ostrander (1984).

6. Christopher & Schlenker (2000).

7. Johannesen-Schmidt & Eagly (2002).

8. Harris, Norman, & Houston (2004).

9. Symonds (2006).

10. Sixty-seven percent of lower-income whites ($N=15$), 71% of lower-income blacks ($N=14$), 31% of affluent whites ($N=13$), and 18% of affluent blacks ($N=11$) said they took a course that addressed social class. Group membership was significantly related to taking a course that addressed social class, χ^2 (3, $N=53$) = 10.61, $p=.014$, Cramér's $V=.45$.

11. Forty percent of lower-income whites ($N=15$), 36% of lower-income blacks ($N=14$), 36% of affluent whites ($N=14$), and 46% of affluent blacks ($N=13$) reported personal sharing by other students that changed the way they viewed social class. Group membership was not significantly related to reports that personal sharing changed the way students viewed social class, χ^2 (3, $N=56$) = 0.41, $p>.05$, Cramér's $V=.09$.

12. Based on $N=54$ responses, 76% of students spoke of having formed a close friendship with a person from a very different class background. When further asked whether they had learned something about social class through this cross-class relationship, 77% of lower-income whites ($N=13$), 89% of lower-income blacks ($N=9$), 67% of affluent whites ($N=9$), and 79% of affluent blacks ($N=7$) reported that they had. Responses from three students who formed a close friendship with a person from a very different class background than their own could not be determined.

13. Eighty percent of lower-income whites ($N=15$), 64% of lower-income blacks ($N=14$), 71% of affluent whites ($N=14$), and 62% of affluent blacks ($N=13$) reported having meaningful, honest conversations with students about issues of social class. A χ^2 test was not calculated because four cells have expected values less than five.

14. Forty percent of lower-income whites ($N=15$), 29% of lower-income blacks ($N=14$), 14% of affluent whites ($N=14$), and 23% of affluent blacks ($N=13$) said they discussed class issues at least once a week.

15. In the fall interviews, 79% of lower-income blacks ($N=14$) and 47% of lower-income whites ($N=15$) felt that they had a contribution to make based on their social class background, versus 50% of affluent whites ($N=14$) and 7% of affluent blacks ($N=14$). Group membership was significantly related to perceptions of having a contribution to make based on class background, χ^2 (3, $N=55$) = 14.60, $p=.002$, Cramér's $V=.51$. In the spring interviews, 40% of lower-income whites ($N=15$), 69% of lower-income blacks ($N=13$), 14% of affluent whites ($N=14$), and 23% of affluent blacks ($N=13$) felt that they had contributed something special based on their class background. A χ^2 test was not calculated because two cells have expected values less than five.

16. Seventy-three percent of lower-income whites ($N=15$), 64% of lower-income blacks ($N=14$), 64% of affluent whites ($N=14$), and 31% of affluent blacks ($N=13$) reported that their experience at Amherst living and interacting with people from different class backgrounds had changed the way they saw people of their own social class or other social classes. Group membership was not related to whether living at Amherst changed the way students viewed social class, χ^2 (3, $N=56$) = 5.88, $p > .05$, Cramér's $V=.32$.

17. See Brewer & Brown (1998); Fiske (1998).

18. See Stuber (2008).

19. Fiske (1993); Gurin, Peng, Lopez, & Nagda (1999). The less powerful, by contrast, have more to gain by attending to those in power.

20. Contact that meets Allport's (1954) four conditions has been found to produce these outcomes (Pettigrew, 1998a, p. 70).

21. Ortner (1991, p. 168) describes social class as "a set of differential positions on a scale of social advantage."

22. See Bettie (2000) for a discussion of "performing" class.

23. Twenty-nine percent of affluent whites ($N=14$), 31% of affluent blacks ($N=13$), 33% of lower-income whites ($N=15$), and 43% of lower-income blacks ($N=14$) held jobs. Two of the affluent students and two of the lower-income students held jobs off campus rather than on it. Group membership was not related to holding a job, χ^2 (3, $N=56$) = 0.74, $p > .05$, Cramér's $V=.12$.

24. See Stuber (2008).

25. Until the present, lower-income white and first-generation students have been given no real admission advantage at elite colleges, in contrast to minority students, athletes, and legacies (Bowen, Kurzweil, & Tobin, 2005).

CHAPTER 8: NEGOTIATING RACIAL ISSUES

1. See Willie (2003).

2. At the end of the year 85% of lower-income blacks ($N = 13$) and 69% of affluent blacks ($N = 13$) reported that their race opened up social opportunities, versus 20% of lower-income whites ($N = 15$) and 7% of affluent whites ($N = 14$). Group membership was significantly related to perceptions that race opened up social opportunities, χ^2 (3, $N = 55$) = 23.33, $p < .001$, Cramér's $V = .65$.

3. Cross, Strauss, & Fhagen-Smith (1999) discuss the importance of bonding for many blacks. Tatum (1997) argues that black adolescents seek the support of other blacks who understand their perspectives and share common concerns. Racial minority students who leave home for residential colleges have been found to seek new bases to support their racial identities by linking themselves with other ethnic minority students (Ethier & Deaux, 1994; Saylor & Aries, 1999). Datnow & Cooper (1996) found that African American students at elite independent schools identified their formal and informal black peer networks as "one of the most important factors in helping them cope in the predominantly White environments of their schools" (p. 62).

4. See http://www.amherst.edu/~aas/clubs/black_students_union/, retrieved August 19, 2007.

5. Twenty-nine percent of lower-income blacks ($N = 14$) and 31% of affluent blacks ($N = 13$) reported not feeling comfortable with some of the blacks on campus. For blacks, being affluent or lower-income was not significantly related to feeling comfortable with some blacks on campus, Fisher's Exact Test, $p = 1.00$. A χ^2 test was not calculated because two cells have expected values less than five.

6. See Tatum (1997).

7. Graham (1999), p. 184.

8. The centrality of race—that is, the extent to which race is a stable, core dimension of self-concept and significant to self-definition—is one of the key dimensions of racial identity (Sellers, Shelton, Cooke, Chavous, Rowley, & Smith, 1998). Some blacks form identities that accord only minor significance to race, while for other blacks race holds major significance (Cross, Strauss, & Fhagen-Smith, 1999). Students of color highly identified with their racial identities have been found to associate more with members of their same race and less with whites (Gurin, Peng, Lopez, & Nagda, 1999).

9. Means and standard deviations on the importance of race to identity were as follows: for lower-income blacks $N = 14$, $M = 5.43$, $SD = 1.45$; for affluent blacks $N = 14$, $M = 4.71$, $SD = 1.77$. The difference between the groups was not statistically significantly, t (26) = 1.17, $p > .05$, $r^2 = .05$.

10. Twenty-nine percent of lower-income blacks ($N = 14$) and 43% of affluent blacks ($N = 14$) gave importance ratings of 3 or 4 to race.

11. Fifty-seven percent of lower-income blacks ($N = 14$) and 46% of affluent blacks ($N = 13$) reported feeling pressure to be with other blacks. Being affluent or lower-income

was not significantly related to feeling pressure to be with other blacks, χ^2 $(1, N = 27) = 0.03$ with Yates' correction for continuity, $p > .05$, Cramér's $V = .11$.

12. Omi & Winant (1994), p. 55.

13. Banks & Eberhardt (1998), p. 55.

14. Banks & Eberhardt (1998). Racial categorizations have served as ways to separate people and to allocate differential statuses. Race is "a *fundamental* axis of social organization" (Omi & Winant, 1994, p. 13; emphasis in original) and has profound implications for the differential, racist treatment of blacks.

15. Willie (2003), p. 6.

16. Willie (2003), p. 7 (emphasis in original).

17. Willie (2003), p. 5 (emphasis in original).

18. Tatum (1997).

19. Similar patterns exist among Asian students on campus, where Asian students question one another's authenticity as Asians according to whether they speak or read an Asian language or whether they look "Asian enough" if they are mixed race.

20. For lower-income blacks $N = 14$, and for affluent blacks $N = 13$. Being affluent or lower-income was not significantly related to blackness being questioned, χ^2 $(1, N = 27) = 0.05$, $p > .05$, Cramér's $V = .12$.

21. Graham (1999), p. 1. See also Hunter (2005).

22. Hunter (2005); Klonoff & Landrine (2000).

23. Willie (2003), p. 102.

24. Hunter (2005).

25. See Bergin & Cooks (2002); Fordham & Ogbu (1986); Neal-Barnett (2001); Suskind (1998). Fordham & Ogbu (1986) claimed that fear of "acting white" undermined black academic achievement. Research results, however, have been mixed. A number of studies have found that high-achieving blacks are accused of "acting white," but that the accusation does not inhibit academic achievement (e.g., Bergin & Cooks, 2002; Horvat & Lewis, 2003). Tyson, Darity, & Castellino (2005, p. 600) found that: "Students in all racial and ethnic groups confront similar dilemmas of high achievement, and they also tend to use similar strategies of downplaying achievement."

26. Many blacks felt that they were "bicultural" and could change their speech, dress, and patterns of interaction as they moved between blacks and whites. Cross, Strauss, & Fhagen-Smith (1999) refer to such changes in speech, dress, or behavior as "code switching" or "fronting." Code switching allows people to temporarily accommodate to the norms of another group.

27. Hunter (2005, p. 95) found that one cost of having lighter skin was "having to prove oneself as an authentic or legitimate member of the ethnic community." Lighter-skinned blacks were accused of not being black enough.

28. See Neal-Barnett (2001).

29. Stephan & Stephan (1985).

30. Thirty-seven percent of lower-income blacks $(N = 14)$ and 15% of affluent blacks $(N = 13)$. For blacks being affluent or lower-income was not significantly related to hearing whites make insensitive or ignorant comments about race, Fisher's Exact test, $p = .39$. A χ^2 test was not calculated because two cells have expected values less than five. In a study of a predominantly white university, Feagin, Vera, & Imani (1996) found that the majority of black students had faced some racial discrimination on campus.

31. A similar phenomenon most likely occurs, for example, when a student is the only male in a classroom during a discussion of gender, or the only Latino during a discussion pertaining to Latinos.

32. Feagin, Vera, & Imani (1996), p. 91.

33. Watson, Terrell, Wright, Bonner, Cuyjet, Gold, Rudy, & Person (2002) similarly found that minority students lamented being expected to be spokespersons for their racial and ethnic groups.

34. Feagin, Vera, & Imani (1996), p. 91. Nathan (2005, p. 60) also reports that students of color report "being continually expected to educate whites about minority issues or speak 'as a representative of their race.'"

35. Fifty percent of lower-income blacks ($N=14$) and 69% of affluent blacks ($N=13$) had heard racist comments framed as jokes, versus 20% of lower-income whites ($N=15$) and 14% of affluent whites ($N=14$). A χ^2 test was not calculated because one cell had an expected value less than five. Fine & de Soucey (2005, p. 9) characterize of the use of humor in groups as "essential in the desire for social lubrication in that its message is—whatever discord looms—that 'this is not serious,' 'this does not mean what it appears to mean on the surface,' and that 'we have been through this before and have remained friends.' Joking constitutes an established frame that rescues interactions from friction. It smoothes relationships and causes the flow of discourse within the group to become more widely agreeable and acceptable."

36. This joking is an example of what Bourdieu (1984, p. 183) wrote of as "the art of making fun without raising anger, by means of ritual mockery or insults which are neutralized by their very excess and which, presupposing a great familiarity, both in the knowledge they use and the freedom with which they use it, are in fact tokens of attention or affection, ways of building up while seeming to run down, of accepting while seeming to condemn—although they may also be used to test out those who show signs of stand-offishness."

37. Fine & de Soucey (2005).

38. Margolis & Romero (1998) found that many graduate student women of color felt stigmatized as "affirmative action" students. They spoke of feeling that they were "let" in, not that they "got" in.

39. Feagin, Vera, & Imani (1996), p. 68.

40. See Kennedy (2002) for a historical perspective on the use of the word "nigger."

41. Cross (1991).

42. Hardiman & Jackson (1992; 1997) describe five stages, which they label *Naïve, Acceptance, Resistance, Redefinition,* and *Internalization.* The stages of acceptance and resistance take first a passive and then an active form. Hardiman & Jackson acknowledge that a person does not actually move neatly from one stage to another, but may live a mixture of social identities (Hardiman & Jackson, 1992). Cross (1991) also describes five stages of black racial identity development: *Pre-encounter, Encounter, Immersion-emersion, Internalization,* and *Internalization-commitment.* In contrast to Hardiman & Jackson, Cross does not discuss the possibility that a person might hold beliefs representative of several stages simultaneously, or that different stages may come to ascendance in different situations. Cross places a higher valuation on the later stages, seeing some forms of racial identity as superior to others.

43. Hardiman & Jackson (1992), p. 23.
44. Cross, Strauss, & Fhagen-Smith (2001).
45. Tropp (2006).
46. Cross, Strauss, & Fhagen-Smith (1999), p. 31.

CHAPTER 9: AS THE YEAR ENDED

1. Seventy-three percent of lower-income whites ($N=15$), 57% of lower-income blacks ($N=14$), 93% of affluent whites ($N=14$), and 77% of affluent blacks ($N=13$) felt that their race had not made a difference academically. A χ^2 test was not calculated because four cells have expected values less than five.

2. Overall 13% of students felt that class background had contributed to their being less prepared academically: 33% of lower-income whites ($N=15$), 7% of lower-income blacks ($N=14$), 7% of affluent whites ($N=14$), and 0.0% of affluent blacks ($N=13$). A χ^2 test was not calculated because four cells have expected values less than five.

3. For lower-income whites, $N=15$, $SD=.26$; for affluent whites $N=13$, $SD=.26$. The effect of class on GPA was not significant, $F(1, 49)=0.33$, $p>.05$, $\eta^2=.01$, and the race by class interaction was not significant, $F(1, 49)=1.23$, $p>.05$, $\eta^2=.03$. The mean cumulative GPA at the end of the 2006 spring term for students at the college was 3.44. The lack of an effect of class on GPA was not attributable to the college policy that allows first-year students to drop one course without academic penalty for educational reasons in either the first or second term. Thirteen percent of lower-income whites ($N=15$), 7% of lower-income blacks ($N=14$), 0.0% of affluent whites ($N=13$), and 36% of affluent blacks ($N=11$) dropped a course without penalty. A χ^2 test was not calculated because four cells have expected values less than five.

4. Academic self-confidence is representative of a construct psychologists refer to as academic self-efficacy, or the "self-evaluation of one's ability and/or chances for success in the academic environment," and is a psychological predictor of college grades (Robbins, Lauver, Le, Davis, Langley, & Carlstrom, 2004, p. 267). At the end of the year, for academic confidence: lower-income whites $N=15$, $M=5.08$, $SD=.55$; lower-income blacks $N=14$, $M=5.18$, $SD=1.09$; affluent whites $N=14$, $M=5.65$, $SD=.70$; and affluent blacks $N=13$, $M=5.21$, $SD=.81$. The effect of race was not significant, $F(1, 52)=0.65$, $p>.05$, $\eta^2=.01$. The effect of class was not significant, $F(1, 52)=1.95$, $p>.05$, $\eta^2=.04$. The race by class interaction was not significant, $F(1, 52)=1.62$, $p>.05$, $\eta^2=.03$.

5. For lower-income blacks $N=14$, $M=3.19$, $SD=.41$, and for affluent blacks $N=11$, $M=3.14$, $SD=.40$. Whites had significantly higher GPAs than blacks, $F(1, 49)=19.86$, $p<.001$, $\eta^2=.29$.

6. Bowen & Bok (1998) similarly found in their study of elite colleges and universities that students with lower SATs attained lower ranks in class.

7. See Bowen & Bok (1998). In an analysis of 11 highly selective colleges and universities, Vars & Bowen (1998) found SAT scores predictive of college grades for both blacks and whites, although this relationship was stronger for whites than blacks. They found that whites had a GPA of 3.30, and blacks 2.80.

8. The lack of difference between affluent and lower-income students in GPA in this study (reported in note 3) is not consistent with findings by Walpole (2003) based on a sample of over 12,000 students from 209 four-year institutions nationally. Walpole found lower SES college students had lower GPAs than high SES students.

9. Feagin, Vera, & Imani (1996).

10. For whether race made academic integration easier or more difficult: lower-income whites, $N=15$, $M=3.93$, $SD=.19$; affluent whites $N=14$, $M=3.76$, $SD=.50$; lower-income blacks, $N=14$, $M=4.24$, $SD=.38$; affluent blacks $N=13$, $M=4.13$, $SD=.89$. There was a significant effect of race, $F(1, 52)=5.44$, $p=.024$, $\eta^2=.10$. There was no significant effect of class, $F(1, 52)=0.96$, $p>.05$, $\eta^2=.02$, and no significant race by class interaction, $F(1, 52)=0.05$, $p>.05$, $\eta^2=.001$.

11. For whether class made academic integration easier or more difficult, overall $N=56$, $M=3.99$, $SD=.67$. There was no significant effect of race, $F(1, 52)=2.14$, $p>.05$, $\eta^2=.04$, no significant effect of class, $F(1, 52)=2.37$, $p>.05$, $\eta^2=.04$, and no significant race by class interaction, $F(1, 52)=0.92$, $p>.05$, $\eta^2=.02$.

12. Watson, Terrell, Wright, Bonner, Cuyjet, Gold, Rudy, & Person (2002, p. 69) similarly found that minority students were concerned "about their assigned responsibilities as spokespersons for their respective minority community and for their race."

13. No significant effects of race or class were found for these five variables. For psychological health overall $N=56$, $M=5.14$, $SD=1.42$; for social life overall $N=56$, $M=5.54$, $SD=1.08$; for growth as a person overall $N=56$, $M=5.43$, $SD=.93$; for finding a place at the college overall $N=56$, $M=5.39$, $SD=1.51$; for feelings of confidence in relation to peers overall $N=56$, $M=5.19$, $SD=.68$. These five measures were combined into a single measure of overall social well-being (Chronbach's alpha $=.70$). Overall $N=56$, $M=5.34$, $SD=.79$. There was no significant effect of race, $F(1, 52)=0.01$, $p>.05$, $\eta^2=.00$, no significant effect of class, $F(1, 52)=0.32$, $p>.05$, $\eta^2=.006$, and no significant race by class interaction $F(1, 52)=0.15$, $p>.05$, $\eta^2=.003$.

A regression was run to predict students' ratings of their overall social well-being at the end of the school year from gender, race, and class. The base group for the regression was an affluent white male. Dummy variables for gender, race, and class were entered into the regression. The adjusted $R^2=-.045$. None of these variables were statistically significant predictors of students' assessments of social well-being: black ($\beta=-.01$), female ($\beta=-.08$), and lower-income ($\beta=-.08$).

14. A low rating was defined as a score below the scale midpoint of 4 on any of these scales. Eleven percent gave low ratings on psychological health, 5% on social life, 4% on feelings of comfort and inclusion in relation to peers, 2% on having grown as a person, and 16% on having found a place at Amherst.

15. For ratings of the impact of class on getting invited to social events, overall $N=56$, $M=3.79$, $SD=.80$. There was no significant effect of race, $F(1, 52)=0.16$, $p>.05$, $\eta^2=.003$, no significant effect of class, $F(1, 52)=1.12$, $p>.05$, $\eta^2=.02$, and no significant race by class interaction $F(1, 52)=0.003$, $p>.05$, $\eta^2=.00$. For the impact of race on getting invited to social events, overall $N=56$, $M=3.86$, $SD=.75$. There was no significant effect of race, $F(1, 52)=0.002$, $p>.05$, $\eta^2=.00$, no significant effect of class, $F(1, 52)=0.002$, $p>.05$, $\eta^2=.00$, and no significant race by class interaction $F(1, 52)=0.00$, $p>.05$, $\eta^2=.00$.

16. For ratings of the effect of social class on social integration and comfort, overall $N=56$, $M=3.72$, $SD=.68$. There was no significant effect of race, $F(1, 52)=0.18$, $p>.05$, $\eta^2=.003$, no significant effect of class, $F(1, 52)=0.12$, $p>.05$, $\eta^2=.002$, and no significant race by class interaction $F(1, 52)=0.003$, $p>.05$, $\eta^2=.00$.

17. Blacks reported that race made social integration and comfort significantly more difficult than whites did, $F(1, 52)=5.90$, $p=.019$, $\eta^2=.10$. There was no significant

effect of class, $F(1, 52) = 0.40, p > .05, \eta^2 = .01$, and no significant race by class interaction $F(1, 52) = 0.01, p > .05, \eta^2 = .00$. For lower-income whites $N = 15$, $M = 3.60$, $SD = .49$; for affluent whites $N = 14$, $M = 3.60$, $SD = .58$; for lower-income blacks $N = 14$, $M = 4.12$, $SD = .53$; and for affluent blacks $N = 13$, $M = 4.08$, $SD = 1.08$.

18. For mean number of extracurricular activities joined, $N = 55$, $M = 2.02$, $SD = 1.15$.

19. For "gotten to know people well of different social class backgrounds," overall $N = 56$, $M = 5.18$, $SD = 1.47$. There was no significant effect of race, $F(1, 52) = 0.01, p > .05$, $\eta^2 = .00$, no significant effect of class, $F(1, 52) = 0.84, p > .05, \eta^2 = .01$, and no significant race by class interaction $F(1, 52) = 1.64, p > .05, \eta^2 = .03$. For "gotten to know people well of different races," the overall mean was $N = 56$, $M = 5.45$, $SD = 1.37$. There was no significant effect of race, $F(1, 52) = 0.06, p > .05, \eta^2 = .001$, no significant effect of class, $F(1, 52) = 0.54, p > .05, \eta^2 = .01$, and no significant race by class interaction $F(1, 52) = 2.06, p > .05, \eta^2 = .04$. Eighteen percent gave ratings below the scale midpoint on having "gotten to know people well from different class backgrounds," and 11% on having "gotten to know people well of different races."

20. Means and standard deviations for class making it easier or more difficult to go home for family visits were as follows: lower-income whites $N = 15$, $M = 4.80$, $SD = 1.97$; lower-income blacks $N = 14$, $M = 5.14$, $SD = 1.29$; affluent whites $N = 14$, $M = 2.50$, $SD = 1.40$; affluent blacks $N = 13$, $M = 3.31$, $SD = 1.44$. Lower-income students found that social class made going home for family visits significantly more difficult than affluent students did, $F(1, 52) = 24.56, p < .001, \eta^2 = .32$. There was no significant effect of race, $F(1, 52) = 1.90, p > .05, \eta^2 = .04$, and no significant race by class interaction, $F(1, 52) = 0.31$, $p > .05, \eta^2 = .01$. For class making it easier or more difficult to have parents or family members visit campus: lower-income whites $N = 15$, $M = 5.07$, $SD = 1.87$; lower-income blacks $N = 14$, $M = 5.21$, $SD = 1.37$; affluent whites $N = 14$, $M = 2.50$, $SD = 1.23$; affluent blacks $N = 13$, $M = 3.38$, $SD = 1.66$. Lower-income students found that social class made visits to campus by family members significantly more difficult than affluent students did, $F(1, 52) = 27.88, p < .001, \eta^2 = .35$. There was no significant effect of race, $F(1, 52) = 1.54, p > .05, \eta^2 = .03$, and no significant race by class interaction, $F(1, 52) = 0.78$, $p > .05, \eta^2 = .02$.

21. For whether race made it easier or more difficult to go home for family visits, overall $N = 56$, $M = 3.91$, $SD = .75$. There was no significant effect of race, $F(1, 52) = 2.63$, $p > .05, \eta^2 = .05$, no significant effect of class, $F(1, 52) = 2.81, p > .05, \eta^2 = .05$, and no significant race by class interaction $F(1, 52) = 0.03, p > .05, \eta^2 = .001$. For whether race made it easier or more difficult for family members to visit the campus, overall $N = 56$, $M = 3.96$, $SD = .89$. There was no significant effect of race, $F(1, 52) = 1.39, p > .05, \eta^2 = .03$, no significant effect of class, $F(1, 52) = 3.54, p > .05, \eta^2 = .06$, and no significant race by class interaction $F(1, 52) = 0.89, p > .05, \eta^2 = .02$.

22. Eighty percent of lower-income whites $(N = 15)$, 88% of lower-income blacks $(N = 14)$, 100% of affluent whites $(N = 14)$, and 85% of affluent blacks $(N = 13)$ talked with their families "at least once a week." A χ^2 test comparing the four groups on frequency of talking with parents ("at least once a week"/"a few times a month or less") was not calculated because four cells have expected values less than five.

23. Twenty percent of lower-income whites talked on the phone with family members daily, 40% did so two or three times a week, and 20% did so once a week. Lower-income blacks showed a similar pattern: 14% talked on the phone with family members daily, 50% did so two or three times a week, and 20% did so once a week.

24. Forty percent of lower-income whites, 43% of affluent whites, 46% of affluent blacks, and 27% of lower-income blacks were in e-mail contact with families at least once a week. Group membership was not significantly related to e-mail contact "at least once a week" versus "less than once a week," χ^2 (3, $N = 56$) = 1.01, $p > .05$, Cramér's $V = .13$.

25. Twenty-seven percent of lower-income whites ($N = 15$), 43% of lower-income blacks ($N = 14$), 7% of affluent whites ($N = 14$), and 31% of affluent blacks ($N = 13$) felt such pressures. A χ^2 test was not calculated because four cells have expected values less than five.

26. Seventy-one percent of lower-income whites ($N = 14$), 43% of lower-income blacks ($N = 14$), 21% of affluent whites ($N = 14$), and 39% of affluent blacks ($N = 13$) reported that family members were vicariously living through them. The relationship between group membership and reports that family members were vicariously living through students approached significance, χ^2 (3, $N = 55$) = 7.35, $p = .06$, Cramér's $V = .37$.

27. In the on-line survey, for "how much you feel you have changed in order to fit in at Amherst College," overall $N = 56$, $M = 3.16$, $SD = 1.64$. There was no significant effect of race, $F(1, 52) = 0.48$, $p > .05$, $\eta^2 = .01$, no significant effect of class, $F(1, 52) = 0.73$, $p > .05$, $\eta^2 = .01$, and no significant race by class interaction $F(1, 52) = 0.03$, $p > .05$, $\eta^2 = .001$. In the face-to-face interview, 67% of lower-income whites ($N = 15$), 54% of lower-income blacks ($N = 13$), 64% of affluent whites ($N = 14$), and 85% of affluent blacks ($N = 13$) indicated that they had not changed to fit in at Amherst. A χ^2 test was not calculated because four cells have expected values less than five.

28. See Almanza (2003); Aries & Seider (2005); Kuriloff & Reichert (2003); Megivern (2003); Stewart & Ostrove (1993); Sullivan (2003); Zweigenhaft & Domhoff (1991).

29. In a study of minority students who took part in A Better Chance, students reported having acquired the ability to feel comfortable with wealthy people, to "talk with anyone about anything" (Zweigenhaft & Domhoff, 1991, p. 107).

30. See Lareau (2003); Lareau & Weininger (2003).

31. Going on to higher education puts lower-income students "on a trajectory of class mobility, which is experienced as a painful dislocation between an old and newly developing habitus, which are ranked hierarchically and carry connotations of inferiority and superiority" (Baxter & Britton, 2001, p. 99).

32. See Lubrano (2004).

33. Thirty-three percent of lower-income whites ($N = 15$), 36% of lower-income blacks ($N = 14$), 7% of affluent whites ($N = 13$), and 0.0% of affluent blacks ($N = 12$) felt that they were juggling two worlds. A χ^2 test was not calculated because four cells have expected values less than five. See Almanza (2003); Aries & Seider (2005); Dahlberg (2003); Lubrano (2004); Zweigenhaft & Domhoff (1991).

34. Forty-seven percent of lower-income whites ($N = 15$), 7% of lower-income blacks ($N = 14$), 7% of affluent whites ($N = 14$), and 8% of affluent blacks ($N = 13$) were experiencing difficulties maintaining connections with friends at home. The relationship between group membership and experiencing such difficulties was statistically significant, χ^2 (3, $N = 56$) = 8.70, $p = .034$, Cramér's $V = .39$.

35. In a study of predominantly white elite independent schools, Datnow & Cooper (1996) found that blacks were caught between two peer cultures. Blacks struggled with being accepted by black peers outside of school and white peers at school.

36. Blacks confront frustrations due to tokenism and subtle or obvious discrimination as they enter white-collar and professional occupations (Cole & Omari, 2003).

37. Bowen & Bok (1998).

38. See Steele & Aronson (1995); Steele, Spencer, & Aronson (2002) for a discussion of stereotype threat.

39. Robbins, Lauver, Le, Davis, Langley, & Carlstrom (2004).

40. Robbins, Lauver, Le, Davis, Langley, & Carlstrom (2004).

41. See Cross, Strauss, & Fhagen-Smith (1999).

CHAPTER 10: MEETING THE CHALLENGES OF DIVERSITY

1. Forty percent of lower-income whites ($N = 15$), 36% of lower-income blacks ($N = 14$), 21% of affluent whites ($N = 14$), and 23% of affluent blacks ($N = 13$) reported learning from both race *and* class. An additional 40% of lower-income whites, 29% of lower-income blacks, 43% of affluent whites, and 15% of affluent blacks reported learning from either race *or* class.

2. Tropp (2006, p. 183) writes that "implementing optimal conditions within the contact situation may not necessarily be enough to ensure positive contact outcomes among members of both minority and majority status groups."

3. In the year she spent enrolled as a freshman at her own university, Nathan (2005) found that every minority student she interviewed had some experience with racism, be it a racist comment heard in the classroom, a rude remark, or a hostile look.

4. See Crosby, Iyer, Clayton, & Downing (2003).

5. Other suggestions pertaining to race included more funding for the Black Student Union and bringing more black students to campus. These suggestions were made by lower-income blacks. The suggestion given by two affluent blacks was that families like theirs should qualify for financial aid.

6. Major & Eccleston (2005, p. 76) report that the respect derived from other in-group members becomes more important than the groups' position in society. Connections to in-group members provide "opportunities for self-validation, sharing of experiences, and social support, all of which may help buffer the stigmatized from stigma-based exclusion."

7. Appel, Cartwright, Smith, & Wolf (1996). See also Feagin, Vera, & Imani (1996); Nathan (2005).

8. These findings contrast with studies by Watson, Terrell, Wright, Bonner, Cuyjet, Gold, Rudy, & Person (2002), and Feagin, Vera, & Imani (1996).

9. Sixty-four percent of lower-income whites ($N = 15$) and 50% of lower-income blacks ($N = 14$) offered positive comments about their overall experience.

10. The other suggestions included making the financial aid process "a little easier" and changing the policy of charging all students in a dormitory for dorm damage when those responsible were unknown, a policy that was much harder on lower-income students.

11. See Major & Eccleston (2005) for the benefits listed in note 6 above.

12. Institutional support for diversity is found to be an "especially important condition for facilitating positive contact effects" (Pettigrew & Tropp, 2006, p. 766). Appel, Cartwright, Smith, & Wolf (1996) report that the perception of students that an institu-

tion values diversity is associated with college satisfaction and the cognitive development of students. Members of minority groups are more likely to feel welcomed and accepted if they perceive that diversity is valued (Tropp & Bianchi, 2006).

13. Until the present, lower-income white and first-generation students have been given no real admission advantage at elite colleges, in contrast to minority students, athletes, and legacies (Bowen, Kurzweil, & Tobin, 2005).

14. See Pettigrew (1997); Pettigrew & Tropp (2006).

15. See Bauman, Bustillos, Bensimon, Brown, & and Bartee (2005); Hale (2003); Milem, Chang, & Antonio (2005); Niemann & Maruyama (2005); Tierney (1988); Williams, Berger, & McClendon (2005).

16. Feagin, Vera, & Imani (1996), p. 70.

17. See Nagda, Gurin, & Johnson (2005).

18. For a discussion of the importance of the role played by leadership, see Bolman & Deal (2003); Schein (1992).

19. King (1991), p. 142.

20. A letter could go out to students before they arrive on campus urging them to use moderation in what they bring out of consideration for less affluent dorm-mates.

21. Pope, Miklitsch, & Weigand (2005, p. 53) argue that "it is vital for all first-year students to be educated about the value of diversity. Teaching first-year students the attitudes and skills necessary to form meaningful relationships with individuals who may be culturally different from them will prepare them to enter the workforce after college and make important contributions as citizens."

22. Programming on class has now been added to the orientation.

23. See Nagda, Gurin, & Johnson (2005).

24. Amherst has begun to better address problems faced by lower-income students in a variety of ways. For example, a brochure has been prepared for students on how to open checking accounts. Arrangements have been made with a local bank to enable students to cash financial aid checks from the college without being required to have an account there. A shopping trip is now organized during orientation to stores in the area where students can buy inexpensive winter clothing.

25. Programming for the Thanksgiving break was not in place for students in this study during their first year. The college has begun offering a meal plan for lower-income students staying on campus over the Thanksgiving break and has arranged for faculty and staff to host students for Thanksgiving dinner. For students reluctant to be hosted, funds were made available for the first time in 2007 to purchase food and cook a Thanksgiving dinner together. Such plans are also highly beneficial to international students who cannot afford to leave campus during these breaks. A similar type of meal plan could be made available to lower-income students and international students who have to remain on campus during the spring break in March.

26. To take another example, the college plans a wonderful Family Weekend in the fall, but not all families can afford to visit campus. Some lower-income students are left on the sidelines as affluent families arrive, meet their children's friends, perhaps watch some of their activities, and take their children out to dinner. Programming is needed to address students who are left on the margins at such times or to facilitate a campus visit by their family members. The college is exploring the possibility of offering families a travel voucher for one trip to the campus over the four years their child is at the

college. In 2007 the college offered families from New York with high financial need two round-trip bus tickets to enable family members to take a day trip to campus for Family Weekend. Discussion continues on how to expand this program.

27. As this book was completed, the only additional information available about these students pertained to retention. In the spring of 2008, at the end of their junior year, only one of the 58 students in the study had dropped out of the college, a lower-income white. That student was eligible to return. The three students who were on leave at the time of the second freshman-year interview had returned to campus. One lower-income white was on leave from the college for the academic year, but was expected back in the fall of 2008.

28. Feagin, Vera, & Imani (1996) also describe variability in the degree and manner in which black students experienced and responded to racial barriers.

References

Adair, V. C., & S. L. Dahlberg (Eds.). (2003). *Reclaiming class: Women, poverty, and the promise of higher education.* Philadelphia: Temple University Press.

Allport, G. W. (1954). *The nature of prejudice.* Garden City, NY: Doubleday.

Almanza, L. (2003). Seven years in exile. In V. C. Adair & S. L. Dahlberg (Eds.), *Reclaiming class: Women, poverty, and the promise of higher education in America* (pp. 157–165). Philadelphia: Temple University Press.

Appel, M., Cartwright, D., Smith, D., & Wolf, L. E. (1996). *The impact of diversity on students.* Washington, DC: Association of American Colleges and Universities.

Argyle, M. (1994). *The psychology of social class.* London: Routledge.

Aries, E., & Seider, M. (2005). The interactive relationship between class identity and the college experience: The case of lower income students. *Qualitative Sociology, 28,* 419–443.

Aries, E., & Seider, M. (2007). The role of social class in the formation of identity: A study of public and elite private college students. *The Journal of Social Psychology, 147,* 137–157.

Astin, A. W. (1993). *What matters in college? Four critical years revisited.* San Francisco: Jossey-Bass.

Banaji, M. R., & Greenwald, A. G. (1995). Implicit gender stereotyping in judgments of fame. *Journal of Personality and Social Psychology, 68,* 181–198.

Banks, R. R., & Eberhardt, J. L. (1998). Social psychological processes and the legal bases of racial categorization. In J. L. Eberhard & S. T. Fiske (Eds.), *Confronting racism: The problem and the response* (pp. 54–75). Thousand Oaks, CA: Sage Publications.

Banks, W. (1970). The changing attitudes of black students. *The Personnel and Guidance Journal, 48,* 739–745.

Bauman, G., Bustillos, L. T., Bensimon, E. M., Brown, M. C., II, & and Bartee, R. D. (2005). *Achieving equitable educational outcomes with all students: The institution's roles and responsibilities.* Washington, DC: Association of American Colleges and Universities.

Baxter, A., & Britton, C. (2001). Risk, identity and change: Becoming a mature student. *International Studies in Sociology of Education, 11*, 87–102.

Bell, L. A. (1997). Theoretical foundations for social justice education. In M. Adams, L. A. Bell, & P. Griffin (Eds.), *Teaching for diversity and social justice* (pp. 3–15). New York: Routledge.

Bergin, D. A., & Cooks, H. C. (2002). High school students of color talk about accusations of "acting white." *Urban Review, 34*(2), 113–134.

Bettie, J. (2000). Women without class: Chicas, cholas, trash, and the presence/absence of class identity. *Signs: Journal of Women in Culture and Society, 26*, 1–35.

Bolman, L. G., & Deal, T. E. (2003). *Reframing organizations: Artistry, choice, and leadership* (3rd ed.). San Francisco: Jossey-Bass.

Bourdieu, P. (1977). Cultural reproduction and social reproduction. In J. Karabel & A. H. Halsey (Eds.), *Power and ideology in education* (pp. 487–511). New York: Oxford University Press.

Bourdieu, P. (1984). *Distinction.* Cambridge: Harvard University Press.

Bourdieu, P., & Passeron, J. (1979 [1964]). *The inheritors: French students and their relation to culture.* Chicago: University of Chicago Press.

Bowen, W. G., & Bok. D. (1998). *The shape of the river: Long term consequences of considering race in college and university admissions.* Princeton: Princeton University Press.

Bowen, W. G., Kurzweil, M. A., & Tobin, E. M. (2005). *Equity and excellence in American higher education.* Charlottesville: University of Virginia Press.

Bracey, J. R., Bámaca, M. Y., & Umaña-Taylor, A. J. (2004). Examining ethnic identity and self-esteem among biracial and monoracial adolescents. *Journal of Youth and Adolescence, 33*, 123–132.

Brewer, M. B., & Brown, R. J. (1998). Intergroup relations. In D. T. Gilbert, S. T. Fiske, & G. Lindzey (Eds.), *The handbook of social psychology* (4th ed.) (pp. 554–594). Boston: McGraw-Hill.

Brewer, M. B., & Miller, N. (1984). Beyond the contact hypothesis: Theoretical perspectives on desegregation. In N. Miller & M. B. Brewer (Eds.), *Groups in contact: The psychology of desegregation* (pp. 281–302). New York: Academic Press.

Campbell, M. E., & Eggerling-Boeck, J. (2006). "What about the children?": The psychological and social well-being of multiracial adolescents. *The Sociological Quarterly, 47*, 147–173.

Cantor, N. (2004). Introduction. In P. Gurin, J. S Lehman, & E. Lewis, with E. L. Dey, G. Gurin, & S. Hurtado (Eds.), *Defending diversity: Affirmative action at the University of Michigan* (pp. 1–16). Ann Arbor: University of Michigan Press.

Cantor, N. E., & Prentice, D. A. (1996). The life of the modern-day student-athlete: Opportunities won and lost. Paper presented at the Princeton Conference on Higher Education.

Carter, R. T. (1997). Is white a race? Expressions of white racial identity. In M. Fine, L. Weis, L. C. Powell, & L. M. Wong (Eds.), *Off white: Readings on race, power and society* (pp. 198–209). New York: Routledge.

Chang, M. J. (2001). The positive educational effects of racial diversity on campus. In G. Orfield (Ed.), *Diversity Challenged: Evidence on the impact of affirmative action* (pp. 175–186). Cambridge, MA: Civil Rights Project, Harvard University, Harvard Education Publishing Group.

Childs, E. C. (2005). Looking behind the stereotypes of the "angry black woman": An exploration of black women's responses to interracial relationships. *Gender & Society, 19*, 544–561.

Christopher, A. N., & Schlenker, B. R. (2000). The impact of perceived material wealth and perceiver personality on first impressions. *Journal of Economic Psychology, 21*, 1–19.

Cole, E. R., & Omari, S. R. (2003). Race, class and the dilemmas of upward mobility for African Americans. *Journal of Social Issues, 59*, 785–802.

Collins, P. H. (2005). *Black sexual politics: African Americans, gender, and the new racism*. New York: Routledge.

Cooney, T. M., & Radina, M. E. (2000). Adjustment problems in adolescence: Are multiracial children at risk? *American Journal of Orthopsychiatry, 70*, 433–444.

Cozzarelli, C., Wilkinson, A. V., & Tagler, M. J. (2001). Attitudes toward the poor and attributions for poverty. *Journal of Social Issues, 57*, 207–227.

Crocker, J., & Lawrence, J. S. (1999). Social stigma and self-esteem: The rule of contingencies of worth. In D. A. Prentice, & D. J. Miller (Eds.), *Cultural divides: Understanding and overcoming group conflict* (pp. 364–392). New York: Russell Sage Foundation.

Crocker, J., & Major, B. (1989). Social stigma and self-esteem: The self-protective properties of stigma. *Psychological Review, 96*, 608–630.

Crocker, J., & Quinn, D. (1998). Racism and self-esteem. In J. L. Eberhardt & S. T. Fiske (Eds.), *Confronting racism: The problem and the response* (pp. 169–187). Thousand Oaks, CA: Sage.

Crosby, F. J. (2004). *Affirmative action is dead; Long live affirmative action*. New Haven: Yale University Press.

Crosby, F. J., Iyer, A., Clayton, S., & Downing, R. A. (2003). Affirmative action: Psychological data and the policy debates. *American Psychologist, 58*, 93–115.

Cross, W. E. (1991). *Shades of black: Diversity in African-American identity*. Philadelphia: Temple University Press.

Cross, W. E., Strauss, L., & Fhagen-Smith, P. (1999). African American identity development across the life span: Educational implications. In R. H. Sheets & E. R. Hollins (Eds.), *Racial and ethnic identity in school practices: Aspects of human development* (pp. 29–47). Mahwah, NJ: Lawrence Erlbaum Associates.

Dahlberg, S. L. (2003). Survival in a not so brave new world. In V. C. Adair & S. L. Dahlberg (Eds.), *Reclaiming class: Women, poverty, and the promise of higher education in America* (pp. 67–84). Philadelphia: Temple University Press.

Daniel, G. R. (1996). Black and white identity in the new millennium: Unsevering the ties that bind. In M. P. P. Root (Ed.), *The multiracial experience: Racial borders as the new frontier* (pp. 121–139). Thousand Oaks, CA: Sage Publications.

Datnow, A., & Cooper, R. (1996). Peer networks of African American students in independent schools: Affirming academic success and racial identity. *Journal of Negro Education, 65*(4), 56–72.

Devine, P. G., & Vasquez, K. A. (1998). The rocky road to positive intergroup relations. In J. L. Eberhard & S. T. Fiske (Eds.), *Confronting racism: The problem and the response* (pp. 234–262). Thousand Oaks, CA: Sage.

Dews, C. L., & Law, C. L. (1995). *This fine place so far from home: Voices of academics from the working class.* Philadelphia: Temple University Press.

Dixon, J., Durrheim, K, & Tredoux, C. (2005). Beyond the optimal contact strategy: A reality check for the contact hypothesis. *American Psychologist, 60,* 697–711.

Douthat, R. G. (2005). *Privilege: Harvard and the education of the ruling class.* New York: Hyperion.

Dovidio, J. F., & Gaertner, S. L. (1998). On the nature of contemporary prejudice: The causes, consequences, and challenges of aversive racism. In J. L. Eberhardt & S. T. Fiske (Eds.), *Confronting racism: The problem and the response* (pp. 3–32). Thousand Oaks, CA: Sage.

Dovidio, J. F., Gaertner, S. L., Hodson, G., Houlette, M. A., & Johnson, K. M. (2005). Social inclusion and exclusion: Recategorization and the perception of intergroup boundaries. In D. Abrams, M. A. Hogg, & J. M. Marques (Eds.), *The social psychology of inclusion and exclusion* (pp. 245–264). New York: Psychology Press.

D'Souza, D. (1991). *Illiberal education.* New York: The Free Press.

DuBois, W. E. B. (1993 [1903]). *The souls of black folk.* New York: Knopf.

Duncan, G. J., Boisjoly, J., Levy, D. M., Kremer, M., & Eccles, J. (2003). Empathy or antipathy? The consequences of racially and socially diverse peers on attitudes and behaviors. Retrieved August 19, 2007, from http://www.jcpr.org/wp/Wpprofile.cfm?ID=384.

Ethier, K. A., & Deaux, K. (1994). Negotiating social identity when contexts change: Maintaining identification and responding to threat. *Journal of Personality and Social Psychology, 67,* 243–251.

Feagin, J. R., Vera, H., & Imani, N. (1996). *The agony of education: Black students at white colleges and universities.* New York: Routledge.

Field, L. D. (1996). Piecing together the puzzle: Self-concept and group identity in biracial black/white youth. In M. P. P. Root (Ed.), *The multiracial experience: Racial borders as the new frontier* (pp. 211–226). Thousand Oaks, CA: Sage Publications.

Fine, G. A., & deSoucey, M. (2005). Joking cultures: Humor themes as social regulation in group life. *Humor, 18*(1), 1–22.

Fiske, S. T. (1993). Controlling other people: The impact of power on stereotyping. *American Psychologist, 48,* 621–628.

Fiske, S. T. (1998). Stereotyping, prejudice, and discrimination. In D. T. Gilbert, S. T. Fiske, & G. Lindzey (Eds.), *The handbook of social psychology* (4th ed.) (pp. 357–411). New York: McGraw-Hill.

Fordham, S., & Ogbu, J. U. (1986). Black students' success: Coping with the "burden of 'acting white.'" *The Urban Review, 18,* 176–206.

Gaertner, S., & Dovidio, J. F. (1986). The aversive form of racism. In J. F. Dovidio & S. L. Gaertner (Eds.), *Prejudice, discrimination, and racism* (pp. 61–89). San Diego, CA: Academic Press.

Gaertner, S. L., Dovidio, J. F., Nier, J. A., Ward, C. M., & Banker, B. S. (1999). Across cultural divides: The value of a superordinate identity. In D. A. Prentice & D. J.

Miller (Eds.), *Cultural divides: Understanding and overcoming group conflict* (pp. 173–212). New York: Russell Sage.

Gaertner, S., & McLaughlin, J. P. (1983). Racial stereotypes: Associations and ascriptions of positive and negative characteristics. *Sociological Psychology Quarterly, 46*(1), 23–30.

Gibbs, J. T. (1987). Identity and marginality: Issues in the treatment of biracial adolescents. *American Journal of Orthopsychiatry, 57,* 265–278.

Glaser, B. G., & Strauss, A. L. (1967). *The discovery of grounded theory: Strategies for qualitative research.* Chicago: Aldine.

Graham, L. O. (1999). *Our kind of people: Inside America's black upper class.* New York: HarperCollins.

Granfield, R. (1991). Making it by faking it: Working-class students in an elite academic environment. *Journal of Contemporary Ethnography, 20*(3), 331–351.

Gurin, P. (2004). Expert report of Patricia Gurin. *Gratz, et al. v. Bollinger, et al.,* No. 97-75321 (E.D. Mich). *Grutter, et al. v. Bollinger, et al.,* No. 97-75928 (E.D. Mich). Retrieved August 19, 2007, from http://www.umich.edu/~urel/admissions/research/expert/gurintoc.html.

Gurin, P., with Dey, E. L., Gurin, G., & Hurtado, S. (2004). The educational value of diversity. In P. Gurin, J. S. Lehman, & E. Lewis (Eds.), *Defending diversity: Affirmative action at the University of Michigan* (pp. 97–188). Ann Arbor: University of Michigan Press.

Gurin, P., Dey, E., Hurtado, S., & Gurin, G. (2002). Diversity and higher education: Theory and impact of educational outcomes. *Harvard Educational Review, 72*(3), 330–366.

Gurin, P., Nagda, B. A., & Lopez, G. E. (2004). The benefits of diversity in education for democratic citizenship. *Journal of Social Issues, 60*(1), 17–34.

Gurin, P., Peng, T., Lopez, G., & Nagda, B. A. (1999). Context, identity, and intergroup relations. In D. A. Prentice & D. J. Miller (Eds.), *Cultural divides: Understanding and overcoming group conflict* (pp. 133–170). New York: Russell Sage Foundation.

Hale, F. W., Jr. (Ed.). (2003). *What makes racial diversity work in higher education: Academic leaders present successful policies and strategies.* Sterling, VA: Stylus.

Hanson, S. L. (1994). Lost talent: Unrealized educational aspirations and expectations among U.S. youth. *Sociology of Education, 67*(3), 159–183.

Hardiman, R. (2001). Reflections on white identity development theory. In C. L. Wijeyesinghe & B. W. Jackson III (Eds.), *New perspectives on racial identity development: A theoretical and practical anthology* (pp. 108–128). New York: New York University Press.

Hardiman, R., & Jackson, B. W. (1992). Racial identity development: Understanding racial dynamics in college classrooms and on campus. In M. Adams (Ed.), *Promoting diversity in college classrooms: Innovative responses for the curriculum, faculty, and institutions* (New Directions for Teaching and Learning, no. 52, pp. 21–37). San Francisco, CA: Jossey-Bass.

Hardiman, R., & Jackson, B. W. (1997). Conceptual foundations for social justice courses. In M. Adams, L. A. Bell, & P. Griffin (Eds.), *Teaching for diversity and social justice: A sourcebook* (pp. 16–29). New York: Routledge.

Harris, P. B., Norman, M. T., & Houston, J. M. (2004, July). The cost of classism: Income and stereotypes on campus. Paper presented at the Annual Convention of the American Psychological Association, Honolulu, Hawaii.

Hartup, W. W. (1993). Adolescents and their friends. In B. Laursen (Ed.), *Close friendships in adolescence* (pp. 3–22). San Francisco, CA: Jossey-Bass.

Helms, J. E. (1984). Toward a theoretical explanation of the effects of race on counseling: A Black/White model. *Counseling Psychologist, 12*(4), 153–165.

Helms, J. E. (1990). *Black and White racial identity: Theory, research, and practice.* New York: Glenwood Press.

Horvat, E. M., & Antonio, A. L. (1999). "Hey, those shoes are out of uniform": African American girls in an elite high school and the importance of habitus. *Anthropology Education Quarterly, 30,* 317–342.

Horvat, E. M., & Lewis, K. S. (2003). Reassessing the "burden of 'acting white'": The importance of peer groups in managing academic success. *Sociology of Education, 76,* 265–280.

Hoyt, S. K. (1999). Mentoring with class: Connections between social class and developmental relationships in the academy. In A. J. Murrell, F. J. Crosby, & R. J. Ely (Eds.), *Mentoring dilemmas: Developmental relationships within multicultural organizations* (pp. 189–210). Mahwah, NJ: Lawrence Erlbaum Associates.

Hunter, M. L. (2005). *Race, gender, and the politics of skin tone.* New York: Routledge.

Hurtado, S. (2001). Linking diversity and educational purpose: How diversity affects the classroom environment and student development. In G. Orfield (Ed.), *Diversity challenged: Evidence on the impact of affirmative action* (pp. 187–203). Cambridge, MA: Civil Rights Project, Harvard University, Harvard Education Publishing Group.

Jackson, B. W., III (2001). Black identity development: Further analysis and elaboration. In C. L. Wijeyesinghe & B. W. Jackon III (Eds.), *New perspectives on racial identity development: A theoretical and practical anthology* (pp. 8–31). New York: New York University Press.

Jencks, C. (1979). *Who gets ahead? The determinants of economic success in America.* New York: Basic Books.

Jencks, C., & Phillips, M. (1998). The black-white test score gap: An introduction. In C. Jencks & M. Phillips (Eds.), *The black-white test score gap* (pp. 1–51). Washington, DC: Brookings Institution Press.

Johannesen-Schmidt, M. C., & Eagly, A. H. (2002). Diminishing returns: The effects of income on the content of stereotypes of wage earners. *Personality and Social Psychology Bulletin, 28,* 1538–1545.

Johnson, J. D., Lecci, L., & Swim, J. (2006). Predicting perceived racism and acceptance of negative behavioral intergroup responses: Validating the JLS in a college and community sample of Blacks. *Personality and Individual Differences, 40,* 421–431.

Jost, J. T., Banaji, M. R., & Nosek, B. A. (2004). A decade of system justification theory: Accumulated evidence of conscious and unconscious bolstering of the status quo. *Political Psychology, 25,* 881–919.

Karabel, J. (2005). *The chosen: The hidden history of admissions and exclusion at Harvard, Yale, and Princeton.* Boston: Houghton Mifflin.

Kay, A. C., & Jost, J. T. (2003). Complementary justice: Effects of "poor but happy" and "poor but honest" stereotype exemplars on system justification and implicit activation of the justice motive. *Journal of Personality and Social Psychology, 85*, 823–837.

Kennedy, R. (2002). *Nigger: The strange career of a troublesome word*. New York: Pantheon Books.

Kerbo, H. R. (1996). *Social stratification and inequality: Class conflict in historical and comparative perspective* (3rd ed.). New York: McGraw-Hill.

King, J. E. (1991). Dysconscious racism: Ideology, identity, and the miseducation of teachers. *Journal of Negro Education, 60*(2), 133–146.

Klonoff, E. A., & Landrine, H. (2000). Is skin color a marker for racial discrimination? Explaining the skin color-hypertension relationship. *Journal of Behavioral Medicine, 23*, 329–338.

Kuriloff, P., & Reichert, M. C. (2003). Boys of class, boys of color: Negotiating the academic and social geography of an elite independent school. *Journal of Social Issues, 4*, 751–769.

Lamont, M., & Lareau, A. (1988). Cultural capital: Allusions, gaps and glissandos in recent theoretical developments. *Sociological Theory, 6*, 153–168.

Landrine, H. (1999). Race×class stereotypes of women. In L. A. Peplau, S. C. DeBro, R. C. Veniegas, & P. L. Taylor (Eds.), *Gender, culture, and ethnicity* (pp. 38–61). Mountain View, CA: Mayfield.

Lareau, A. (2003). *Unequal childhoods: Class, race, and family life*. Berkeley: University of California Press.

Lareau, A., & Weininger, E. B. (2003). Cultural capital in educational research: A critical assessment. *Theory and Society, 32*, 567–606.

Lawler, S. (1999). "Getting out and getting away": Women's narratives of class mobility. *Feminist Review, 63* (Autumn), 3–24.

Leonhardt, D. (2004, April 22). As wealthy fill top colleges, concerns grow over fairness. *New York Times*.

Lott, B., & Bullock, H. E. (2001). Who are the poor? *Journal of Social Issues, 57*, 189–206.

Lubrano, A. (2004). *Limbo: Blue-collar roots, white-collar dreams*. Hoboken, NJ: Wiley.

MacLeod, J. (1995). *Ain't no makin' it: Aspirations and attainment in a low-income neighborhood*. Boulder: Westview Press.

Major, B., & Eccleston, C. P. (2005). Stigma and social exclusion. In D. Abrams, M. A. Hogg, & J. M. Marques (Eds.), *The social psychology of inclusion and exclusion* (pp. 63–87). New York: Psychology Press.

Margolis, E., & Romero, M. (1998). "The department is very male, very white, very old, and very conservative": The functioning of the hidden curriculum in graduate sociology departments. *Harvard Educational Review, 68*(1), 1–32.

Marx, A. (2004). Amherst College 183rd Commencement Address, Amherst College, Amherst, MA, May 23.

Marx, A. (2006). Opening Convocation Address "To Honor Gerald Penny," Amherst College, Amherst, MA, September 4.

McGuire, W. J., McGuire, C. V., Child, P. L., & Fujioka, T. (1978). Salience of ethnicity in the spontaneous self-concept as a function of one's ethnic distinctiveness in the social environment. *Journal of Personality and Social Psychology, 36*, 511–520.

McGuire, W. J., McGuire, C. V., & Winton, W. (1979). Effects of household sex composition on the salience of one's gender in the spontaneous self-concept. *Journal of Experimental Social Psychology, 15*, 77–90.

Megivern, D. (2003). Not by myself alone: Upward bound with family and friends. In V. C. Adair & S. L. Dahlberg (Eds.), *Reclaiming class: Women, poverty, and the promise of higher education in America* (pp. 119–130). Philadelphia: Temple University Press.

Milan, S., & Keiley, M. K. (2000). Biracial youth and families in therapy: Issues and interventions. *Journal of Marital and Family Therapy, 26*, 305–315.

Milem, J. F., Chang, M. J., & Antonio, A. L. (2005). *Making diversity work on campus: A research-based perspective*. Washington, DC: Association of American Colleges and Universities.

Moore, R. M., III. (2002). Race, gender and intimacy on a college campus. In R. M. Moore III (Ed.), *The quality and quantity of contact: African Americans and whites on college campuses* (pp. 323–344). Lanham, MD: University Press of America.

Moynihan, D. P. (1965). *The negro family: The case for national action*. Retrieved August 19, 2007, from http://onlinebooks.library.upenn.edu/webbin/book/lookupid?key =olbp33085.

Nagda, B. A., Gurin, P., & Johnson, S. M. (2005). Living, doing and thinking diversity: How does pre-college diversity experience affect first-year students' engagement with college diversity? In R. S. Feldman (Ed.), *Improving the first year of college: Research and practice* (pp. 73–108). Mahwah, NJ: Lawrence Erlbaum Associates.

Nathan, R. (2005). *My freshman year: What a professor learned by becoming a student*. Ithaca: Cornell University Press.

Neal-Barnett, A. M. (2001). Being black: New thoughts on the old phenomenon of acting white. In A. M. Neal-Barnett, J. M. Contreras, & K. A. Kerns (Eds.), *Forging links: African American children: Clinical developmental perspectives* (pp. 75–88). Westport, CT: Praeger.

Niemann, Y. F., & Maruyama, G. (2005). Inequities in higher education: Issues and promising practices in a world ambivalent about affirmative action. *Journal of Social Issues, 61*, 407–426.

Omi, M., & Winant, H. (1994). *Racial formation in the United States: From the 1960s to the 1990s* (2nd ed.). New York: Routledge.

Orfield, G., & Whitla, D. (2001). Diversity and legal education: Student experiences in leading law schools. In G. Orfield & M. Kurlaender (Eds.), *Diversity challenged: Evidence on the impact of affirmative action* (pp. 143–174). Cambridge, MA: Harvard Educational Publishing Group.

Ortner, S. B. (1991). Reading America: Preliminary notes on class and culture. In R. G. Fox (Ed.), *Recapturing anthropology: Working in the present* (pp. 163–189). Santa Fe, NM: School of American Research Press.

Ostrander, S. A. (1984). *Women of the upper class*. Philadelphia: Temple University Press.

Ostrove, J. M. (2003). Belonging and wanting: Meanings of social class background for women's constructions of their college experiences. *Journal of Social Issues, 59*, 771–784.

Ostrove, J. M., & Long, S. M. (2001, August). *White women's social class identity and the college experience.* Paper presented at the Annual Convention of the American Psychological Association, San Francisco, CA.

Pettigrew, T. F. (1997). Generalized intergroup contact effects on prejudice. *Personality and Social Psychology Bulletin, 23,* 173–185.

Pettigrew, T. F. (1998a). Intergroup contact theory. *Annual Review of Psychology, 49,* 65–85.

Pettigrew, T. F. (1998b). Prejudice and discrimination on the college campus. In J. L. Eberhardt & S. T. Fiske (Eds.), *Confronting racism: The problem and the response* (pp. 263–279). Thousand Oaks, CA: Sage.

Pettigrew, T. F., & Tropp, L. R. (2006). A meta-analytic test of intergroup contact theory. *Journal of Personality and Social Psychology, 90*(5), 751–783.

Phinney, J. S., & Alipuria, L. L. (1996). At the interface of cultures: Multiethnic/multiracial high school and college students. *Journal of Social Psychology, 136,* 139–158.

Piaget, J. (1975). *The equilibration of cognitive structures: The central problem of intellectual development.* Chicago: University of Chicago Press.

Pinderhughes, E. (1995). Biracial identity—Asset or handicap? In H. W. Harris, H. C. Blue, & E. E. H. Griffith (Eds.), *Racial and ethnic identity: Psychological development and creative expression* (pp. 73–93). New York: Routledge.

Pope, R. L., Miklitsch, T. A., & Weigand, M. J. (2005). First-year students: Embracing their diversity, enhancing our practice. In R. S. Feldman (Ed.), *Improving the first year of college: Research and practice* (pp. 51–71). Mahwah, NJ: Lawrence Erlbaum Associates.

Robbins, S. B., Lauver, K., Le, H., Davis, D., Langley, R., & Carlstrom, A. (2004). Do psychosocial and study skill factors predict college outcomes? A meta-analysis. *Psychological Bulletin, 130,* 261–288.

Rockquemore, K. A., & Brunsma, D. L. (2002). *Beyond black: Biracial identity in America.* Thousand Oaks, CA: Sage Publications.

Rodriguez, R. (1982). *Hunger of memory: The education of Richard Rodriguez.* New York: Bantam Books.

Root, M. P. P. (Ed.). (1996). *The multiracial experience: Racial borders as the new frontier.* Thousand Oaks, CA: Sage Publications.

Rubin, H., & Rubin, I. (1995). *Qualitative interviewing: The art of hearing data.* Thousand Oaks, CA: Sage.

Rudenstine, N. L. (2001). Student diversity and higher learning. In G. Orfield & M. Kurlaender (Eds.), *Diversity Challenged: Evidence of the impact of affirmative action* (pp. 31–48). Cambridge, MA: Harvard Educational Publishing Group.

Ryan, J., & Sackrey, C. (1984). *Strangers in paradise.* Boston: South End Press.

Saylor, E. S., & Aries, E. (1999). Ethnic identity and change in social context. *The Journal of Social Psychology, 139,* 549–566.

Schein, E. H. (1992). *Organizational culture and leadership.* San Francisco: Jossey-Bass.

Sellers, R. M., Morgan, L. M., & Brown, T. N. (2001). A multidimensional approach to racial identity: Implications for African American children. In A. M. Neal-Barnett, J. M. Contreras, & K. A. Kerns (Eds.), *Forging links: African American children: Clinical developmental perspectives* (pp. 23–56). Westport, CT: Praeger.

Sellers, R. M., Shelton, J. N., Cooke, D., Chavous, T., Rowley, S. A. J., & Smith, M. (1998). A multidimensional model of racial identity: Assumptions, findings and future directions. In R. L. Jones (Ed.), *African American identity development: Theory, research, and intervention*. Hampton, VA: Cobb & Henry.

Sennett, R., & Cobb, J. (1972). *The hidden injuries of class*. New York: Knopf.

Skeggs, B. (1997). *Formations of class and gender: Becoming respectable*. London: Sage Publications.

Snow, D. A., & Anderson, L. (1987). Identity work among the homeless: The verbal construction and avowal of personal identities. *American Journal of Sociology, 6,* 1336–1371.

Sommers, V. S. (1964). The impact of dual-cultural membership on identity. *Psychiatry, 27,* 332–344.

Steele, C. M., & Aronson, J. (1995). Stereotype threat and the intellectual test performance of African Americans. *Journal of Personality and Social Psychology, 69,* 797–811.

Steele, C. M., Spencer, S. J., & Aronson, J. (2002). Contending with group image: The psychology of stereotype and social identity threat. In M. P. Zanna (Ed.), *Advances in experimental social psychology* (vol. 34, pp. 379–440). San Diego, CA: Academic Press.

Steele, S. (1990). *The content of our character: A new vision of race in America*. New York: St. Martin's Press.

Stephan, W. G., Boniecki, K. A., Ybarra, O., Bettencourt, A., Ervin, K.S., Jackson, L.A., McNatt, P.S., & Renfro, C. L. (2002). The role of threats in the racial attitudes of blacks and whites. *Personality and Social Psychology Bulletin, 28,* 1242–1254.

Stephan, W. G., & Finlay, K. (1999). The role of empathy in improving intergroup relations. *Journal of Social Issues, 55,* 729–743.

Stephan, W. G., & Stephan, C. W. (1985). Intergroup anxiety. *Journal of Social Issues, 41,* 157–175.

Stewart, A. J., & Ostrove, J. M. (1993). Social class, social change, and gender. *Psychology of Women Quarterly, 17,* 475–497.

Strauss, A., & Corbin, J. (1990). *Basics of qualitative research: Grounded theory procedures and techniques*. Newbury Park, CA: Sage Publications.

Stuber, J. M. (2006). Within the walls and among the students: How white working- and upper-middle-class college students make sense of social class. Unpublished doctoral dissertation, Indiana University.

Stuber, J. M. (2008). Talk of class: The discursive repertoires of white working- and upper-middle-class college students. *Journal of Contemporary Ethnography, 35,* 285–318.

Sue, D. W., Capodilupo, C. M., Torino, G. C., Bucceri, J. M., Holder, A. M. B., Nadal, K. L., & Esquilin, M. (2007). Racial microaggressions in everyday life: Implications for clinical practice. *American Psychologist, 62,* 271–286.

Sullivan, N. (2003). Academic constructions of "white trash" or how to insult poor people without really trying. In V. C. Adair & S. L. Dahlberg (Eds.), *Reclaiming class: Women, poverty, and the promise of higher education in America* (pp. 53–66). Philadelphia: Temple University Press.

Summers, L. (2004, June 10). Harvard University President Lawrence H. Summers Commencement Address. Harvard University, Cambridge, MA. http://www .president.harvard.edu/speeches/2004/commencement.html.

Suskind, R. (1998). *A hope in the unseen: An American odyssey from the inner city to the Ivy League.* New York: Broadway Books.

Symonds, W. (2006, February 27). Campus Revolutionary; Tony Marx has a radical plan to get more poor kids into top colleges, starting with Amherst. *Business Week, 3973,* 64.

Tatum, B. D. (1997). *"Why are all the Black kids sitting together in the cafeteria?" and other conversations about race.* New York: Basic Books.

Tierney, W. G. (1988). Organizational culture in higher education: Defining the essentials. *Journal of Higher Education, 59,* 2–21.

Tokarczyk, M. M., & Fay, E.A. (Eds.). (1993). *Working-class women in the academy: Laborers in the knowledge factory.* Amherst: University of Massachusetts Press.

Tropp, L. R. (2006). Stigma and intergroup contact among members of minority and majority status groups. In S. Levin & C. van Laar (Eds.), *Stigma and group inequality: Social psychological perspectives* (pp. 171–191). Mahwah, NJ: Lawrence Erlbaum Associates.

Tropp, L. R., & Bianchi, R. A. (2006). Valuing diversity and interest in intergroup contact. *Journal of Social Issues, 62,* 533–551.

Tropp, L. R., & Pettigrew, T. F. (2005a). Differential relationships between intergroup contact and affective and cognitive dimensions of prejudice. *Personality and Social Psychology Bulletin, 31,* 1145–1158.

Tropp, L. R., & Pettigrew, T. F. (2005b). Relationships between intergroup contact and prejudice among minority and majority status groups. *Psychological Science, 16,* 951–957.

Turner, J. C. (1982). Towards a cognitive redefinition. In H. Tajfel (Ed.), *Social identity and intergroup relations* (pp. 15–40). New York: Cambridge University Press.

Turner, J. C., with Hogg, M.A., Oakes, P. J., Reicher, S. D., & Wetherell, M. S. (1987). *Rediscovering the social group: A self-categorization theory.* Oxford: Blackwell.

Twenge, J. M., & Campbell, W. K. (2002). Self-esteem and socioeconomic status: A meta-analytic review. *Personality and Social Psychology Review, 6*(1), 59–71.

Tyson, K., Darity, W., & Castellino, D. R. (2005). It's not "a black thing": Understanding the burden of acting white and other dilemmas of high achievement. *American Sociological Review, 70,* 582–605.

van Dick, R., Wagner, U., Pettigrew, T. F., Christ, O., Wolf, C., Petzel, T., Castro, V. S., & Jackson, J. S. (2004). Role of perceived importance in intergroup contact. *Journal of Personality and Social Psychology, 87,* 211–227.

Vars, F. E., & Bowen, W. G. (1998). Scholastic aptitude test scores, race, and academic performance in selective colleges and universities. In C. Jencks & M. Phillips (Eds.), *The black-white test score gap* (pp. 457–479). Washington, DC: Brookings Institution Press.

Veblen, T. (1899). *The theory of the leisure class: An economic study in the evolution of institutions.* New York: The Macmillan Company.

Walpole, M. (2003). Socioeconomic status and college: How SES affects college experience and outcomes. *The Review of Higher Education, 27*(1), 43–73.

Waters, M. (1999). *Black identities: West Indian immigrant dreams and American realities*. New York: Russell Sage Foundation.

Watson, L. W., Terrell, M. C., Wright, D. J., & Bonner, F. A., Cuyjet, M. J., Gold, J. A., Rudy, D. E., & Person, D. R. (2002). *How minority students experience college: Implications for planning and policy*. Sterling, VA: Stylus Publishing.

Williams, D. A., Berger, J. B., & McClendon, S. A. (2005). *Toward a Model of Inclusive Excellence and Change in Postsecondary Institutions*. Washington, DC: Association of American Colleges and Universities.

Willie, S. S. (2003). *Acting black: College, identity, and the performance of race*. New York: Routledge.

Wittenbrink, B., Judd, C. M., & Park, B. (1997). Evidence for racial prejudice at the implicit level and its relationship with questionnaire measures. *Journal of Personality and Social Psychology, 72*, 262–274.

Zweigenhaft, R. L., & Domhoff, G. W. (1991). *Blacks in the white establishment? A study of race and class in America*. New Haven: Yale University Press.

Index

Academic confidence, 22, 155
Academics, 111, 154–156, 179–181; grades, 155, 167; SAT scores, 22, 45, 155
Acting white, 141–143, 152, 168. *See also* Black students, challenges for; Blackness
Adjustment, 156–157, 169–173
Admission: data on participants, 13–14; historical changes in, 1–4; making it to Amherst, 23, 45; race and, 2–3, 7, 89, 148; social class and, 3–4, 45, 117, 129, 167, 175
Affluent students, challenges for: coping with negative stereotypes, 56–57, 112–115; finding ways to be inclusive, 83–84; tensions about greater privilege, 75–76
Affirmative action, 2, 7, 103
African Americans. *See also* Blacks
Allport, Gordon, 5, 6, 8, 11

Bi-racial identity, 105–106. *See also* Black students, challenges for; Blacks
Black community, 37–38, 131–134, 151–152, 166; tensions within, 134–144. *See also* Black students, challenges for; Blacks
Black Student Union (BSU), 39, 133–134, 136–138
Black students, challenges for: being "black enough", 91, 140–144, 152 (*see also* Acting white); bridging two worlds, 166–168; classroom issues, 89, 95, 145–147, 153–156, 180–181; concerns about relating to whites, 38–39, 131; differences in racial self-definition, 136, 139–140, 152; expectations to be with blacks, 39, 134, 136–139; family hopes and expectations, 9, 158–160; inter-racial dating, 39, 103–104, 137; joking about race, 9, 99, 102, 137, 145, 147–153; racial offenses, 144–145, 148–151, 153; representing one's race, 9, 39, 146–147, 153, 156, 179; skin tone differences, 9, 140–141; social class differences, 134–136, speech differences, 141–143; stereotyping, 36, 38, 87–93, 100–101, 106, 108, 142–143, 146–149; summary of findings, 170–171. *See also* Adjustment; Blacks; Blackness; Cross-race relationships
Blackness: 91, 139–144, 147, 152
Blacks: diversity among, 134–136, 151–152; racial identity, 16, 36, 104–108, 136, 139–140, 151–152; self-segregation, 41, 65–67, 85; skin tone, 9, 140–141; social networks, 36–38, 79–80, 132–134, 136–137; stereotypes about, 9, 40, 87–93, 100–101, 108, 142–143. *See also* Black community; Blackness; Black students, challenges for; Race

Bok, Derek, 7, 64, 65, 72, 155
Bowen, William, 3, 7, 64, 65, 72, 155
Bridging two worlds, 158, 162–167

Class mobility. *See also* Social mobility
Classroom diversity: learning about race,
   94–96, 107, 174–175, 179–180; learning
   about class, 115–116, 175–176, 180. *See also*
   Learning from diversity
Classroom issues, class–related, 113–114,
   180–181
Classroom issues, race–related, 89, 95,
   145–147, 153–156, 180–181
Clothes and accessories: as markers of social
   class, 29–30, 34–36, 60, 112–115; as markers
   of race, 90, 141–143
Code-switching, 168
Commonalities across class lines. *See also*
   Learning from diversity
Commonalities across race lines. *See also*
   Learning from diversity
Connections: making new, 9, 80, 162;
   pre–existing, 38, 46, 79–80, 129. *See also*
   Social capital
Contact theory, 5–6, 174
Conversations about race, 101–106, 153,
   177–178
Conversations about social class, 116–119,
   177–178
Cross-class relationships: Bowen and Bok
   findings on, 72; comfort/discomfort in,
   30–32, 54, 59, 71–72, 74, 82, 84;
   expectations for forming, 9, 31–34;
   inclusion in, strategies for, 83–84; learning
   from, 116–129; negotiating, 75–78, 80–84;
   prevalence of, 72–73; prior experience with,
   21–22, 71, 109; valuing of, 71–72; variability
   in who forms, 73. *See also* Learning from
   diversity
Cross-race relationships: Bowen and Bok
   findings on, 64–65; being "race-blind",
   97–98, 107; comfort/discomfort in, 8–9,
   39–42, 67–71; difficulties forming, 6, 8–9,
   38–40, 68–69; expectations for forming, 36,
   38–42;—interracial dating, 39, 103–104;
   learning from, 96–107, 116–130, 149–150;
   negotiating, 144–151, 153; prevalence of,
   64–66, 70, 85; prior experience with, 20–21,
   36, 40; racial offenses and, 144–145,
   148–151, 153; social class and, 65–66, 70;
   valuing of, 69–71. *See also* Inclusion,
   Learning from diversity; White students'
   comfort with blacks

Cultural capital, 7, 30, 45–46, 74, 79, 161–162
Curriculum. *See also* Academics; Classroom
   diversity

Diversity goals, enhancing, 177–183

Economic capital, 7, 25–30, 74–77, 83–84
Entitlement, 51, 113, 162, 176
Exclusion, 74; from activities, 31, 74, 77–79;
   from conversations, 78; from eating out, 31,
   77;—from social groups, 67–68, 79, 81–83,
   141–142; from summer plans, 76–77; from
   trips, 31, 75–76; *See also* Inclusion;
   Self-exclusion
Extracurricular activities, 75, 81; number
   participated in, 157; pre-college, 45, 55, 79;
   race-related, 81, 90, 133–134, 136, 138. *See
   also* Black Student Union (BSU)

Family: changing relationship with, 158,
   161–163, 166; contact with, 157–158;
   parental education, 18–20; parental hopes
   and expectations, 9, 157–160; parental
   occupation, 18, 20, 58
Feagin, Joe, 7, 96, 146–147, 149, 155, 177
Financial aid: application information, 13–14;
   awards, 19, 25, 75, 78, 167; debt, 48, 59;
   feelings about, 50–53, 57–59, 83, 167;
   misperception of recipients of, 34, 92, 135;
   percent receiving, 1–2, 33
Friendships. *See also* Cross-class relationships;
   Cross-race relationships; Same-class
   relationships; Same-race relationships

Gender, 3, 69, 112, 141, 182; attitudes towards
   inter-racial dating, 103–104; inability to
   address in the study, 24, 183
Grade point average (GPA), 155, 167. *See also*
   Academics

Hardiman, Rita, 107–108, 152
Home friends and communities, 20–21, 157,
   162–167

Inclusion: blacks' feelings of, 33, 36, 38, 67;
   feelings of, 75, 81, 156; strategies for, 83–84,
   181–182. *See also* Exclusion
Institutional change: goals for, 177–183; in
   student body, 1–4, 131–132; need for, 108,
   130, 153
Intergroup anxiety: –class–based, 30–32,
   71–72; for blacks, 38–39, 144; for whites,
   39–40, 144

Intergroup interaction. *See also* Cross-class relationships; Cross-race relationships
Internships, 46, 76–77, 80
Interviews, 8, 15–18, 24. *See also* Research methods

Jackson, Bailey, 107–108, 152
Jobs: expectations about future, 48, 158, 162; on campus, 78, 127–128; parental, 18, 20, 49, 58, 127, 163; summer, 76–77, 79–80, 128; to support oneself, 123
Joking about race, 9, 99, 102, 137, 145, 147–151, 153
Joking about social class, 56, 59, 114–115

Learning from diversity, 3–6; about race and racism, 71, 85–86, 93–107, 149–150, 170; about social class, 63, 78, 115–129, 170—
Legacy, 1–3, 9
Lower-income students, challenges for: academic under-preparation, 22, 154–155, 167, 181; changing relationship with family, friends, home communities, 157–159, 162–167; family expectations, 9, 157–160; lack of cultural capital, 7, 30, 74, 79, 161–162; lack of economic capital, 26–30, 74–78; lack of social capital, 79–80, 162; negotiating relationships with affluent students, 31, 74–78, 80–84; representing one's social class, 111, 156; stereotyping, 57–58, 92–93, 110–112, 129; summary of findings, 42–43, 167–168, 172–173. *See also* Adjustment; Cross-class relationships
Lower-income students, character traits and values, 48–55

Nigger or the N-word, 8, 40, 144, 146, 150–151. *See also* Racial terms

On-line surveys, 8, 16–17, 24
Orientation, 15; costs incurred for, 27, 77; issues addressed during, 33, 43, 182

Parents. *See also* Family
Participants, 8, 13–16, 18–23
Possessions, 25–30. *See also* Purchases for college
Prejudice: conditions that reduce, 5–6, 69–70, 94, 96, 115–116, 174; examples of, on campus, 89, 110–114, 144; reduction of, on campus, 116–130; in society, 36, 87–88, 100, 105, 144, 153. *See also* Learning from diversity

Preppy, 23, 98–99, 112–113, 115, 175; attire, 29, 34, 113
Prep schools. *See also* Private high schools and prep schools
—Private high schools and prep schools: academic preparation at, 4, 22, 45, 155; attendance at, 21; college admission and, 2–4, 45; experiences at, 32–33, 45, 47, 67, 79, 98, 122; perceptions and reactions to students who attended, 56, 74, 92–93, 113–114, 120, 147. *See also* Public high schools
Public high schools: 2–3, 21, 45, 117, 155. *See also* Private high schools and prep schools
Purchases for college, 25–28, 34, 84

Race: admission and, 1–3, 7, 89, 148; analytic frameworks for understanding, 107–108, 152, 175, 180; being "race–blind", 97–98; centrality of, to self-definition, 136, 139–140, 152; class divisions and, 135–136; definitions of, 139–140; expectations about, 36, 38–42; prior experiences with and thoughts about, 20–21, 36, 40; representing one's, 9, 39, 146–147, 153, 156, 179; skin tone, 140–141. *See also* Black students, challenges for; Blacks; Cross-race relationships; Joking about race; Racial identity; Racial offenses; Racial terms; Stereotypes
Racial identity, 36, 104, 136, 139–140, 151–152; bi–racial identity, 105–106; model of, 107–108; of participants, 16
Racial joking. *See also* Joking about race
Racial profiling, 36, 94, 104–105, 145
Racial offenses, 144–145, 148–151, 153
Racial stereotypes. *See also* Stereotypes
Racial terms: Nigger or the N-word, 8, 40, 144, 146, 150–151; other racial terms, 137, 146–147, 151
Racism: concerns about, 38, 93, 99–100, 102; in society, 87–88, 107–108; on campus, 132, 144, 148–149, 183; learning about, 94–96, 104–105, 108, 177, 180. *See also* Racial offenses
Relationships. *See also* Same-class relationships; Same-race relationships
Research goals, 2, 8, 169
Research methods: data analysis, 17–18; generalization and limitation of results, 23–24, 183–184; interviews, 8, 15–18, 24; on–line surveys, 8, 16–17, 24; participants, 8, 13–16, 18–23; procedures, 13–17; response rate, 15–16

Same-class relationships: desire for, 31–32, 60–62; prevalence of, 56, 73

Same-race relationships: blacks' social networks, 36–38, 132–134; complexities of, for blacks, 134–143, 150–152; learning from, for blacks, 105; prevalence of, 65–67. *See also* Black students, challenges for

SAT (Scholastic Aptitude Test), 22–23, 45–46. *See also* Academics

Self-exclusion, 41, 81–82. *See also* Exclusion

Self-segregation, 65–67, 70, 123, 128; blacks eating together in the dining hall, 41, 68, 85, 134–135, 138

Social capital, 38, 46, 79–80, 129, 162

Social class: admission and, 1–4, 13–14, 23, 45, 111, 117, 129, 167; analytic frameworks for understanding, 62–63, 130, 180; awareness of privilege by the affluent, 28, 44–46, 121–124; contentment with class position, 44–49, 61; determinants of, 18–20, 25–30, 127–128; difficulties discerning/not attending to differences in, 32–36, 43, 59–60, 121, 128–129; hiding/disguising markers of, 55–59, 117; perceived costs/benefits to being lower–income, 46–55, 61; perceptions of relative class position, 46–47, 128; prior experiences with and thoughts about, 21–22, 31, 44–55, 71, 109; representing one's, 111, 156; reproduction of, 62–63; salience of, 28–32, 59, 74–80, 109, 183. *See also* Clothes and accessories, Cross-Class relationships; Cultural capital; Economic capital; Social capital

Social influence, 80–81

Social integration and comfort, 36, 156–157. *See also* Cross-class relationships; Cross-race relationships

Social justice, 3–4, 117, 129

Social mobility: institutional commitment to, 2–3, 129; in society, 62–63; of participants, 48, 61, 160, 162–166 –

Social support networks: among blacks, 36–38, 79–80, 132–134, 136–137; among lower-income students, 31–32, 60–62. *See also* Same-class relationships; Same-race relationships

Stereotypes, 5–6, 87–88: avoiding, 56–58, 92–93;—breaking down class-based, 116–121; breaking down racial, 93–96, 98–101, 108; joking about, 147–151, 153; of blacks, 9, 36, 40, 87–92, 100–102, 108, 142–143, 146–148; of the poor, 57–58, 110–112, 118; of the rich, 45, 56–57, 74, 112–115; of whites, 92–93, 98–100; socialization of, 87–88. *See also* Learning from diversity

Structured dialogue, 130, 153, 177–178

Travel: by the affluent, 30, 45, 75–77, 113, 183; desire to, by lower-income students, 30, 47–48, 52; inability to pay for, 31, 34, 75–77; inadequacy evoked by lack of, 30; including others in, 83, 125

Tuition and fees, 5, 14–15, 51. *See also* Financial aid

Wealthy students, negative perceptions of, 45, 52, 56–57, 74, 83, 110, 112–115

Well-being, 156–157, 169–171, 173. *See also* Adjustment

White students' racial issues: comfort with blacks, 8–9, 39–42, 68–71; concerns about blacks eating together in the dining hall, 41, 68, 85, 134–135, 138—

Elizabeth Aries is Professor of Psychology at Amherst College. She is the author of *Men and Women in Interaction: Reconsidering the Differences* and *Adolescent Behavior: Readings and Interpretations*